Critical acclaim for first edition of *Get A Life!*:

"*Get a Life!* is well worth reading to learn about what needs fixing, and more important, what we can do to fix it in our community."
Jane Jacobs, author of *The Death and Life of Great American Cities* and *Systems of Survival*

"Congratulations, a great book....Too much of environmental concern is simply a greenwash, trying to put a green face on doing business as usual. This book gets at the deeper issues and tries to give concrete suggestions on how we can remedy the situation."
David Suzuki, scientist and broadcaster

"I started reading *Get A Life!* and was instantly hooked. Get the book!"
Amory Lovins, energy economist

"An irreverent and sassy, but eminently practical, guide book...clean, fresh, all encompassing."
Paul Hawken, author of *The Ecology of Commerce*

"Comes amazingly close to being the definitive eco-manifesto for the '90s."
Bob Hunter, Greenpeace co-founder

"Brilliant, powerful, authoritative and a good read! This book can help change the game of 'economism' into a broader move toward healthier communities and sustainable societies."
Hazel Henderson, author of *Politics of the Solar Age* and *Paradigms in Progress; Life Beyond Economics*

"It's an inspirational book and shows the way forward without talking down to anyone."
Dr. John Todd, author and creator of living machines

"I plan to give away 10 of my 11 copies to share the common sense, and embodied therein, the hope that there is hope."
Mendelson Joe

"Wonderful, simply wonderful!"
Anita Roddick, founder Body Shop International

"The economic professors must be jealous. Only a book this irreverent is able to capture the immense changes in how jobs are created by responding to our new sense of environmental values. Bravo!"
John Sewell, former Mayor of Toronto, author

"*Get a Life!* is well worth getting. It's a kind of self-help manual for ecologically minded contingency workers. Its style is punchy, as in: 'Hometown value-added—turning logs into lumber and lumber into furniture—is as much for job-huggers as tree-huggers."
Richard Gwyn, columnist, *Toronto Star*, Feb.16, 1994

"Over 50 pages of practical projects capable of serving as the basis for small and medium business…. In brash, humourous writing style itself a departure from most environmental books, the authors never miss an opportunity to take a slap shot at political, economic and business policies which have resulted in environmental degradation and economic recession."
EcoLog Week

"*Get A Life!* is probably one of the best pedagogical tools which I have had the pleasure to read in my five years as a professor of co-operative entrepreneurship and community economic development."
Professor Ginette Lafrenière, School of Commerce and Administration, Laurentian University

How To Make A Good Buck, Dance Around The Dinosaurs
And Save The World While You're At It

One hundred and one ways to tread lightly on Mother
Earth, make bags of money, simplify your life, have a blast,
keep fit and save your sanity while everything is crumbling
all around you

Published by Get A Life Publishing House
2255B Queen St. East, Suite 127,
Toronto, Ontario CANADA
M4E 1G3
416-669-6070
Published October, 1995

Canadian Cataloguing in Publication Data
Roberts, Wayne, 1944–
Get a life! how to make a good buck, dance around the dinosaurs and
save the world while you're at it

(Get a life!)
ISBN 0-9697755-1-2

1. Green movement. 2. Economic development—Environmental
aspects. 3. Environmental protection. I. Brandum, Susan. II. Title. III.
Series: Get a life! (Toronto, Ont.)

HC120.E79R63 1995...363.7'058...C95-900894-2

Cover design: Glenn Cameron
Interior design: Ed Martin

Printed and bound in Canada

Dedication

Get A Life! is a home-based, not a house-based business. We have our partners, Lori Stahlbrand and Ed Martin, to thank for that difference and dedicate this book to them.

Preface

With A Little Help From Our Friends

This book is a venture in the new economy. We'll find out if we can turn our passions into a career. Our company has a lot of room for growth, to put a positive spin on it. Don't bother suing us. We have no capital assets. We've got this far by finding openings where our reputation takes us farther than our credit rating. Our printing broker, Tom Scanlon of IS5, trusted us to repay him over six months. Friends and family spotted us loans to do some marketing, which we've guaranteed against lifetime savings. Self-publishing keeps you hustling, helps turn dreams into business plans, and puts marketing fire in the belly of writers who don't normally like sales. It also lets us practice what we preach about putting it on the line for a new economy.

Too small to rate as a small company, too independent to fit with any one organization, we're big enough and interdependent enough to be a virtual corporation. With no budget for libraries, researchers, staff designers, layout artists, printers, merchandisers, accountants, no money for walls, we've linked with others who are trying out the new economy. We made a point of establishing win-win relationships with some real comers: Glenn Cameron, who did our cover, and Ed Martin, who did our interior design, layout and typesetting, and who is travelling the Internet looking for sales contacts, and marketing sage Ross Munroe all gave us grassroots expertise, knowing they will sink or swim with us because they get a percentage of our sales.

A score of friends and well-wishers have sent clippings from their home-town papers, passed on news service items that never made it on the media, or kept us in touch with the action across the continent. The advantage of only having a dime is that you can turn on it. Our only fixed costs are teenage daughter Jaime who told her dad to get a life when he balked at the idea of her backpacking across the continent for a film project on youth activism, and three-year-old Anika who keeps asking her dad when it will be safe to play on the street. Soon baby, I hope, soon.

We're interactive, which means the information flow goes two ways. In our first edition, we pulled together the experiences of the Toronto-based Coalition For a Green Economic Recovery, a group of rebels with a cause who want to do something meaningful while business and political leaders are either still stuck in the denial phase of grieving the passing of old ways, or trying desperately to recreate them. The book sold wherever there were lineups for **Rocky Horror Picture Show** or **On Deadly Ground**. Readers gave us their suggestions, which we did our best to include in this totally revised edition. And, as you'll see from the layout, we're set up for fast turnaround with any new proposals that come back from this run. No need to turn an organization upside-down just to try out a new idea. Ready, fire, aim! is the best way to learn in a world of fast-breaking change, so books as well as organizations need lots of space to fill in the blanks.

With no institutional links to bookstores, brokers, advertisers, universities, or reviewers, we're casting our bread upon the networks, counting on local heroes out there to pass the book on to friends, nieces and nephews ready to try something new. Word of mouth is cheaper and faster than advertising, it comes with stronger endorsements, and entails greater responsibilities. That's a plea. If you like the book, we ask you to buy a box in advance, then use the bulk discount to finance your voluntary activities. Invite us to speak to your organization, so we can learn from you for the next edition.

You can get in touch with us any way you want. We're home-based. Phone us at 416-699-6070 or 416-536-6717, fax us at 416-536-9101. We're international. Write us at 4045 Meadow Gateway, Broadview Heights, Ohio, U.S.A. 44147, or 2225B Queen St. E., Suite 127, Toronto, Ontario, Canada M4E 1G3. We're global. E-mail us at ertin@io.org and we'll direct you to our WWW page. Hope to hear from you.

Wayne Roberts
Susan Brandum

About The Authors

Senior writer Wayne Roberts learned that the environment was about life in cities, not just scenic parks, while studying at Berkeley in the 1960s, days of People's Park and much else. With a Ph.D. in economic history, he has taught at universities and labor colleges, worked as assistant to the president of the Ontario Public Service Employees Union, and has written several books on industrial history. Arrested on a logging blockade in Temagami, Ontario, in 1989, he's since given his time to finding jobs for workers displaced by economic restructuring. He's a featured columnist on green business with the alternative weekly, NOW Magazine.

Co-author Susan Brandum spent her youth in mining towns in Canada before settling down with one family foot in Cleveland, Ohio, and one in Port Elmsley, Ontario. She consults with major companies on energy management, heads the Green Business Fund in Toronto, and is involved in the nitty gritty of building green communities through the Green Communities Initiatives. She is co-chair of the Coalition for a Green Economic Recovery.

Researcher John Bacher, now working on an ecological history of North America, has a Ph.D. in history and is the author of Keeping to the Marketplace: The Evolution of Canadian Housing Policy. A member of the Ontario drainage board, he's also active in farmland preservation in the Niagara Falls area, where he heads the Preservation of Agricultural Land Society, and Friends of Foodland.

Table of Contents

Principle 9

Easy Does It **243**

Applies the power of positive thinking and the concept of "social capital" to new ways of offering public and business services

Principle 10

What a Wonderful Life! **281**

Replaces planned economies with the spontaneity of "community economies" and creates opportunities to take it easy, but take it

Ready When You Are

Introduction

"What we have here is an insurmountable opportunity."
Yogi Berra

This is a book of solutions for a world that is crumbling around us. It's action-packed with projects you can do today, even without big money or government behind you. The ideas come from our trip along the underground railway of the North American Free Trade Agreement, trading freely with local heroes, self-starters, bootstrap entrepreneurs, geeks, flakes, inventors, community organizers, greens, champions, and sharp business operators from across Canada and the United States. It's called prophet-sharing.

Their success stories gave us the scoop on the best-kept secret in economic forecasting: community development and ecological restoration will inspire and ensure tomorrow's promising careers and businesses. Those masterminding NAFTA's, GATT's or palaeolithic conservatism's race to the bottom of global competitiveness won't do it. Instead, the ones to watch are home- and neighbourhood-based ventures that work with nature, with compact technologies and with smart systems that all tap into and give back to community economies, social justice and environmental protection.

We've pulled together more than 101 ready-to-go projects from our travels. Taken separately, they're a dessert tray that individuals looking for more rewarding careers or lifestyles can pick from. Taken together, they foreshadow a citizen-led economic recovery and the next generation of entrepreneurial breakthroughs. Their methods of operation are so distinctive that we devote the first chapter to a discussion of emerging trends as a "fourth wave" of industrialism. In chapters two through 12, we break out 10 trend-setting principles guiding the emerging economic leaders of tomorrow. We present two examples to personify each principle. Each of these chapters also provides a list of bite-size and stand-alone projects that flow from the general principle. The idea is to get some economic leapfrogging going, so new ventures can grow by leaps and bounds, drawing on, adapting and extending successes elsewhere.

Before we get down to the hard-headed and technical stuff that assures the future of the new growth companies, we need a sense of the spirit underlying them. Whether they're making good in agriculture, the food industry, health care, waste management, construction, crafts, energy conservation, tourism, the civil service or neighborhood improvement organizations, thriving new entrepreneurs share a common social-psy-

chological profile. They practice economics with an attitude, which
we call Get A Life! It's a can-do, up yours, no time for doom and gloom,
no truck with the analysis-paralysis of the chattering classes, an "if you
can't join them, beat them," attitude. Everybody has to adopt a stance
that matches their own personality. Some might pre-fer Drop Dead!
Others might opt for Barney in Construction Boots. A Finnish family,
the Siiralas, likes to take a sauna by the pond behind the converted
barn where they stitch their coveted Wrinkles dolls in Carnarvon,
Ontario, and thinks the right term is Get a Loofah! Some variant of
this attitude is a precondition for success at the cutting edge, where
the new economy is pushing up against the corporate and government
old guard.

The most effective of the new entrepreneurs also share some essential
business and social skills that help them win from the margins. Indeed,
we'd go so far as to argue that the scarcity of these skills is the biggest
single obstacle to the new economy's triumph in the immediate future.
Even without media play, elite endorsement, expensive advertising, or
well-organized distribution networks, some new companies are already
grabbing market share or winning contracts from open-minded government agencies. Even with government subsidies and trade deals prop-
ping up the old clunker monopolies, the advantages of alternative
production and service systems already on-line are so outstanding—
return on investment of anywhere from 30 to 1,000 per cent is normal,
savings to individuals and governments in the range of 25 per cent is
commonplace, with lots of positive job, community and environmental
spinoffs to boot—that new businesses would be at the top of the heap
today if sheer rational calculation had anything to do with the
economy.

Promoters of new business opportunities might have the right ideas,
but as Jim Lang notes curtly in **Make Your Own Breaks,** "ideas without
entrepreneurship are like the sound of one hand clapping." What's missing is more catalysts who exert what Loblaws food chain vice-president
Patrick Carson calls the Power of One, leaders who are ready for what
futurist John Kettle calls "management in the future tense," and executives who will risk becoming what **Fortune Magazine** calls champions,
given that "in most organizations, the future doesn't have a lobbying
group." In their absence, North American business remains socially

challenged and disabled, to use the politically correct terms, and unable to rise to the occasion of new opportunities.

Even at this early stage, it's possible to identify the complex of skills, styles and stances that make effective new entrepreneurs tick. Here's our checklist of the qualities that will fetch a high premium as the new economy gathers force. Success without college, success despite college.

The Body Shop has a department of "social inventions," which develops innovative products and gutsy partnerships with suppliers. Many of the deals, like the one with at-risk youth from a Baltimore ghetto who produce Body Shop soap dishes, are well off the beaten path. Most of the deals are mutually profitable. That's one way of giving the middle finger to the business-as-usual crowd, with their pat refrains that this is the way of the world, there's not much anyone can do about it, that's not what they taught us at Harvard, it was tried before and didn't work, and my daddy doesn't agree either.

The new entrepreneurs are a willful bunch because they believe where there's a will, there's a way. They'll give new ideas a try before rejecting them out of hand. Economics R Us. It's as subject to human need and choice as any other social activity. When economics is fatalistically accepted as out there, an external set of unchangeable laws, it leads to brain damage, says solar age futurist Hazel Henderson. "I can't imagine a more screwed-up notion than that human beings must be sacrificed to serve economics," says Dr. David Suzuki, the geneticist who hosts a TV series on science and the environment that's watched throughout the world. "Economics is fundamentally warped because economics is divorced from the things that keep us alive."[1]

Reinventing economics as a life science, refocussing on an economy we can live with, returns the discipline to its origins as a field within moral philosophy that highlights human rights, needs, values and choices. That starts to get the proportions of problems right by putting first things first. "We have to start growing economic and environmental solutions from the inside out," says Steve Hall, a transportation consultant with the Washington-based International Institute for Energy

Conservation. "Instead of working backwards from the needs of planners and technocrats—figuring out whether buses, street rail, or cars are the best way to transport people along grids—we need to let solutions flow from the human spirit and impulse to live, create and reach out, which makes transportation part of personal and community development and land use."

Sandra Marks leads West End Ventures, an Ottawa, Ontario self-help group for low-income mothers who want to start their own businesses. "We are in the hope business," she says, after landing a six-figure contract to train local residents with good social skills to handle home visits marketing energy-efficiency renovations. Since she gave up social work in an agency for Ventures, she says, "we don't do needs assessments any more. We do strength assessments."

The new economy is a whine-free, take-charge zone. Government and big business stack the deck against many people. So what else is new? All that means is that government and big business aren't likely to solve their problems. Those who would be free must themselves strike the blow. Since 1992, the people of Kapuskasing, behind the spruce curtain of northern Ontario, have been running their own paper mill at a handsome profit. Paper giant Kimberly-Clark wanted to close the mill, but townspeople "weren't prepared to give the right of decision to someone else," says Peter Goth, general manager of Kapuskasing Community Futures. "Once the ownership of the problem was established, the formulation of a resolution—a community buyout—wasn't far behind."

We don't have a crisis of unemployment, poverty or racism, Frances Moore Lappé and Paul Dubois argue in **The Quickening of America.** "The crisis is that we as a people don't know how to come together to solve these problems." Their book presents proven problem-solving strategies from communities across the United States. They all require a comfort level with both conflict and conflict resolution, confrontation and negotiation. They all require leadership that can move from opposition to proposition, from critique to partnership. The new entrepreneurs don't back off from a fight, but feel, like the old suffragist slogan had it, "I will not waste my life in friction when it could be turned into momentum."

It takes all kinds to grow the new economy, one of the reasons why the term partnership is bandied around so often these days. "Criticism is important, but it can't change a light bulb," says Keith Collins, the civil servant who started up Ontario's Green Community Initiative, a runaway success of local economic development paired with energy conservation. Collins brought together unlikely partners—from gas and electric utilities to renovators, building suppliers, bankers, diehard greens and residents' associations—to do $500-million worth of conservation retrofits that saved or made money for everyone. The fit among the partners wasn't always perfect, noses were often out of joint, and arms were sometimes twisted, but in the end there was a win for everyone.

Conflict, it sometimes turns out, is more apparent than real. Corporations rant on about the $200 billion a year they pay to get their pollution emissions down to government standards. Someone should tell them that it costs less than that to move the entire economy toward clean production. The corporations' best bet is to hire "insultants" who'll work through their problems with them, help them move their money from the back end of cleanup to the front end of new products and methods. Corporate failure to do that has less to do with their bottom line than with outmoded structures and hierarchies that can't pick up new possibilities on their radar. The big PR flaks and lobbying firms are only too happy to indulge the fright of big companies and enlist them in a war against regulations. But greens may be better off doing an end-run on the PR firms, who can politically outgun them anyway, and help companies overcome the real problem. "The challenge," says energy conservation consultant Alex MacDonald, "is to set up horizontal relationships with organizations that are structured vertically." That might involve, for instance, partnering a utility, usually run on top-down engineering lines, with community groups that can deliver neighborhood buy-in for conservation programs that reduce residents' costs and boost utility returns by avoiding the need for new energy supply. Those who prefer dragging out blood feuds might consider other professions, such as university teaching or lawyering.

It's easier to be for the working class than in the working class. Those who prefer being lone wolves are better suited as inventors, not entrepreneurs.

Michelle and Pierre Geoffrion run a small and charming inn called L'Aubergine in Quebec's Eastern Townships. They cater to Vermont, New York and Quebec skiers and hikers. The word-of-mouth trade based on their award-winning maple sugar pie and French cuisine keeps them hopping. "We have to distinguish ourselves with our meals because we can't afford to put Jacuzzis in the rooms," is how they explain their business strategy.

Small may or may not be beautiful. For the moment, there's no alternative. As long as the big companies stick to pollution as usual, the new economy will come through the small- and micro-business sector. New entrepreneurs are comfortable with both the limits and opportunities of breaking ground in a genuinely equal opportunity sector of the economy, where, to put a positive spin on it, upstarts and boot-strappers have the field to themselves. But it takes a mindset obsessed with re-engineering. When they have to go to the FFA (family, friends and acquaintances) for a start-up loan, they whittle away at business plans until costs hit rock bottom. They work with equalizers, high talent and high design. They avoid the factors that disqualify them, high tech and big bankrolls. That's a better use of time than holding your breath for the government or bank loan to come through. Daydreamers who prefer the abstractions of the big picture, or who don't like getting down and dirty, are well-served by a variety of sustainable development round tables.

In the midst of an angry farmers' protest against politicians and consumers driving down food prices, Dan Wiens was taken aback by the sight of his own clenched fist waving in the air. What am I doing denouncing consumers, the Winnipeg, Manitoba farmer asked himself. That's when he got the idea to try out community support agriculture, a method of linking farmers directly to customers. Consumers agree to pre-buy a share of a farmer's crop, usually for a little less than what they'd pay for the same quality at a supermarket, but for a lot more than the farmer would get from a broker. The environment also wins because the food travels less and food scraps go back to the farm field, not on to the garbage dump. "What we need to do is not shake our fists," Wiens says, "but offer viable alternatives within our areas of competency."

New entrepreneurs are more into demonstration projects than demonstration protests. "We need the threat of a good example," says Ottawa social investment consultant George Brown. Blaming is as useless as a moral means test. For every evil member of the bourgeoisie, there are 50 McLosers among what H.L. Mencken called the booboisie, who chalk up one-quarter of North American pollution scarfing down fat food, near-bread and krap cheese, driving muscle-head cars, powerboats and weedwhackers, living in monster homes with plastic broadloom inside and pink flamingoes on herbicide-sprayed lawns outside. For every member of the pollutocracy who's made a killing on toxic chemicals, there's a champion of the people who won subsidies for struggling farmers and fishers, unwittingly driving them into chronic overproduction, personal bankruptcy and destruction of their resource base. Making economic amends is not for the vengeful. "Would that the task of decontamination were as simple and pleasurable as decapitation," Andrew Ross notes wryly in **The Chicago Gangster Theory of Life**. CEO turned economic theorist Paul Hawken, author of **The Ecology of Commerce**, taught us that "environmental destruction is not an intention problem, but a design problem." Giving the priority to design, not intent, highlights the needs for talking heads, not falling heads, and points to ongoing learning and action-based dialogue that can overcome shared ignorance, not evil.

Dr. Dean Ornish has a best-selling book and busy clinic that take the new economy to heart. Best-known for his low-fat diet and exercise plan that reverses heart disease at a fraction of the cost of bypass surgery, he also plugs a lifestyle that's high in spirit. The number one killer in North America "is not just physical heart disease," he says. "It's what I call emotional or spiritual heart disease. There's a real hunger for a sense of community and connection."

Like America's beloved Depression-era president FDR, new entrepreneurs are happy warriors. Cheer leaders, they know laughter is the best medicine, and that good on you goes further than good for you. David Engwicht, a former window-washer who turned himself into the world's leading expert on traffic-calming and living streets, says that "the business of change is about giving people a positive experience." He now gift wraps his traffic management strategy as community art. The new transportation planning is as low in guilt trips as it is in costs and pollution.

Cities built for a human scale will "make walking a total delight," says Bob Burco, who planned Portland, Oregon's acclaimed street-rail system on the basis of his people-watching experience sipping wine in European cafés. Now at the Rhode Island School of Design, he promotes public transit that's "more like a cruise ship and less like a sardine can. Big Brotherism isn't successful," he says. "I work hard to make things fun," and he isn't above organizing "bus loads" on fire trucks or hay wagons. John McKnight, Chicago's apostle of grassroots organizing, turned from social work to matchmaking. Instead of labelling clients by their problem, he introduces them around by saying "I have somebody with a gift and I'm looking for a place for the gift to be given." There's no power in negative thinking. Guilt saps energy, joy spreads it, says India's foremost development economist, Vandana Shiva. "If the world is to be conserved for survival," she says, "the human potential for conservation must be conserved first."

In Portland, Oregon, business developers with Ecotrust have come up with 101 little schemes to create jobs while restoring the forest and fishery. Here's one: instead of spraying replanted areas with toxic herbicides to kill off alder, a "weed tree," they let the pioneer tree species do its work, fixing nitrogen in exhausted soil. That saves companies $1,000 an acre on spraying, and saves drinking and fishing water from poisoning. As well, says Ecotrust's Allana Probst, alder are turning out to be "the next paneling fashion, featuring the beauty of the flaw." Not a big deal, but a good deal. It comes from being centered.

Whatever gets us through the decade, the new entrepreneurs are happy to do their little bit, and eager to get on with the first steps. They're not into fire and brimstone threats about global warming judgment days and ozone apocalypse. Most people have a mortgage or rent to pay first and turn off the background noise.

Scare tactics overpower, rather than empower. Panic breeds silly slogans such as "think globally," when it's local thinking that has to be improved. We shouldn't equate world views that have run out of ideas with a planet that has run out of time. The image of a world careening toward disaster sidetracks public discussion into a war of the scientists, those who believe and don't believe the globe is really warming, rather than a dialogue about changes that should be made for their own sake and on their own merits. "It may be better to think of it as an emergency, from which new ideas emerge as a basis for social change," Andrew Ross writes, "rather than as a crisis, for which one finds a solution which is more likely to be expediently exploited in the name of the status quo."

Crisis mongering leads into the arms of central government, the one agency with the power to impose draconian solutions from on high. Whatever your philosophy about a role for government, we can't control that right now. Waiting for Godot is an action-packed thriller compared to Waiting for Government, never mind Waiting for Lefty. New entrepreneurs don't ask what government can do for them, but what they can do without government. The next generation of social advance will come from changes in civil society, not the state.

It's the beginning, not the end, that is nigh, and the next step is to take the next step. "Practice 'rapid inch-up'," advises **Fortune Magazine**. "Take enough tiny steps and pretty soon you outdistance the competition." Like all isms, the lust for final solutions comes from the closed-system thinking that has dominated the first three waves of industrialism, the all-pervasive assumption that manipulation of a few variables will let us conquer the problems of an open-ended and co-evolving world. Conservative voodoo economics, as much as Soviet command economies, are part of the debacle of that push-button fantasy. The new world will not be built, as the great old labor anthem had it, from the ashes of the old. It will come from the cracks and spaces of the old, and spread from there. "Ring the bells that still can ring," singer Leonard Cohen implores in his **Anthem of the 1990s**. "Forget your perfect offering. There's a crack in everything. That's how the light gets in."

Critics should keep to the sidelines, where the going is easy. "The environmental movement has made its reputation in the public mind by stopping things," says David Orr, director of environmental studies at Oberlin College in Cleveland, Ohio. "But now we have to turn the page, and we have to show how the environmental discussion and ecological intelligence can be woven into communities that work better than industrial-technological communities."[2] Turning the page means getting comfortable with the mess of progress. New entrepreneurs know that the perfect is not the enemy of the good. They also have that same confidence in the face of adversity that Alexander Graham Bell had when he was tinkering with inventions to help the deaf, and stumbled on a clue that led him to design the telephone. "When one door closes, another opens," he said. "But we often look so long and so regretfully upon the closed door that we do not see the one which has opened for us."

Buddy Can You Paradigm?
The Fourth Wave and How to Surf It

"In order to live and succeed..., you're going to have to color outside the lines."
Newfoundland Manufacturer's Association[1]

This is a catalogue of opportunities for careers, lifestyles and communities that are healthy, wealthy and wise. You can leaf through it like any other catalogue, looking for items that catch your fancy among more than 101 tried-and-true success stories of bootstrap operations that made good by making a difference. Or you can plunge in, beginning with this chapter, which lays out a problem-solving strategy for identifying and inventing careers that restore the environment (natural capital), heal communities (social capital) and boost productivity (human capital) in one fell swoop.

There's no real need to coin phrases such as corporate re-engineering or community economic development to describe our strategy, not when J.B. Say's 200-year-old definition of the entrepreneur still says it all: the person who "shifts economic resources out of an area of lower and into an area of higher productivity and greater yield." Green community economic development is just a current translation. In a nutshell, it's:

- Green, because the new entrepreneurs substitute services for commodities and talents for toxins.
- Community, because a good neighbor policy replaces import-export grids with home-town partnerships.
- Economic, because the new entrepreneurs go beyond competitiveness to effectiveness and productivity
- Development, because they stretch abilities, not assets.

The force is with this new generation of entrepreneurs. For the time being, they're held back by unfair competition from deadbeat corporations kept on life support with billions of dollars a year in government subsidies.

The new economy is riding the surf of a fourth wave of technical and social change. It will do to Wall Street what rock and roll did to the Andrews Sisters, the computer to the typewriter, the calculator to the slide rule, the compact disc to the vinyl LP, jeans and T-shirts to the dress code, and the Internet to government and corporate monopolies over information and communication.

"Wave," often overworked as a metaphor for change, is helpful here. Wave as in a rough-edged pulse of energy that gathers force while colliding with and absorbing receding waves, with no fixed beginning or end. Wave as in subject and object of such a complex of forces

that it can't be wished into being, manipulated or held back by utopi-
ans, planners or embezzlers. Wave as in wake and undertow, deep cur-
rents with carrying capacity that outlasts the roar and froth of the
tossing surf.

Here's a quick rundown on the four waves of industrialism, with
enough examples to portray the drift of macro-level changes. Though
we think our categories cast new light on overlooked dimensions of
economic change, our purpose is to situate the future that new entrepreneurs are inventing, not conduct a snorefest in economic history.

The first wave, over-rated in standard history texts as The Industrial
Revolution dating from the late-1700s to the late-1800s, had more to
do with marketing and social changes than transformations of manufacturing technology. Its mascots were the railroad and the steam-
boat, which outdistanced horse and wind power, and made long-haul
trade in humdrum objects—not just fine silks, spices and furs—
viable. But the product line of the first industrial revolution was centered on textiles. Slave labor tended the cotton, and child labor
turned it into cheap ready-to-wear for the mass market. The infa-
mous "dark, satanic mills" relied on an impersonal market of casual
labor to displace the skill of cottage-industry crafts with narrow specialties, quickly learned. But this intense division of labor only
worked for soft and shoddy goods with a ready mass market. Services,
such as women's work in the home, were unaffected. The first wave
barely penetrated the metal or building trades, where precision still
required master artisans to handle heavy and durable materials.
That's why the industrial revolution is remembered more as an era of
mean-spirited, iron-fisted scrooges and robber barons than brilliant
inventors.

The second wave, which historians of work call Fordism, continues
to exert a pervasive influence, especially in the organization of governments. Mass production and the assembly line were adapted to a
wide range of new products, thanks to the flexibility in machine
placement and precision tooling brought on by electricity at the turn
of the century. This was the era of smokestack industries, when the
bending and shaping of heavy metals required the smoke and stench
of molten ores. Financed by merchant bankers, the new captains of
industry churned out thousands of standardized products geared to an

impersonal market of consumers for whom name brand meant a corporation, not a person. Unlike the first industrial revolution, many of the new products were destined for the home market, as canned foods and household goods brought the market home. Next to the car, pasteurized and homogenized milk was the quintessential Fordist product. Sterility and uniformity were guaranteed by linear production flows, and by government regulations issued under President Teddy Roosevelt's aptly named Square Deal, even though producers and consumers lived in worlds apart.

By the 1950s, the Indian summer of Fordism's merger with New Deal liberalism, mass production was buoyed by mass consumption brought on by government spending, aggressive advertising and the extension of credit to ordinary people. A chicken in every pot, a car in every garage, two parents and two kids in every suburban home, seemed within reach of all, as the first wave's social pyramid—a few at the pinnacle and many at the bottom—was turned into a beehive, with many in the middle. Until the early 1970s, according to economist Ravi Batra, the happy days rested on a tripod: tariffs that protected home-market wages and profits from international competition, antitrust and public safety laws that protected consumers from abuse by protected corporations, and social legislation and unions that protected workers from abuse by protected companies.

The legs were knocked out from under this tripod by the third wave, commonly referred to as the post-industrial, knowledge-based, or service economy. The third wave continues to define the economy and politics today. Plastic is its synthetic emblem. It's a product of automated process technologies that came on the scene during the 1950s, requiring little in the way of assembly or workers. Plastic can be formulated and controlled in labs, not rowdy steel mills. Made from cheap petrochemicals, it frees corporations from the unpredictable risks and price shocks of materials harvested by decentralized primary producers—of natural cotton, wool and rubber, for instance. Light, flexible and cheap enough to throw away after one use, plastic packages are made for the long-distance, one-way transportation and marketing systems of the few monopolies that can handle the set-up and overhead costs of high-volume production.

McDonalds symbolizes the changes wrought by the retail and service
sectors of the plastic economy. Services once carried out at home,
part of the "love economy"—nothin' says lovin' like somethin' from
the oven, the jingle went—became marketed commodities. Semi-
skilled workers who once enjoyed the income and security befitting
job-specific production savvy were transferred to a McJobs sector,
where the wages and conditions are as low as the learning curve.

McDonalds, along with supermarkets and superstores, is at the forefront of a retailing revolution that dovetails with post-industrialism.
Name-brand manufacturers, mainly hold-overs from the second wave,
have their prices and standards set by third-wave retail giants. The
name in their name brand is no longer worth much of a margin, and
they have to squeeze suppliers and producers to be considered for
shelf space. Computers, which went from oddity to fixture inside of
two decades, supply the data needed by post-industrialism, speeding
up the circulation of goods to feed the maw of corporations with
enormous appetites for cash flow.

Post-industrialism, in short, is the name we give to an economy that
pushes land, farmers, factories and workers to the breaking point so
they can carry a non-productive majority. Lawyers, PR flaks and the
like make up the 26 per cent of the labor force that economists Arjo
Klamer and Donald McCloskey call "sweet talkers."[2] Then come the
speculators and brokers and their hangers-on. That level of parasitism
reinforces the centrality of petrochemicals in the third-wave economy. Farm fertilizers and pesticides, for instance, part of the 80-fold
increase in fossil fuel additives to food over the century, according to
Vaclav Smil's **General Energetics: Energy in the Biosphere and
Civilization,** squeeze more productivity from the land while squeez-
ing skilled tenders off it. The Affluent Society has been replaced by
the new world odor of the Effluent Society. Petrochemicals intensify
the pace of exploitation of resources, and reduce the need for labor-
intensive production methods.

The third wave broke free from the social contract of the second during the 1980s. Unlike second-wave monopolies and production
methods that could co-exist with a government-regulated economy,
third wave-firms in North America opted for a wide-open, deregulat-
ed playing field. They had to deal with the Fordist hangover of high

wages for semi-skilled labor, a challenge they might have met by adopting "dynamic flexibility" and "continuous improvement" strategies that involved workers in their own upgrading in return for stable working conditions. That's what several European countries have done, with the result that they now take productivity as something of a gauge for equality. North American companies, by contrast, opted for the "static flexibility" of cutting costs through layoffs and wage concessions.[3] A chainsaw generation of "denominator managers" slashed staffing costs to jack up short-term profits, without considering long-term impact on the numerators of productivity, assets and net income, Gary Hamel and C.K. Prahalad argue in **Competing For the Future**. "American management on the whole," wrote Edwards Deming, the quality control guru whose ideas were spurned in North America but embraced in Japan, "has a negative scrap value."[4]

On top of the world, multinationals worked the ends of two worlds of development against the middle. From the colonial Third World, they took cheap labor and virgin resources. From the industrial first world, they took cheap infrastructure, such as libraries, schools and cultural institutions, that skilled a sophisticated workforce at public expense. The biggest raid on public infrastructure took the form of government subsidies for cheap energy, which made new lengths in both globalization and automation viable. When gasoline is cheaper than Perrier, there's no reason to wonder why machines are cheaper to feed than workers, or why cheap labor, not closeness to markets, determines where corporations locate. Global production and marketing released corporations from traditional obligations to sustain domestic resources and purchasing power, since they could now buy and sell anywhere. Big corporations went from being tax payers to tax recipients, and by 1986, the conservative **Economist** calculates, lost revenues from industry tax breaks "exceeded the government's entire receipts from the personal income tax."[5]

At the same time, fierce international competition set the pace for lean and mean shedding of middle-income workers. The backbone of Fordist prosperity was broken when some 40 million North American industrial jobs disappeared, and a majority of the workforce suffered a 20-per-cent reduction in income.[6] Deregulation and privatization humbled monopolies that once balanced guaranteed blue-chip profits with decent wages. The beehive social structure of the 1950s and '60s became the hourglass of the 1990s, with a tiny funnel in the middle to let crumbs from the engorged top—the richest one per cent of Americans own 42 per cent of the country's wealth, while the same group in Canada owns 25 per cent[7]—trickle through to the bulging bottom. A detailed study of Massachusetts job creation, for instance, reveals that eight of 10 high-growth occupations offer severely substandard wages, while two enjoy incomes far above average. "There's growth at the high end," says Paul Harrington, who conducted the survey for Northeastern University's Center for Labor Market Studies, "even more growth at the low end and not much in the middle tier."[8]

It's now clear that the third-wave economy is going nowhere fast. Global sourcing has decoupled productivity from competitiveness, and turned trade into a game of musical chairs, with the taxpayers always left standing to pay for the transportation and energy infrastructure along which that great sucking sound travels. Three of Canada's top export sectors to the U.S. are also among its top five importers. We sell you what you used to make, you sell us what we used to make, and this is called competitive. Keep on truckin'. In the process, the productivity of natural and community systems has been ruptured, requiring expenditures on sorry substitutes such as prisons, police and the toxic Superfund.

Not to worry that Third World imports are destroying traditional jobs and communities, the guru of globalization, Milton Friedman, writes in **Fortune.** When cheap imports cause prices to fall, "people can have more —more movies, more income tax software or accountants, more lawsuits, more courses at community college—all requiring more workers," writes Friedman. "People's tastes and wants are infinitely expansible. If you don't have anything to do with people, every man can have his own private psychiatrist."[9] This is a script for social de-skilling that creates an economy based on the charms of the Bundies, the dysfunctional TV family in **Married With Children.** In this knowledge economy from hell, taxpayers spend as much on police and jails as on education; governments tax ignorance with gambling casinos; and universities graduate four times more lawyers than engineers.[10] The **Nation,** counting a million-and-a-half Americans wasting away in prison, calls it "gulag Keynesianism."[11]

Even the big companies can't shake static cling. Business consultants are raking in $17 billion a year, three times their earnings in 1985, putting executives on the couch.[12] Judging from the results, the advice seems to be "if it ain't broke, break it." Many renewal strategies seem like wild goose chases. Companies want loyal and keen employees who'll take risks, and they want to fire any who make mistakes. They talk up "customerizing" their operations, but think customers like playing hide and seek with sales staff and hanging in for the duration at the switchboard: "Your call is important to us,...if you want to talk to an operator, push Z." They want to flatten and lay off middle management, but suffer for want of a bridge within the corporation and with traditional clients.[13] They want to be decentralized after they've absorbed yet another mega-merger, imitating the patterns of bulimics. They want managers to see the big picture, while top executives, clearly missing a few bytes, spend six weeks a year in their paper-full offices hunting up lost files that have been photocopied an average of 19 times.[14] This may be why the North American economy has been clogged by persistently low growth rates and poor increases in productivity since the third wave took over the show in the early 1970s. The U.S. growth rate has averaged 2.4 per cent a year since 1973, a full percentage point below the average for the century before, while productivity rates have crept ahead at one per cent a year.[15]

Computers, on which $1 trillion were spent during the 1980s,[16] compete with bio-technology as the non-smarters of the third-wave knowledge economy. Bio-technology hasn't got much beyond growing tomatoes with the shelf life of Twinkies or crossing seed companies with chemical monopolies which breed plants that take to their pesticides. Harnessed to the information and communications needs of top-heavy corporations, computers can't duplicate the productivity, accessibility or service development they provide to solo operators. Computers have helped dumb-size big corporations, which now churn out 23 trillion pages of paper a year, which take up 60 per cent of corporate time to shuffle.[17] This is pushing the envelope, but not much else.

It seems that computers can't undo the curse of bigness, the law of geometric proportions that Kirkpatrick Sale calls "the beanstalk principle." It was a snap for Jack to outrun the giant, because the giant needed a heart and legs 10 times stronger than Jack's to carry the dead weight of five extra feet in height. Likewise, the formula in Sale's **Human Scale** shows, the transaction costs of one 1,000-person company require 999,999,000 more bits of information than 100 companies with 10 employees each. The bigger they are, the harder they fall, but at least their demise will be well-documented. All that's postponing the collapse of corporate giants under their own weight is the mass of government subsidies to their resource, research, just-in-time and transportation infrastructure.

Government job creation, environmental protection and income maintenance programs are caught in the same bind, throwing money down the black hole of damage control. Government spending used to be almost self-financing, due to the multiplier effect of money passing through local economies—as when pensioners spent their checks at neighborhood retailers, providing a customer base that let retailers and suppliers afford taxes for pensions. But this "pump-priming" has almost no spill-over effect in an economy that functions like a leaking pail—as when pensioners spend their checks on imports at the Price Club. This explains the collapse of political support for programs now deemed to help only the poor, but which once trickled up to the benefit of everyone, and the shift to thinking about welfare spending in terms of dependency, not interdependence. The mid-1990s swing to neo-conservative politics will finish off the last bastion of Fordism, the government bureaucracies still mired in the one-rule-fits-all command and control social engineering of a bygone era. Otherwise, neo-conservatism has as much to do with an opportunity society as Wal-Mart has to vibrant downtowns.

Third-wave governments are hooked on cross-addictions, subsidizing cheap raw materials at one end and recycling at the other, spending taxpayers' money to underwrite both the costs of automation and the unemployment that comes from it. The right hand doesn't know what the left is doing. The best the cross-addicts can do is trumpet environmental industries as a $200-billion-a-year bonanza for inventors who can clean up after the mess. "We might as well celebrate cancer as a growth industry," Paul Hawken writes. "Business must add value to the economy and the society in order to make a positive contribution," he argues. "Reducing the harm caused by growth is a self-canceling contribution at best."18

If the term "knowledge economy" shows the conceit of those who trade in junk bonds, currencies and derivatives, the sure sign that third wavers don't know what's coming down the pike is the term "information highway." Highways move people and goods in one of two directions. The Internet moves ideas in all directions. Highways are engineered for controlled access and speed. Internet exchanges crisscross all boundaries and controls, save for those informally agreed to as "netiquette." The best surprise on a highway offramp is virtual food at some nowheresville chain. The best surprise at the end of the Internet is the fourth wave, protected from predators by the "information briar patch."

When the Internet was still a toy of the military, the next generation of entrepreneurs was already foreshadowing the fourth wave. The most hopeful business story of the last two decades, it is also the most under-rated, partly because it flew in outside the radar of third-wave stereotypes. Who would have thought that 1960s hippies, peaceniks and radicals would have anticipated a new economy? Rejecting the conformity of Fordism at dusk, the sterility of the third wave at day-break, and a war that symbolized what the best and brightest of both waves could sink to, the counter-culture tuned into nascent forces that prefigured the fourth wave—solar power to get off the utility grid, and new sets of simplified needs and communal relationships to get off the consumer grid.

After a decade of big chills, the counter-culture spawned the rock climbers of the fourth wave, who defied the laws of economic gravity by finding toeholds in tiny niches and defining the critical features of the fourth wave—diversity, interdependence, co-evolution and balance in healthy ecosystems and markets alike. Alternative newspapers became fixtures in most cities, providing launching pads for the talents and savage wit of runaway successes such as **Roger And Me** and **The Simpsons.** Crunchy granola, yogurt and red zinger made it on supermarket shelves, while sandals, jeans and T-shirts became dress clothes. Frances Moore Lappé's **Diet For A Small Planet,** and Ithaca's co-op Moosewood restaurant and cookbooks put beans and grains back in the shopping cart. **The Whole Earth Catalogue** led the way in mail-order. Ben and Jerry cornered the market for premium ice cream with the taste of real chunks and social justice. With 360,000 members, Mountain Equipment Co-op, founded by west coast '60s backpackers, thrives at the high end of sports equipment retailing, and sets the standard for quality, customer service and environmental responsibility across the industry.

Pete Camejo, one of Berkeley's foremost '60s radicals and once a socialist candidate for the U.S. presidency, now uses his organizing skills as CEO of Progressive Asset Management, one of several ethical investment houses that handle $600 million in assets, mostly at an above-average rate of return.[19] His counterparts from Canada, Ian Angus, author of the red-hot **Canadian Bolsheviks,** and Dan Tapscott, once the socialist candidate for Edmonton's mayoralty, now ply their skills in radical analysis as the most sought-after consultants in the field of telecommunications, worker empowerment and the "virtual economy." A score of socially conscious credit card and long-distance brokers secure customer loyalty with competitive prices and values-added services, provoking the recent fad of social marketing, now the dominant form of corporate sponsorship across the continent.

While the counter-culture's niche markets provided shelter from second-wave, name-brand monoculture, a series of new social movements gave sharp entrepreneurs a head start working with insights that could take knowledge-based economics to new heights. Former physicist, Friend of the Earther and arms race critic Amory Lovins retrained to become the world's leading thinker on the "soft energy path." He re-conceptualized energy as a service, not just a commodity, and laid the basis for a hard-nosed look at, and highly profitable take-up of, alternative energy. From his back-to-the-land retreat in pastoral Prince Edward Island, John Todd trained the promoters of California's wind-powered utilities, which now supply 15 per cent of the state's electricity market. Todd also nudged the Age of Aquarius into the Age of Aquariums with "living machine" greenhouses that recover nutrients from sewage and lay the basis for agriculture as an urban industry. Get your shit together, indeed.

The mild bunch switched from dope to rope, and turned heads by rediscovering ancient uses of hemp as an alternative to petrochemical-based cording, textiles, plastics and fuels. Richard Rose of Sarah's Natural Foods started with soy-based foods "when most people thought tofu was a martial art," and now, as CEO of one of the fastest-growing companies in America, flogs "deliciously legal" hempeh burgers and "barely legal" hemp cheese, while pushing for the legalisation and re-industrialization of a crop that will turn North America's family farmers into agro-chemical producers.

By the late-1980s, these forms of re-engineering and re-invention hit the mainstream corporate world. Body Shop configured itself as a "multi-local," lending its good name and marketing outlets to rain forest harvesters and Baltimore ghetto manufacturers alike. Body Shop showed how companies with a mission based on core competencies rather than old-line products could open up new markets. The giant Weston food chain, which pioneered green and President's Choice no-name brands, is now preparing to follow suit by using its large consumer base to stimulate jobs in the surrounding economy.

Recycling, which now diverts about 22 per cent of what used to be garbage,[20] re-invents waste as a resource and turns rags into riches, transforming many have-not communities into haves—new paper mills are being built close to the "urban forest" of recycled newsprint, not endangered wilderness, while booming mini-steel mills locate close to already-processed tin cans, not raw iron ore. Unless the old companies would rather fight than switch, counting on Rush Limbaugh's "I'd rather be polluting" dittoheads for sales and piddling away their assets on multi-million dollar lawsuits, they'll also figure out that wise use means re-engineering around core mandates and skills, not outdated products.

Having shown the way in re-engineering, fourth-wave companies are also moving in as "category killers." Aveda's pure fumes and herbal personal care products, marketed in high-end salons and spas, blur the lines between vanity cosmetics and paramedical health support. "Our salons are wellness and beauty centers, not just places to go for a haircut," says Aveda chair Horst Rechelbacher. New wave "naturalistic" medicine, which is where the real health-care reforms of the future lie, has a following among one-third of Americans, involving them in new partnerships that turn patients into producers of their own health through proper eating and exercise. Community Support Agriculture takes customerizing to the limit, providing fresh food direct to the consumer, knocking out brokers and supermarkets, and pocketing their fees to sustain family farms that use organic methods.

The new "neo-traditional" town planning looks to vibrant "main streets," not thoroughfares, as the way to encourage social and economic access, as distinct from mobility. "If you want mobility, build a merry-go-round," street-calming expert David Engwicht tells traffic engineers who haven't caught on to the new categories in urban development. Home-based businesses combine quick turnaround times and personalized service that only individuals can offer with the access to information and communication devices that only huge corporations could once afford.

Community economic development takes re-engineering to down-scale markets. When the going gets tough, the tough stay put, and CED has become the talk of the town in marginalized ghettoes and threatened ghost towns, promising a future based on neighborhood substitutions for imports and welfare. It expresses what Canadian CED theorist Mike Lewis calls the "new partnerships" and "social scaffolding" that underlie entrepreneurship of the future, what the Chicago Center For Neighbourhood Technology calls the "new environmentalism." It's based, Valjean McLenighan argues in **Sustainable Manufacturing: Saving Jobs, Saving the Environment,** on improving efficiency of resource use through "an inclusive process that promotes cooperation among a broad range of players, each with a different agenda, and many of whom are new to the team."

There are hundreds of stories like these in the fourth-wave economy. They're products of wishful thinking, to be sure, or at least of creative and artful thinking, but they're not about mindbending our way out of economic depression with Prozac. Above all, the new entrepreneurs have their fingers on new strategies for productivity that are part of a distinctive technological, economic, social and intellectual web. What's happened to date is only a prelude to what the entrepreneurs of Generation X and Y-not will be able to accomplish once the 10 key features of fourth wave economics take hold.

Nature's Call

Principle 1

Heeds the call of the wild by designing technologies and organizations that evolve in harmony with both the simplicity and the "chaos" of natural systems

*"It's not that humans don't learn faster than nature,
it's just that nature's been at it a lot longer."*
Wes Jackson, Land Institute

"More critically, what the natural infrastructure provides is not products or resources, but functions (like photosynthesis or respiration) whose precise pattern is constantly shifting. The ultimate reason why we should value a high level of biodiversity is that a multi-species system which can draw on the capacities of a large range of different organisms is better able to adapt, by forming new patterns, to its own internal evolution, or to environmental shocks and changes (whether natural or anthropogenic), than is one containing only a limited range of organisms."

Review of Green Imperialism: Colonial Expansion, Tropical Island Edens and the Origins of Environmentalism, 1600 – 1860[1]

Just say know is the prime directive of the new economy, which substitutes resourcefulness for resources by working in harmony with natural systems. Ecological engineering applies the intelligent systems underlying natural cycles to infrastructure that creates new wealth. Its foremost practitioner, John Todd, the Thomas Edison of fourth-wave inventors, grows smart "living machines."

Strolling through his space-age greenhouse in Frederick, Maryland, John Todd looks more like a landscape gardener than a doctor of zoology who's won top scientific and design awards. The greenhouse takes in about 30,000 gallons of raw sewage a day and transforms it into drinkable water within a week. With a staff of two and a capital cost of $472,000, it costs less to build and operate than a conventional sewage disposal plant because it isn't a sewage disposal plant. It's a resource retrieval service that uses the nutrients in human waste to feed millions of animals and plants. After breaking down for a day in an enclosed pool, an airless "bio-reactor" loaded with scavenging bacteria, the water cascades through a series of tanks where algae, duckweed, pennywort, ginger, mint, papyrus, orchids, cypress trees, snails and minnows feast on the remains. Then the water is "polished" in a marsh and gravel bed until it flows out clean.

Todd explains how the intricate root systems of his water-borne plants—their surface area, contact points for the bacteria, is "10,000 times greater than anything we can engineer," he says—convert potential pathogens into elements of a healthy food chain. And a healthy economic chain too, because the plant feeding frenzy turns a cost center of urban living into a profit center. The duckweed can be sold as pig feed, the cypress for Christmas trees, the papyrus for fine art paper, the minnows for fish bait, the orchids to flower shops.

Living machines come from a new brand of stewardship at the center of the emerging scientific paradigm. Ecological engineering is a "convergence of biology and materials science," Todd says. This understates his revolutionary blending of ultra-modern building materials with the latest scientific revelations about the universe.

Chaos theory and the Gaia hypothesis are today's equivalents of the law of gravity or theory of relativity. They have not had the social or economic impact usually attached to scientific breakthroughs, probably because they've fallen on the stony ground of entrenched superstition. According to creation theologians such as Thomas Berry and Matthew Fox, western religion has been driven since the fourth century by other-worldly obsessions linked to notions of original sin and the fall from Eden into a hostile planet that had to be tamed and overcome.[2] The Renaissance-era fathers of modern science, Francis Bacon and René Descartes, came from this tradition when they set out formal, linear methods to conquer the external world by manipulating laws governing inanimate objects.[3] Likewise for modern sewage systems laid out in grids to evacuate the city's "filth," monuments to a scientific culture that dis-aggregated cycles of life and decay in order to triumph over disorder.[4]

Rejecting that tunnel vision, Todd embraces James Lovelock's Gaia hypothesis, which holds that all elements on the planet are alive and co-evolving in dynamic relationships. He also follows chaos theory, which works with the surprises of a universe with a "mind" of its own. The new wisdom doesn't treat earth like dirt, just another input to be upgraded with chemicals, but as a living entity with hundreds of thousands of micro-organisms per square inch. Nor does post-Age of Reason science treat the environment as something to be cleaned up, or pollution as a problem that can be beaten. Todd prefers the term ecology to environment, since it implies living connections. This is where he's coming from when he defines ecological engineering as a "new design science for the post-petroleum era," based on "a careful meshing of human purposes with the larger patterns and flows of the natural world." Thus, living machines, powered by the sun and the natural cycles of life and decay.

The toilet-trainer of the new economy, Todd has perfected his greenhouses to the point where they can finance a bottom-up reconstruction of production systems. As incidentally as plants turn potential pathogens into safe food, Todd's engineered gardens get around the exporting of sewage and the importing of food. With living machines alchemy, a problem becomes a solution. Sewage plants become grounds for urban agriculture and aquaculture, with a nutrient base and economy of space that allow city neighborhoods to become self-reliant in food production.

"Sustainable agriculture is a design dance with the natural world."

North Carolina landscape designer Chuck Marsh

The best fertilizer on a farmer's field, it's been said, is the farmer's footstep. Bringing nature's cycles back full circle takes more than scientific design. It requires intensive management by skilled workers who follow through with their work. Sixty dairy farmers and 40 staff with the CROPP co-op in Lafarge, Wisconsin, are putting that culture back into agriculture, and making knowledge the only additive in their food.

Harriet Behar finished university at Madison, Wisconsin, in the 1970s and decided to become a back-to-the-lander. Since 1989, she's been marketing director for Organic Valley milk products, sold for a premium price across the continent. The co-op helps members beat the odds in a state where three dairy farmers a day end up in bankruptcy.

For organic dairy farmers, back to the land means letting their cows out of the barn and onto pasture. Unlike conventional dairy operations that deliver silage to cows cooped up in the barn, CROPP herds feed on fresh grass. As farmers turn their attention to growing quality grass, they find that "the real gold that comes off a farm is manure," Behar says, because it's the secret to prime soil and feed. The grass is greener on the outside of the barn. The added bonus is that the cows are less stressed in their natural environment and need less veterinary care and antibiotics. Altogether, that keeps costs down to the point where low volumes can still produce a decent income.

For organic dairy farmers, back to the land also means doing their own research. They find that rotational grazing allows new grass to recover quickly, that cats do a better job on mice than poisons, that wasps eat the worms that attack their orchards, that setting aside habitat for "beneficials" (natural predators of pests) is cheaper and healthier than spraying pesticides. To mimic natural cycles, "you have to be an open-minded observer, and let the land and your friends teach you," Behar says. That extra knowledge fetches them a premium price, especially for cheeses and cultured butters made without toxic cleaners or fumigants. "Value-added is the quality of the finished product, as close to pure as we can get," says Behar.

Back to the land extends to customer relations, since co-op members see themselves as raising food, not turning out commodities. "Farmers and consumers working together for a healthy planet" is the co-op's motto. "I have 60 marketing assistants," Behar says of dairy farm members, who handle in-store promotional tastings, and bring along pictures of their homesteads to show off their family-farm brand. "The customers fawn on them, and they love it. It gives them such pride," she says. And they bring their knowledge about retailing and marketing back to the land. The co-op invites the public to six field days a year, each drawing about 300 people. Lafarge, once the second-poorest county in the state, has become a tourist destination, and plans are afoot to build a model farm where travelers and students can connect to where their food comes from.

"We're challenged as mankind has never been challenged before to prove out maturity and our mastery, not of nature, but of ourselves."

Rachel Carson[5]

Mimicking nature's economy means learning to extract the fullest value from natural and human cycles. That means laying off commodities, not workers. Here are some trends to watch for as the economy moves toward "add skills and stir."

The Great Indoors

A new $40-million high-rise in downtown Toronto has re-invented the wall. The entrance to Canada Life Assurance's office tower features a tropical floral mural as breathtaking in its potential to revolutionize the building industry as in its beauty. It's referred to as a "breathing wall." Water trickles down lava rock where some 8,000 ferns and mosses hang into an aquarium that hosts water lilies, orchids, lilies, bamboo, fish, frogs and snails. The kaleidoscope of 250 plant and animal species is an experiment in bringing the great outdoors to corporate headquarters, where it can clear the jungle breath known as indoor air pollution, said by the Environmental Protection Agency to be the fourth largest environmental threat to Americans. Often as much as 10 times thicker than the air outside, the poor quality of office air—tight buildings commonly seal in off-gases from petrochemicals in rugs and furniture, fumes from toxic toners, inks and cleaners, as well as harmful bacteria and dust mites that flourish in mechanical ventilating systems—is a plague in many office towers.

David House, lead hand in the construction, thinks the experiment will clear the air for a new way of financing office buildings. If absenteeism and other costs go down over the life of the building, cutting edge developers, as in Japan, will be able to warranty their properties and regain some of the up-front money they spent doing the job right. "True economy is not just more miles to the gallon; it's more years to the car," says House. If the experiment continues to succeed, it can be adapted to heritage buildings, homes, even cars, he says. This will confirm the experience of NMB Bank in Amsterdam, which incorporated a bright tree- and plant-filled atrium in its head-quarters to breathe oxygen into the building. Combined with other people-friendly designs, the atrium reduced energy use by 40 per cent and employee absenteeism by 25 per cent.[6]

For breathing wall designer Wolfgang Amelung, the beauty of his living mural stands on its own merits. It's a showcase for the com-pany. It will be used as a board room for meetings that promote brainstorming, not the linear thinking that comes from think tanks featuring sensory deprivation. And it shows off his philosophy that "art and science are merging. The best science is the most creative art, proof that we're so in touch with nature that we can dance with it."

The breathing wall is more than a pretty rock face. Grown over vol-canic rock, the tropical garden draws nutrients from the air, not soil — which sidesteps problems of mold from soil microorganisms fes-tering in the warm indoors. Some plants were selected because they're known to absorb specific toxins. NASA researchers have identified a host of common plants that thrive on elements that are toxic for humans, and can remove as many as 70 per cent of indoor poisons.[7] Chrysanthemum and Peace Lilies filter benzene, for in-stance, while philodendron and poinsettias filter formaldehyde.

However, the scientific advance comes from designing an ecosystem with a stability of its own. It's the very vitality and complexity of the rock garden and aquarium that "will be the engine of an air-cleaning machine," says Guelph University greenhouse expert Mike Dixon, who's monitoring the system. A wizard of the secret life of plants, Amelung is not interested in "turning plants into another slave tech-nology." He's designing an ecosystem with the ability to work out its own way of handling impurities in the air, even if we can't trace this back to a particular cause. His theory is that the more complex an ecosystem, the stronger its immune system, the more able it is to check, counter, marginalize, absorb or neutralize turbulence, in this case polluted air.

Amelung is a devotee of chaos theory. Chaos is why computer-laden meteorologists can't predict the weather any better than farmers' almanacs. At about the time that Bob Dylan decided you don't need to be a weatherman to know which way the wind blows, mathematician Edward Lorenz came to the more mind-blowing conclusion that weatherpersons didn't know which way the wind would blow. There's too much information to codify, and an error at the 20th decimal overtakes the data base after 20 events. In his famous metaphor, Lorenz said that butterflies flapping their wings precipitated a chain of events sometimes culminating in hurricanes.

Chaos theory deals with the fact that the world is not linear—calling chaos "non-linear science" is like calling zoology "the study of non-elephant animals," remarked an early evangelist of disorder, Stanislaw Ulam—and, therefore, the world is not subject to the straight-arm methods of western science. It turned the mathematics and physics worlds upside down during the 1970s, according to James Gleick's standard work,[8] and began influencing biology and medicine, as well as physics. But the realities chaos portrays have been spurned by professions that see the random unemployment written on the wall, most notably economists, personnel managers and building engineers. Building systems, from high-rises to sewage pipes, are still designed according to the time-honored scientific methods, which exclude the disorder of the outside world in order to maximize control over the inside world. It's a jungle out there, the engineers say. Bring the jungle indoors, replies Amelung.

Working The High End

One of Wolfgang Amelung's specialties with high-end customers is landscaping yards so swimming pools don't have to be chlorinated. Chlorine is expensive, stings the eyes, and creates risks of toxic emissions, even when handled properly. When improperly handled, we're reminded why it was first used as poison gas during World War I. Leakage also speeds thinning of the ozone layer, when Pacman-style chlorine molecules gobble up the protective layer in the upper atmosphere. When put properly in the pool, new research indicates, chlorine causes higher than normal rates of asthma among competitive swimmers.[9] When handled legally afterwards, and dumped into sewers rivers and lakes, volatile chlorine hooks up with industrial toxins in long-term poisonous relationships called persistent organochlorines.

The pervasiveness of chlorine sterilization, Amelung says, reflects the dominance of low-order thinking, the sign of minds trained to seek one-dimensional solutions to complex, multi-faceted problems. The sterile mindset aims to eliminate algae, the mark of a low-order ecosystem inhospitable to diverse life forms, by rendering the system even more sterile, using chlorine to leadeth us to still waters. The syndrome is hard to break out of. "There are three types of mistakes," say two leading popularizers of chaos theory, Jack Cohen and Ian Stewart. "Errors made within the model are the easy type to spot. Harder are the errors made in the explicit assumptions that lie behind the model. The hardest of all to spot are the implicit assumptions in the world view that suggested the model."[10]

Amelung follows a strategy of aiming high. Where chlorine conquers nature by creating artificially lifeless water vulnerable to algae slime the moment the death-support system is turned off, Amelung works with nature to create diversity and movement—the secret to how nature keeps lakes clean without chlorine. For about $10,000, he links the pool to a pond about 20 feet round. The pond has a "reaction chamber," an anaerobic planter box stuffed with mud and water plants that break down unhealthy bacteria. The chamber can't be seen for plants and flowers on the surface, which suck up nutrients from below, creating nutrient-deficient, that is, clear water. The more species the merrier, says Amelung, since diversity increases the stability of an ecosystem, its own capacity for "intelligent" adaptive behavior. As chaos theorists would predict, the dynamics of complex systems lead to their own self-regulating simplicity, and they do it for free.[11]

There are some intriguing parallels here. Pasteurization performs for milk and juice what chlorine performs for water, kills off the harmful bacteria. Milk is a livelier medium than water. That's why it goes bad if it's not sterilized, refrigerated or, weird idea that it is, drunk fresh. Pasteurization got around the problem of a long-distance food system by boiling every living thing out of live food, killing off the harmful bacteria before they spread, but also the enzymes and serum proteins which make digestion and assimilation of nutrients easier.[12] As it turns out, the pasteurization agenda, outlined in Bruno Latour's **The Pasteurization of France,** had less to do with making milk safe than it did with wresting control over city infrastructure from social reformers, who sought social and economic solutions to the problems of urban overcrowding. That control was handed over to labs, where scientists isolated germs, "finally made smaller than the group of men who can then dominate them," Latour says. Chlorine was welcomed for similar reasons, since it solved the problems of water-borne infections in turn-of-the-century cities without requiring a rethink of engineered alternatives to dumping human sewage into water supplies in the first place.

The other obvious instance of low-order control mechanisms is the workplace. What passes for scientific management brings order out of chaos by imposing top-down rules that keep people in their places. The workplace becomes a low-order ecosystem, protected from the outside world by massive injections of compartmentalization. As the 1980s showed, however, organizations that live by the rule book die by the rule book. Way back in the 1970s, the late Eric Trist, a brilliant theorist of industrial democracy, envisioned self-regulating teams of multi-skilled workers highly adaptable to "turbulent environments" as the pathway to high-order problem-solving. His views are now being extended by the Santa Fe Institute, and gaining a corporate hearing.

"We have to start taking responsibility for building higher order systems," says Amelung. "They're like a fountain of youth for us."

Your Swamp Or Mine

A thousand flowers are blooming in the field of naturalized sewage treatment, confirming and extending the basic principles of natural restoration systems. They all offer beautiful and chemical-free alternatives that come in far below the typical cost of $3,750 per user hooked up to conventional sewage and toxic treatment methods.

In Bear River, Nova Scotia, about 90 miles northwest of Halifax, Todd's methods have been applied to replace a system of individual septic tanks. Duckweed and iris thrive in tanks and the roots of willow, dogwood, banana and fig trees dangle in water supported by floating nets. "People keep asking why we haven't done it earlier," manager Carole Armstrong said on hearing the town won the 1995 Sustainable Communities Award.[13]

Retired Cornell University environmental physicist Edgar Lemon is developing an outdoor system that can function even during the winter, when plants and animals are dormant, opening the door to better treatment in the thousands of sewage lagoon systems across North America and for isolated northern communities. Lemon and the Friends of Fort George have built an exiperimental add-on to a sewage lagoon system that treats the effluent of 1,100 Niagara-on-the-Lake residents. The project is called SWAMP—the Sewage Waste Amendment Marsh Process. Instead of adding alum and chlorine in a $7-million plant—with results that are still toxic to Lake Ontario—an expanded SWAMP method would release cleaner water for $2 million. The sewage liquid flows into open-air lagoons, then through boxes called cells which contain bulrushes, weeds and a layer of soil peculiar to the area, which has been found to be a potent cleanser. In warm weather, the fauna and flora take up sewage nutrients and produce oxygen, critical in the breakdown of bacteria. In the winter, the layer of soil does the work, converting and storing the food (including phosphorous, nitrogen and ammonia) until the plants and micro-organisms can use it again in their rush of spring feeding. A particular pulsing schedule floods the cells deep below the soil surface, in unfrozen ground, and causes oxygen to be pulled into the bed throughout the year, without any need to heat a greenhouse. The water produced from this system is clean, drinkable and surpasses government water quality standards, accolades that few conventional systems warrant. Nevertheless, the intellectually challenged in the regional government insisted on the $7-million-dollar non-solution, rather than extending the innovative wetlands over 10 acres.

Inventors are also perfecting their use of natural materials and systems to clean up nasty toxins in the ground. In Burlington, Vermont, there's an experiment using worms to digest and neutralize sewage sludge. And the University of Waterloo's Robert Gillham has found that tons of sand and iron filings can handle chlorinated solvents that are threatening ground water. The "magic sand" seems to break down the compounds into harmless chlorides and ethanes. The U.S.

military is actively considering using this patented method to clean up its mess.[14] And, in various brownfield sites across the U.S., vegetation is being tried out as a means of removing toxins from the soil. In a process called phytoremediation, poplars, goldenrod, fescue, duckweed, arrowroot, hornwort, parrot feather, Eurasian milfoil and some types of algae are put to work doing what comes naturally to them.[15]

In reviewing his own 20 years' of work, Todd says "I'd like you to keep in mind that you're basically looking at Univacs. These were the 1955 computers where they knocked out the sides of buildings so that the computer could fit in to run the insurance company. And keep in mind the laptop of today and the great differences of only a few decades."[16]

An Apple A Day

Natural healing systems will renew medicine as much as engineering, perhaps by returning the profession to the words of its founder, Hippocrates, who said "let food be your medicine and medicine your food."

Western doctors have long resisted the view that illness comes from nutritional deficiency and the consequent breakdown of the body's immune system. Before Pasteur put germs at the center of treatment strategies, doctors were into bleeding and surgery. Since Pasteur, they've been into germ-killing drugs and surgery. It was military, not medical, officers who happened on vitamin C as the cure for scurvy—whence the term "limey" to describe British sailors who sucked limes as a cure. Medical schools remain slow learners. Nutrition is now offered as a separate course at all of 34 medical schools in North America. That's 34 more than a decade ago.[17]

Food is not what the doctor ordered. You eat food when you're well, you take medicine when you're sick. "In our western tradition, we segment everything," says Maine herbalist Corinne Martin.[18] That way, professional boundaries can be maintained, and farmers, nutritionists and holistic health promoters aren't competing on the same turf. Food doesn't lend itself to patents or prescriptions. There's no body part diagnosis that can be pinned on "feeling lousy." There's no advanced specialty associated with the immune system like there is with feet, ear, nose and throat, face lifts or breast enlargements—likely accounting for the slow medical start on AIDS. No blood, urine or stool tests, no X-rays to shoot before advising patients to eat their veggies. But a big role to play as teacher or advocate. Nutrition informs a distinct and alternative medical strategy, which Nobel laureate Linus Pauling called orthomolecular, working to strengthen the body's capacity by meeting its nutrient needs. Pauling referred to conventional drug-based medicine as "toximolecular."[19]

The food industry logically stands to gain from selling nutrition, though government regulators keep the barrier between food and medicine high by forbidding ads that promote healing qualities of foods. That legal barrier could be jumped as easily as any others, except that food companies also prefer drugs over honest food. With mass production methods, it's cheaper to refine nutrients out of coarse foods, then inject an alphabet soup of vitamins, than to use slow-grinding millstones. Vitamin E and essential fatty acids go rancid quite quickly, and reduce shelf life. Chemicals stay fresh for so much longer.

The pill people have as little to gain from nature-sourced health. Pills bespeak the reductionist mentality, taking a complex food down to its simplest ingredient, hopefully one that can be duplicated in a lab and stored on a shelf. But, as chaos theory would suggest, there's more to food than superstar minerals and vitamins. There's taste, which triggers saliva. There's timed release, as complex carbohydrates are digested and broken down. There are phytochemicals, which ensure that vitamins and minerals are assimilated and balanced.[20] "We don't know the active factors or ingredients" in vegetables that prevent cancer, says National Cancer Institute researcher Regina Ziegler. "We don't know what to put in the pills."[21]

To boot, pills cost more than most of the foods that meet the body's requirements. There are several standard books that list food constituents, with enough options for any taste buds or budgets.[22] As a general rule, the cheaper the food is, the better it is for you. That's the only advantage to a food system that degrades food to entertainment and filler. Food has other advantages over pills. The package is recyclable. The wrappings, potato skins for instance, are often nutri-

tious, which can't be said for popular sugar-coated pills, or the Vitamin E pills used in the famous study that debunked E's curative
powers—the coating was laced with carcinogenic coloring.[23]

Medical science is fast catching up with consumer interest. Every
week, a prestigious medical journal reports a new study linking nutrition and disease prevention. An orange a day reduces stroke rates
among seniors.[24] Garlic, now the catsup of intellectuals, knocks rates
of stomach cancer and heart attacks down a full level.[25] Vitamin E,
easily available in wheat germ, lowers the rate of coronary disease by
at least 58 per cent.[26] Beans and barley lower cholesterol levels. The
list keeps getting longer, and the evidence is irrefutable. Dr. David
Jenkins put epidemiological research behind his **New England
Journal of Medicine** report that beans are good for the heart. "With
restricted health budgets, it's becoming terribly important for people
to have means of controlling disease in their own hands," he says.[27]
Patient, heal thyself.

A few corporate executives are also catching on. Robert Schad,
president of Husky Injection Moulding Systems, the world technical
leader in plastic fabrication, is also a health enthusiast. The company
cafeteria subsidizes vegetarian meals. Spinach and ricotta cheese
crèpes or vegetarian moussaka with rice and salad sell for $3.95, a
dollar less than meat dishes. The incentive pays off. Drug costs for
Husky employees average $154 a year, one-third the norm for indus-
trial operations, while absenteeism averages 2.4 days a year, a quarter
of the industrial norm.[28]

Treating foods as medicine, and farmers as health workers, should
help overcome North American stinginess when it comes to paying
for quality food. We now spend less than 15 per cent of our disposable income on food,[29] then pay for cheap food with our lives.
Paying doctors and pharmacists less, and farmers more, is a big part of
what in-your-face economics is about. It will be second nature in the
new medical ethos.

Over-The-Counter Foods

There's a difference between cures for illnesses and drugs. With drugs, the pushers want your repeat business. Supermarkets and drug stores have got repeat business down pat. One set of aisles has junk that gets you coming. The next set of aisles gets you going with laxatives, antacids and hemorrhoid treatments.

When the body won't expel the crap you've ingested, it's cheaper to go to the right food aisle and skip the drugs. There's no reason to be spending $300 million a year on laxatives, when the cure can be as easy and safe as eight glasses of water a day, snacks of high fiber crackers, and lots of fruit.[30] Vitamin E ointment applied topically heals broken skin better than Preparation H, according to Linus Pauling.

Over-the-counter drugs are another scam. Frequent use of painkillers —three or more times a week—actually induces grinding headaches and migraines, leading Canadian medical researchers have found, because they suppress the release of the body's natural painkillers.[31] Health Action International, backed by the World Health Organization, charges that four-fifths of cough and cold remedies are ineffective.[32] There's no evidence that they relieve children's colds, the **Journal of the American Medical Association** reports.[33] And drug warnings that say "Keep medicine out of reach of children" should warn "Keep this medicine out of reach of everyone," Pauling said. Many of these remedies repress symptoms that are part of the body's healing strategy such as fevers that pasteurize harmful bacteria or runny noses that drain them.

Foods are more reliable over-the-counter cold warriors. Garlic is widely respected as a broad-spectrum infection fighter. Colorado herbalist Stephen Buhner says bacteria haven't developed resistance to garlic, as they have to lab-made formulas, because garlic's chemistry is so complex, with 33 sulfur compounds, 17 amino acids and a dozen other compounds that confound germs. A few extra cloves of garlic also keep other people from getting close enough to breathe in your germs. Hot peppers, sometimes called "nature's version of Robitussin," clear congestion. Chicken soup has won folk and scientific acclaim as a flu remedy.[34] Feed a cold, starve the drug companies.

Farmaceuticals

A classic children's story, Heidi, tells of a girl who couldn't be cured by expensive drugs, doctors and bed rest, but cured herself on the cheap with whole foods, clear mountain air and sun. Though the medical majority hasn't banned the book from libraries, it treats the message as a fairy tale and continues on its search for synthetic drug cures.

Reductionist medicine and the petrochemical industry have been an item since the turn of the century. Reductionism, a legacy of the ancient Greeks' faith in the power of reason to delve to the abstract essence of messy realities and extract the one causal element, is a match made in heaven for the petrochemical industry, which can isolate the carbon in coal and oil to duplicate or mimic the active ingredient in plant chemistry. But like platonic love, this leaves out a few active ingredients, enzymes and energies.

The steps in the economic carbon chain are pretty simple: doctors gain a monopoly over issuing prescriptions, and naturalistic practitioners are branded as quacks; the drug companies gain a monopoly over research that churns out cures in centralized labs; the government issues patent protection and a legal go-ahead for the drug; the drug companies shower freebies on doctors and medical journals and buy into hospitals that retain doctors who issue prescriptions; the government pays the drug costs for the biggest customers, seniors.[35] And Greens think ecosystems work in tight circles!

Tramping through a field of weeds outside his home in Carnarvon, Ontario, Dr. Gord Smith points out plantain, a good expectorant, and burdock, good for eczema. A weed is just a herb whose virtues have yet to be discovered, he says, citing Emerson. "They can knock out the pharmaceutical industry because they're low-cost, decentralized, and don't need a doctor's prescription," he says. Like most naturopaths, Smith looks for plants that can fortify the body's capacity to ward off illness by giving an assist to cleansing organs such as the liver and kidney. This is in keeping with the views of the great medical researcher and ecologist René Dubos, whose research opened the doors to the "miracle drugs" of the 1930s and '40s. Dubos repudiated the name given to those drugs, "antibiotics," literally meaning "against life." Dubos called the drugs anti-bacterial, and fought to focus medical attention on bolstering the body's own capac-ity to counteract harmful bacteria. He likened the "conquering mentality" behind magic-bullet drugs to the vigilante-thinking behind cowboy pulp novels. "In the crime-ridden frontier town the hero, single-handedly, blasts out the desperadoes who were running ram-pant through the settlement," he wrote. But, "the death of the villains does not solve the fundamental problem, for the rotten social condi-tions which had opened the town to the desperadoes will soon allow others to come in, unless something is done to correct the primary source of trouble."[36]

After decades of neglect, herbal remedies are making a comeback, opening up new health specializations and training, spawning a range of new personal care companies. There are several explanations for the renewed interest. People with chronic problems looking for an-other opinion and parents of kids with recurrent ear infections, are finding their way to alternative cures. Multiculturalism, that threat-ening form of globalization, introduces the wisdom of disparaged cul-tures with a heritage of folk medicine. The AIDS crisis highlights the centrality of fortifying immune systems. Greens, on the lookout for a health or economic angle to rain forest protection, have publicized the value of wild medicines that proliferate there. Edward Wilson, author of **The Diversity of Life,** wants to see chemical prospecting for cures replace logging in the tropical forests.

Meanwhile, the magic bullets in the corporate drug arsenal are losing their potency. And broad-spectrum antibiotics have got the same problem as chlorine. They kill the good guys as well as the bad guys, so yeasts and other infections aren't checked, leading many people to check out alternative medicines.[37] "Superbugs" are riding the natural selection curve, increasingly easy when antibiotics are not treated as a precious resource with a limited time horizon—livestock account for half the antibiotic use in North America, and provide an oppor-tunity for superbugs to pop up whenever they're misused. Dr. Calvin Kunin of Ohio State University says the antibiotic era will be over by 2020, when antibiotics won't work on traditional childhood diseases such as pneumonia and bronchitis. "We must husband these valuable antibiotics as carefully as possible and use them only when needed, properly and then we can prolong their usefulness,"[38] he says.

Herbal medicine is fast gaining scholarly stature as well as public acceptance. Echinacea, produced from the Purple Coneflower of the western plains and standard in traditional Native medical kits, has made the hit parade of cold cures.[39] Marijuana, referred to as **The Prohibited Medicine** by Harvard professors Lester Grunspan and James Bakalar, has proven abilities to treat glaucoma and reduce the side effects of chemotherapy. Dr. Michael Jenike, affiliated with the Harvard Medical School, favors St. John's Wort to treat depression.[40] Crushed and rubbed on the skin, basil is a non-toxic mosquito repellent.[41] Ginseng is highly regarded as a tonic.[42] Raspberry leaves are commonly used to strengthen uterine muscles for infant delivery.[43] The five-century reputation of feverfew for heading off migraines is deserved, says Dr. Marek Gawell of Toronto's Sunnybrook Hospital.

Botanicals, as they're often called, are helping new-age drug companies bloom. Santa Fe Botanical Research and Education Project sells herbal drops of dandelion root for constipation, feverfew for migraine, oats and ginseng for stress, and juniper berries for bladder inflammation, for example. While there are research and equipment costs, production is easier to decentralize than for petrochemical drugs. Once the medical research has been done, distillation technology that extracts essential oils is the basic equipment. Since herbal remedies give pride of place to energy from the soil and sun, they're a boon for licensed wild-craft harvesters, organic farmers and folks with small acreage. Ginseng is already a $1-billion-a-year export industry.[44] The 1995 convention of the American Society for Horticultural Science showcased Quebec's experiment employing 50 farmers to grow five of the herbs used in a popular tonic by Matol, which previously imported all its herbs from Europe, where the soil is contaminated by heavy metals after centuries of industrial pollution.[45] Farmers will be the main beneficiaries of the new economy's war on drugs.

Labor-Savers

Working with natural cycles can't start too early. Birthing, as practiced in hospital delivery rooms, has been described by cultural anthropologist Robbie Davis Floyd as a "technocratic rite of passage." Multiple ultrasounds are a highly questionable use of $1 billion a year, according to leading scientific bodies.[46] So are various forms of "labor augmentation," including unnecessary cesareans. The system is high on short-term technical interventions to overcome the "inadequacies" of women's bodies, and low on continuous care and bedside manners that enhance bodily flows. Of 60 million birth-related visits to specialists each year, 70 per cent take less than 15 minutes.[47] "Through these procedures, the natural process of birth is deconstructed into identifiable segments, then reconstructed as a mechanical process," says Davis Floyd. "Birth is thereby made to appear as though it conforms, rather than challenges, the technocratic model of reality."[48]

By contrast, says Vicki Van Wagner, who helped win recognition for midwives as an independent profession in Ontario, "what we try to do is give really good human support, so people don't go for cesareans or epidurals or give up on breast-feeding because they didn't get enough human help." Scores of studies in many countries confirm that midwives provide excellent care at a fraction of the standard medical cost. That's partly because of preparatory work with the parents beforehand, which reduces the numbers of epidurals and cesareans, and partly because their fees are lower than doctors. Savings from midwifery are commonly estimated at more than $2 billion a year across North America.[49] The savings also create jobs. In place of inappropriate technology, Florida expects to employ 950 midwives when it reaches its goal of 50 per cent midwife deliveries by the turn of the century.[50]

Laying On Of Hands

An increasingly popular hands-on healing method is chiropractic, which features exercises and manipulations that restore alignment of the skeletal system, without the use of drugs. According to health economist Pran Manga's comprehensive study for the Ontario health ministry on **The Effectiveness of Chiropractic Management of Low-Back Pain,** the province of 10 million people could save $600 million a year on medical visits and $1.4 billion in lost work time by recognizing chiropractors' expertise and giving them gatekeeper status for back problems.

As openness toward the healing traditions of other cultures increases, there will be more opportunities for health professionals and para-professionals who specialize in enhancing the body's latent curative powers. The World Health Organization approves acupuncture, which pinpoints locations controlling bodily functions, for relief of pain, asthma and constipation. The University of Alberta offers the only university-sanctioned acupuncture training on the continent, and is fully booked with students into 1998.[51] At the para-professional level, massage by trained practitioners works out kinks in back and neck muscles better than doctors' dispensing of pain- or inflammation-suppressing drugs, which only mask the symptoms.

Therapeutic touch is now recognized as part of a healing strategy by the Ontario College of Nurses.[52] Preemies who are gently stroked three times a day gain more weight and leave hospital earlier than those who aren't, says Dr. Tiffany Field, professor at the University of Miami School of Medicine and founder of the Touch Research Institute. She has also confirmed that massage can improve sleep, relieve depression and help young women with eating disorders.[53]

You have to wonder how touching ever got forgotten. Maybe parents' power to kiss their kids' cuts and bruises better will soon leave the world of quack folk remedies, and come to be studied in learned journals that will startle the medical world with the news that body and mind are related.

There's a reason why this recognition is late in coming, and why it comes from outside the dominant medical professions. The bias against touchy-feely runs deep in the western medical tradition, says New York psychologist Matthew Fried, a specialist in mind-body therapies. Ever since the ancient Greeks, those who work with their hands have been looked down on, as when a teacher describes little Jonny as good with his hands and really means he's stupid. Thus, with the exception of surgeons, who once doubled as barbers, professionals don't work with their hands. Professional schools teach the importance of maintaining clinical distance. Likewise, Fried says, western religions have entrenched the division and antagonism between body and soul, the world of flesh and spirit. So it has come to pass that "medical specializations are sortings of people that are actually distortions. We haven't been able to find the similarities among the differences, or the differences among the similarities."

Physical therapist Millie Waldman, who shares an office with Fried, says the new healing paradigms challenge fee-for-service doctor-patient relationships based on passive consumerism of expert prescriptions. Alternative or holistic medicine relies on informed patients who take charge of their health and get in touch with diet, exercise and lifestyles that align mind and body. "Type A personalities are threatened by the self-awareness required," she says, but embracing empowerment is key to the cure of many ills. "Powerlessness, the inability to feel you can make a difference, starts when you stop trusting your own body and have to go to experts to make up for the inadequacy," Waldman says. "Rejecting that makes you as much a threat to the system as a revolutionary."

What's called evolutionary or Darwinian medicine is also entering its stride. This latest twist in learning from the wisdom of the body, or Palaeolithic correctness, has hit the bookstores with Dr. Randolph Nesse's **Why We Get Sick,** and Dr. S. Boyd Eaton's **The Palaeolithic Prescription.** The argument is that the body was bio-engineered in tough and demanding stone-age times before doctors and drug companies got into the act. "We're Stone Agers in the fast lane," says Eaton, but our eating and healing habits aren't in touch. Stone age diets, rich in fiber and low-fat wild meat, kept cholesterol levels low. Fevers were the body's way of turning the heat up on harmful bacteria and killing them off. Morning sickness was a defense against tainted foods that could damage the fetus, it's also speculated, and there are risks to drugs that suppress it.[54]

Eco Stations

Other than PR hacks with water utilities, everyone knows that North American water isn't fit for human consumption. One look at the black swill of melted snow on city streets, a quick mental note that this is tomorrow's drinking water, and greens don't have to bring in a scientist to prove the municipal water supply isn't good for you. The EPA rates three per cent of the water supply as safe for drinking.[55] Some of it's little better suited for cleaner fluid or developing photos.

Water that's not fit to drink tells us something is wrong. For starters, there are about 350 persistent industrial toxins in the Great Lakes basin,[56] most with the capacity to cause birth defects or cancer, a measure of the progress we've made replacing water-borne bacterial infections at the turn of the century with water-borne degenerative diseases today.[57] Then come the conquering agents. Chlorine kills and disinfects harmful bacteria, but leaves a queasy feeling in the pit of Dr. John Stockner's stomach. "What's really frightening," says the Canadian federal fisheries scientist stationed in British Columbia, "is the idea that it's healthy to kill the bacteria in water with chemicals, and then drink the chemicals."[58] In July, 1992, the **American Journal of Public Health** confirmed chlorinated water increases the risk of bladder cancer by 21 per cent and of rectal cancer by 39 per cent.[59] Fluoride, another standard additive, has helped cut cavities,[60] a technical fix that substituted for brushing teeth after each meal and cutting sugar and steel-ground refined grains from the diet. Dental associations now urge parents to go light on their kids' fluoride intake.[61] Fluoride has the power to discolor teeth enamel, as the blotches on many kids' teeth suggest. Fluoride is implicated in high rates of osteoporosis, says Duff Conacher, a member of Ralph Nader's research team that broke the bad news on fluoride in the late 1980s. Alum, or aluminum sulfate, is a double dare because it's often added twice, in both water and sewage treatment. Alum is possibly implicated in high levels of Alzheimer's disease, says Dr. William Forbes, a gerontologist at the University of Waterloo. In a 35-year study of 2,000 men, Forbes found memory loss was up to 10 times higher in areas of Canada with high levels of aluminum in the water.[62]

Then there's the $2-billion-a-year designer water solution. Company names may say Clear Spring Water on the label, but it's just a company name, not a promise. It's an odds-on bet that rural spring water has been contaminated by pesticides or manure.[63] And the energy to package and transport melted acid rain from the Alps to North America is a no-brainer.

It will be a while yet before the sins of pollution are washed off. This provides a business opportunity that delivers sparkling water while starting the process of regeneration. A natural system water greenhouse, using beds of mineralized soil for taste and purification after plants have done the brunt of the cleaning, can be up and running in a reasonably-sized backyard for under $75,000. A Harvard Business School grad can do the calculations: 1,000 neighborhood customers, $2 per week per customer, and the owner gets soaking rich in year two. The water supply comes from rainfall. To get adequate supplies, the eco-station operator provides free rain barrels to all customers, thereby saving on expansion of sewage mains to carry off storm water. Since customers are all close by, containers can be returnable.

Green Collar Workers

Green companies need green workers. The coming construction boom, for instance, will center on customized renovations, where the tight margins of high-performance contracting—the builders' fees are based on the owner's savings—will be the norm. Toronto building trades union leader John Cartwright, recognizing that Canadians are already spending $3 billion a year more on renovations than new construction, has seen the writing on the wall of conventional high-rise and convention centre megaprojects, and is pressing unions to come behind what he calls "this decentralized megaproject."

"This is not just about jobs," says Toronto building trades researcher David Sobel. "This is about the dignity of labor." Construction workers of the future will have to be multi-skilled and self-directed, he says, because slapdash, sub-contracting methods don't square with the demands of healthy or energy-efficient buildings. It's not enough, for instance, to fill in cracks with insulating foam. Slathered on too thick, the foam can lock in indoor air pollution or moisture that rots beams. Builders need a feel for the "house as a system." They also have to adjust their approach to the region. Different types of super-windows, different matches of super-windows with other home features, have to be chosen with the local climate in mind, the number of cloudy, sunny, hot and cold days. No two walls are alike when a builder is looking for thermal lag, the ability of materials to passively store heat when it's hot outside and release the heat when it's cool. Attention to trade-offs is another must, again unique to each situation. There's not much use saving money on heating bills with materials that are made with ozone-depleting CFCs or HCFCs, or materials that have a high energy content in their production or transportation, or materials that cause health problems for occupants.

Again, the need for tradespeople with deep reserves of skill comes to the fore. They're the ones who can advise on adobe walls in the southwest, or straw bale construction in the windy north, matching local resources to climatic conditions. They're the ones who can turn thumbs down on prefab materials. The general rule, Sobel says, is that the more materials are poured—cement instead of bricks, glue instead of nails, plastic instead of metals—the higher the embodied energy and toxicity of the materials, and the lower the skill level of the work force.

Working with natural systems will revolutionize work standards in the industry, Sobel says, which may be why the powers that be in the industry aren't rushing in. "Changing behavior is a greater threat to the system than changing windows," Sobel notes.

Cheap is Beautiful

Principle 2

Features the saving graces of "soft path" strategies that simplify and enrich lifestyles by doing more with less

"There must be more to life than having everything."
Children's author Maurice Sendak[1]

"We need a breakthrough that gives us low production costs and high wages that sustain a domestic market. I'm constantly looking for low-cost alternatives in transit, garbage and energy use that have an environmental benefit, that generate employment, and that create enough savings to finance high wages."

Toronto city councillor Peter Tabuns

Economics for a small planet features a new business sector that sells savings, creating boundless job opportunities in a finite world. The maxim is efficiency, doing more with less, not cutbacks, getting by on less. Paybacks of less than three years make energy saving investments the easiest money a person or company never had to earn. "When all else fails, try money," says Amory Lovins, savior of an economy that lives by its wits.

Described by **Wired** magazine as "one part Buckminster Fuller, one part Ralph Nader and one part Mr. Peabody," Amory Lovins is the hotdogger of energy efficiency on the slopes of Snowmass, Colorado, where his Rocky Mountain Institute shows off a new economy that saves the planet by saving money.

Perhaps the worst punster in North America—"negawatt" and "we can't have archaic and eat it too" are just two of his contributions to the English language—he has a mind that's mastered high order physics and theoretical economics, but is equally fascinated with low-flush toilets and compact fluorescent light bulbs.

On staff with Friends of the Earth in the 1970s, crusading against the threats to health and peace posed by nuclear power, he quickly repositioned the entire debate around cost-effectiveness. Perhaps it's because he is, as his friend Alex MacDonald puts it "insufferably agreeable," but he developed a language that's pushed the debate toward consensus on the savings and profits to be made from what he calls the "soft energy path."[2]

Lovins got conservationists to talk in hard-headed terms about efficiency, and utility executives to talk in soft-headed terms about energy services. After all, he argued, consumers don't want electricity, gas
or oil. They want cold beer, hot showers and comfy rooms. That settled, it's a practical matter of finding the best means to an end-use.
Using electricity, high-grade energy produced at thousands of degrees
of heat, to produce lukewarm water and air "is like using a chainsaw
to cut butter," he says. Enough warm water and air can come from
solar water heaters, low-flow showerheads, high-efficiency windows
and furnaces to reserve electricity for computers, radios, TVs and
light appliances, about four per cent of our energy needs. Likewise,
consumers don't care where the work done by watts or thermal units
comes from—a new power plant or savings from efficient appliances.
Since savings are cheaper than coal, oil or uranium, it makes sense to
buy negawatts and pocket the difference.

When Lovins first started promoting his ideas, he compared energy
efficiency to eating a lobster—a little at a time, and a lot of morsels
in the claws and joints. Then he found the comparison lacking.
When it comes to energy efficiency, there is no such thing as a free
lunch, he says. "This is a lunch you get paid to eat." Many savings
are cheaper than free. Compact fluorescents in offices not only save
electricity on lighting, they save on air conditioning, since they give
off less waste heat than incandescents. They also save on operating
costs since they only need to be changed one-fifth as often. High efficiency furnaces and air conditioners not only save on fuel. They're so
much smaller that they provide free extra office space, a boon for any
company that's renting by the square foot. Spot and natural lighting
not only cut electric bills. Workers are more productive and less
spaced out. Lovins recently completed a study of the Las Vegas post
office, which through sheer serendipity paid off a $300,000 renova-
tion investment in one year instead of five, thanks to a jump in
worker productivity.

Lovins now guesstimates there are $300-billion-a-year-worth of yearly
savings to be had from profitable conservation in the U.S.[3] That
translates to 600,000 permanent jobs. Then there's the ricochet ro-
mance factor, as savings bounce off each other. Conservation money
employs local workers, and gets local multipliers going, as builders
buy from bakers who buy from farmers. Conservation is labor-, not

capital-intensive, which means that money goes to people in local communities, who spend it on goods and services. Conservation spending pays for work that's being done, not a project that may come on-line in five years, so there's no capital punishment or loss of money to interest payments. And conservation cuts the cost of doing business, which draws in new business. In Osage, Iowa, for instance, a conservation-minded utility went debt-free while lowering rates five times over five years, spurring two factories to relocate there.

Lovins is now pushing the "hypercar," based on the GM Ultralite concept car that wowed the Detroit auto show in 1992. Designed and built by 50 technicians in 100 days, the car seats four comfortably and maintains good speeds at 200 miles to the gallon, meaning a tankful will take you across the continent. The secret is new materials, such as carbon and glass composites, new production methods which lend themselves to the simplicity and flexibility of composites, and new efficiencies in aerodynamics and motor design. The electric hybrid motor runs moving parts with electricity generated from clean, farm-grown ethanol fuels, and doesn't have the drawback of all-electric cars, heavy batteries. Perhaps the car-makers of tomorrow, like the Macintosh computer makers of yesterday, are tinkering away in some garage, gearing up to take a stodgy industry by storm when it's least expected.

To counter car proliferation, Lovins favors the same kinds of market innovations he proposed to end nuclear proliferation. Again, the issue is service—that is access, not mobility. Negatrips can be generated if employers who give workers who bike, walk or car-pool their share of savings on the cost of a parking space—about $25,000. Condo developers can do the same, and avoid the costs of an underground parking space by giving away free transit passes. Insurance companies can have collision insurance tacked onto the cost of a gallon of gas, removing the up-front cost that has to be paid whether the car is used or not. Municipalities can provide mass transit for less than the cost of a road-widening. They can also allow land-use plans that keep essential services within walking distance of residents.

Staffers with Amory and Hunter Lovins' Rocky Mountain Institute are now taking this message out to hard-hit communities looking for fresh ideas on how to save money and create jobs. "We found that by combining advanced technology, creative use of market forces, aikido politics, and Jeffersonian community organizing," says Lovins, "we can solve many problems at once without making new ones, and can usually protect the environment, not at a cost, but at a profit." He hopes that conservation may also restore the social capital North America is fast frittering away. "I'm not nearly so concerned about the depletion of nonrenewable resources such as oil or copper," he says, "as about the depletion of things that ought to be renewable but are being mined, such as topsoil, biodiversity, social tolerance, traditional culture, civic virtue and morality."[4]

"The best way to get unhooked from the hedonic trap of consumerism is to get hooked on activities that we find enjoyable and meaningful."[5]
Michael Jacobson and Laurie Ann Mazur

The future ain't what it used to be, and everyone knows that the hype about a high-tech economy creating the leisure society hasn't panned out. The economy is smoking more, and we're enjoying it less. But matching means to ends, Lovins' prescription for energy efficiency without self-denial, also applies to saving time. Joe Dominguez and Vicki Robin have laid out a personal time-saving plan for financial independence.

Joe Dominguez and Vicki Robin haven't worked a day since 1969, when they retired from stock broking and acting while still in their youth. In 1984, they set up the New Road Map Foundation, based in Seattle, to spread the word about acquiring financial independence from money. In 1992, they published **Your Money or Your Life,** which charts some of the routes to valuing life by living on the cheap.

To be blunt, money is a waste of time. "Money is something we choose to trade our life energy for," they say. When life, like any resource, is too cheap, we squander it, put in too much for what we get back. When the true costs of a 40-hour workweek are tallied up, their book shows, we spend 30 extra hours and one-third of our income just to earn a paycheck. Add in the time and cost of commuting, of clothes and dressing up, of eating away from home, of cooling out after work and buying things to make up for lost time, and suddenly an $11-an-hour job turns into $4 an hour. Factor in child care, and the bill for stress-related prescription drugs, about $200 billion a year, and the minimum wage starts to look pretty good.

Once hidden costs are brought out in the open, living better becomes a matter of finding the best way of making or saving the equivalent of less than $4 an hour. Moving closer to work and selling your car, for instance, saves having to earn about $10,000 in pre-tax income a year, enough to trade in for a sabbatical every three or four years. Moving to the country, living off the interest from the higher sale price of your city home and the produce from your garden, might also make ends meet.[6]

Their book presents over a hundred options to match means to ends by acquiring financial independence from money. They all require frugality, which the book defines as "enjoying the virtue of getting good value for every minute of your life energy." Being frugal is not about being a miser. "To be frugal means to have a high joy-to-stuff ratio," they say. In the new economy, "frugal, man," will become "the cool, groovy way to say 'far out' in the nineties. Surfers will talk about frugal waves. Teenage girls will talk about frugal dudes. Designers will talk about frugal fashions."

Most public opinion polls confirm that people of all ages and incomes are open to these choices, willing to swap a cut in pay for more free time. It's a good trade, especially when it improves living standards. "Living below your means is the cheapest way to be rich," says North Carolina landscaper Chuck Marsh. In the new economy, savings will replace consumption as the motor of prosperity, and time power, not purchasing power, will set the standards for the pursuit of that old revolutionary goal: life, liberty and the pursuit of happiness.

"Decreasing throughput is the only job-creation strategy there is."
                                    Green entrepreneur Paul Hawken

You have to spend money to save money. But that creates many more jobs, and a lot more good for companies, communities and the environment, than the equivalent amount wasted on operating costs. Here are some trends to watch for as new entrepreneurs break from habits that developed when we had more money than brains.

No Money Down

There's an accounting barrier to the new economy. True, compact fluorescents and efficient fridges cost less over time, but, as is often the case with quality, they have a higher sticker price. On any given day, there are any number of people who will break your knees if you spend your extra money for long-term savings instead of paying off your debts. Once we know what the problem is—high up-front costs—it's easy to get around it. "The problem with green products is not cost, but financing," says energy consultant Alex MacDonald. A new breed of fourth-wave business, an energy saving company or ESCO, handles the problem the same way a new home-buyer, government, utility, furniture store or car lot does. It goes to the bank for a long-term loan to finance the renovations, which the customer gets for no money down. Then the ESCO charges the customer a monthly rate to cover services rendered, plus interest charges. The guarantee is that the combined monthly fee and reduced utility charges will be less than what the customer would have paid out for energy and water if the renovations hadn't been done. Once the debt is repaid, usually in less than five years, the customer keeps all the savings. Pain free, risk free.

ESCOs will be a strategic sector of the new economy, employing at least five per cent of the workforce, according to Howard Geller of the American Council for an Energy Efficient Economy. They've got their work cut out for them. In Canada, where 14 per cent of homes are uninsulated and 2.9 million homes are heated with electricity, there's a $15-billion industry waiting to happen just high-grading the golden pickings at the surface.[7] For less than $3,000 work per unit, global warming emissions can be cut by five per cent while profiting renovators and home owners. Federal buildings in Canada can save $1 billion a year once the cost of renovations are paid off in three years. In the U.S., according to the Boston-based Citizens Conservation Corporation, there are 14 million low-income housing units with almost double the energy expenditures of regular homes, blowing some $13 billion in yearly government subsidies up the chimney. The Alliance to Save Energy claims there are $4.2-billion-worth of profitable savings to be had in U.S. federal buildings.

Municipalities are ahead of other levels of government. From Barrie, Ontario to New York, cities of all sizes find it pays to give away water-saving showerheads and toilets and avoid the higher costs of expanded water filtration plants.[8] In Edmonton, former councillor Tooker Gomberg showed how to turn energy conservation into a boot-strap operation. In 1994, he got the city to establish a $1-million revolving fund for energy retrofits. In the first year, $309,050 was allocated to upgrade public buildings such as arenas, pools and fire halls. This saved taxpayers $137,130 and reduced carbon dioxide emissions by 978 tons. The savings from each year are rolled over to finance next year's renovations in other buildings. "With a return on investment of 44 per cent, it's almost unbeatable," says Gomberg. "You usually don't get that kind of profit on anything unless it's illegal." Even volunteer groups find ESCOs affordable. In Alberta and British Columbia, Mary Ferguson's Destination Conservation works with elementary school students to upgrade their schools. They've saved $5 million at 200 schools over the past five years.[9]

Civic leaders and the private sector are about to embark on the single largest municipal retrofit program in the world in Toronto, where the goal is to bring every building in the city up to top energy and water efficiency standards. Toronto has committed itself to reducing its own greenhouse gas emissions by 20 per cent of 1988 levels by 2005, a loftier goal than the international agreement to stabilize greenhouse gas emissions at 1990 levels by 2005. In a pilot project geared to figuring out financing problems, three levels of government will invest a total of $12 million, with the private sector picking up the city's share of $4 million (to retrofit an initial 30 public buildings) and putting another $18 million into a pot to be accessed by private landlords (to retrofit another 60 buildings) for a total investment of $30 million. Within the two or three years of the pilot project, $12 million is expected to be paid back immediately, $4 million to the ESCOs, which will have completed the work on performance contracts, and $8 million into a revolving fund that will be used either to retrofit more buildings or to leverage additional funds for larger retrofits. Public funds to kick start the project will amount to only $8 million, sure to be saved in reduced energy consumption costs and deferred water and sewage treatment capital expansion.

ESCOs are also a nice way to put construction union pension funds to work. The job dollar goes a long way. According to the New York state energy plan, for instance, the installation of reflectors on office ceiling lights costs 1.07 cents per kilowatt hour saved, one-seventh of electricity charges, but generates 23.1 jobs per $1 million spent, about five times more than money spent producing power.

Tax Relief

If politicians wanted to help people save, they could give tax points for money invested in energy savings, or at least even out the playing field by not giving tax breaks to energy pigs. Energy-efficient equipment, a safer source of new energy supply than megaprojects, would have rapid depreciation status, allowing companies to write off the costs of efficiency the same way they write off the operating costs for energy that goes through the roof. Likewise, buildings that "produced" new energy supply through efficiency or solar methods would be registered as micro-utilities, and write off their equipment as a capital cost. These measures lower the barrier of high entry costs for efficient equipment. Such tax write-offs can be financed by scrapping the rapid depreciation tax breaks that now go exclusively to energy guzzling. Yearly tax deductions for oil and gas drilling in the U.S., just one of the ways politicians reward the wasting of money, come to about $3 billion.[10]

Hidden Profit Centers

When the Loblaws food chain took the lead in helping to commercialize the "Terminator 2," it reckoned it would save $9 million throughout its chain. The Arnold Schwarzenegger of supermarket freezer systems reduces ozone-depleting freon leaks by 72 per cent, electric bills by 25 per cent, and maintenance costs by 15 per cent. But the old-style accountants had it wrong. Since Loblaws, like all other grocery chains, only makes one cent on the customer dollar, it saved the equivalent of $900 million in sales.

Patrick Carson, Loblaws' vice-president of environment, is now introducing Michael Davidson's successful green box shopping system throughout the chain. The system replaces plastic bags and corrugated cardboard boxes and makes use of a uniquely designed shopping cart. "Davidson is fast on his way to becoming a millionaire eco-preneur," says Carson. It's estimated the returnable container industry will be worth $100 billion over the next decade.

The multiplier effect of savings is a big deal when most manufacturers and retailers face shrinking markets, and savings are a big part of what they get to keep. Opportunities aren't hard to come by. Most companies waste so much energy and water, says Canadian Manufacturers Association environment representative Blake Smith, "that there's still a lot of low-lying fruit here." Fuels rush in where managers fear to tread, and very few expenditures can match the typical 33 per cent return on investment from conservation measures, the smartest money around. All it takes is to see conservation as an investment.

"J.M. Schneider is a meat company, not a waste management company," says Brad Erhart, waste and environment manager for the $800-million a year corporation's Kitchener, Ontario factory in southwestern Ontario. "I have to sell an investment in waste management to my superiors as more productive than the purchase of a new meat cutter, so paybacks have to be better than a year."

He's been making his case since 1989, when the company launched a continuous improvement program. "The old school was to check your brain at the door, management has all the answers. That meant that only five per cent of the staff thought about advancing the company, while the people who did and knew the jobs were never asked how to solve the problems," he says. "Without continuous improvement, peo-ple are only concerned with their own function, but continuous im-provement forces managers and workers to integrate decision making."

The new management style led to new approaches to resource use, previously seen as the cost of doing business, not a variable that could be improved. In the first year, he and co-workers saved 500,000 gallons worth of water bills and $400,000 on waste disposal fees by improving methods for showering down carcasses and composting unused parts. "It was quick gold. Every rock you turned over was another fortune," he says. Since then, they've cut water use in half and waste haulage by 80 per cent. Each year, he says, the improvements get "more difficult, but not more expensive." Last year, 22 new initiatives, from reusing printer cartridges to replacing cafeteria styrofoam with mugs, chalked up nearly $2 million in savings. "That's $2 million out of $7 million total profit on $800 million of sales, so it makes a big difference in the profitability of the company," he says. "So I'm sold."

The numbers are now coming in on steel-making giant Stelco's $346,000 investment in an ultrafiltration system that recycles alkali cleaners used to prepare steel for processing at its Hamilton, Ontario plant. Composite savings, including avoided purchases, avoided waste disposal and avoided health and safety problems, come to $900,000 a year. The company also has a new technology to sell. And the Great Lakes benefit from smaller doses of chlorine and caustics.[11]

Can someone please remind us why it is that business puts up such a stink about limiting pollution, when pollution prevention pays off so well? Maybe it's the term, and the F-word—flake—it conjures up. Maybe it's fear of regulation. Maybe it's ignorance made stubborn by company executives hanging tough together to fight off its thankless critics. Maybe it's the memory of old slogans about pollution being the smell of money, when it's just the smell of money burning. Or maybe the professional anti-environmentalists are playing business executives for suckers. At any rate, pollution should be called by its right name, which is Managerial and Professional Incompetence. This might help make the problem more manageable than a no-fault inert term like pollution. It will also make for more interesting pollution index reports: "The MPI level in Cincinnati today is 24. It's the ecology, stupid."

The Road Less Traveled

The easiest way to increase profits by issuing pink slips to resources and green slips to workers is to hire a transportation co-ordinator for every hundred employees. Without slashing one tire, the co-ordinators make it easy for workers to leave their cars at home. They pass around a sign-up sheet for car-poolers so people from the same area can be introduced to one another. They lobby supervisors to space out assignments so they can be done at home one day a week. They promote corporate wellness programs and a corporate culture that celebrates walking or biking to work as a way to keep fit and arrive with juices pumping and mental faculties on an upswing. They fund and pay for shower facilities for bikers and joggers, perhaps at a nearby gym happy for the in-and-out morning business. They give away transit passes or bikes to workers who give up their parking spaces. They organize express shuttle buses and vans to areas with high concentrations of employees, perhaps partnering with other companies in the same building to get enough passengers to make it worthwhile. They rent satellite offices for groups of workers who commute from outlying areas.

Odd as it seems at first, the transport co-ordinator quickly becomes a profit center in a large organization. It's very expensive to leave workers to fend for themselves in getting to work. It's often cheaper to take jobs to the workers than to bring workers to the job. IBM slashed $40 million a year from its Canadian head office rental fees when it transferred workers to satellite offices closer to home, at suburban rental rates.[12] Fitness achieved through walking or biking to work pays dividends in enhanced mental performance and reduced absenteeism. A study at Brigham Young University, for instance, shows that obese workers are off sick twice as often as the slim and trim. This led researcher Larry Tucker to suggest self-financing corporate wellness programs as a positive way to trim fat from the organization.[13] Purdue University researchers found that men and women who walked regularly for exercise enjoyed a host of psychological advantages over couch potatoes, including reduced anxiety, increased motivation, enhanced self-image and sharper decision-making powers.[14] And, the **British Medical Journal** reports that male office workers, their testes squeezed against a chair for too long each day, reduce their risk of testicular cancer by half when they exercise 15 hours a week. That's a low-hanging saving for companies that pay workers' compensation premiums and health benefits.

It's often cheaper to give workers free bikes or transit passes than to subsidize their parking, a common practice everywhere and almost universal in the U.S., at a yearly cost estimated at well over $40 billion.[15] Underground parking spots commonly cost well over $20,000 to build. The interest alone makes it worthwhile for the developer to offer free transit passes to all tenants and put underground space to more profitable use, as warehouse space for tenants and nearby businesses, for example. Government treasuries benefit too, since free parking is an untaxed benefit, denying access to over $12 billion in yearly income tax revenue.[16] If governments rebated the value of that tax deduction to workers who gave up their parking space, we'd be getting somewhere, and without cars. One U.S. report estimated that such a range of initiatives could eliminate 76 million car miles a year, saving the costs on 4.5 million gallons of gas and the damage from about 48 million tons of global warming emissions.[17]

Transportation co-ordinators don't have to limit their line of vision to head office commuters. The Calgary, Alberta cattle yards used telemanagement to come up with a new way of doing its $225-million-a-year business. In the old days, ranchers had to transport cattle to the stock yards, a big expense in fuel and time and a hard trip for the cattle, which usually lost weight during the ordeal. The rancher didn't have much choice but to sell at whatever prices were going that day. Now, two-thirds of cattle yard bids are handled through an electronic auction with TV hook-ups. Cattle are then shipped directly to the processor.[18]

Living Off The Interest

The politicians are wasting our time scrimping on public services to cut taxes. At best, this will cut taxes, not expenses, and save the government money, not us. They should save the rhetoric, pay attention to demand-side management, and get over their fixation with old-hat, supply-side solutions. Demand-management savings are usually of such orders of magnitude that they cancel the capital cost of megaprojects, and are carried by savings on interest to cover them.

This may not seem like a big deal at first, because politicians aren't in the habit of announcing future interest or operating charges when they cut the ribbons and dig the first shovel-full of a favored scheme. The line items that get buried under that first shovel are the real killers in the public debt. When economic forecasters, fortune-tellers in pinstripes, say a road expansion will cost $100 million, it doesn't sound too bad. If they said the road will cost $8 million a year in bank payments and another $8 million in upkeep to prevent depreciation, people might ask how the actual debt ever gets paid down. Transport experts are coming up with answers that make the capital cost vanish, strategies that extend Amory Lovins' concept of nega-watts to negamiles, what the International Institute for Energy Conservation calls Integrated Transport Planning. Maybe they should back a constitutional amendment prohibiting governments from going into debt. A contract on roads.

To make a fair fight out of funding alternatives that live off the carrying charges, we need above-ground accounting of all the carrying charges that are now buried in other department budgets or simply forgotten about. The $1 billion a year Ontario gives to banks for old roads,[19] for instance, is just a flag for the $7.2 billion a year that, according to costings by Tom Samuels of the Better Transportation Coalition, go to policing highway traffic violations and providing highway accident victims with emergency health services. Then come the private costs. The yearly loss in property damage and sick time from collisions is $9 billion. There's a personal and economic loss from the fact that people are three times more likely to be done in by a car than a murderer. Other hidden costs that have to be made good by someone include crop damage inflicted by car smog—$8.8 million a year in the Vancouver area alone, for instance—and health costs of 1,500 to 30,000 cancers a year attributed to car smog, as well as import costs arising from the loss of three million acres of prime farmland to pavement.[20]

Then come the opportunity costs. The gas New Yorkers waste cooling their jets in traffic jams burns a $1.35-million-a-day hole in the local economy for fuel imports. If half that money went to local construction workers laying track for rapid public transit, congestion would be lowered and so would the costs of keeping able-bodied workers on welfare. Every day, New Yorkers lose a million hours of potentially productive time, their feet on the brakes as they curse rush hour and construction delays.[21] The only people making money on that time are the psychologists who've taken to charging $175 an hour for counseling hard-pressed executives on the drive to work.[22] If this time were spent more therapeutically tending gardens, the Big Apple could cut its food imports by a third.

The value put on time lost in California traffic jams is $5 million a day.[23] Wolfgang Zukerman, author of **End of the Road,** costs all the time lost to traffic jams in the U.S. at $150 billion a year. Road subsidies cause the North American version of former Soviet lineups for meat rations. "When prices are too low to equate supply and demand—whether the commodity is sausage or space on roads—rationing takes place in other, almost always more frustrating ways," writes the **New York Time's** Peter Passel.[24] And don't forget to value the time lost by non-drivers in an auto-cratic transportation system when they cool their heels at under-serviced bus stops, or stare into someone's armpit while practicing tai chi in the subway, or accompany their kids to school because side streets have too many cars racing by. British traffic expert John Whitelegg claims car-centered infrastructure "steals time" from non-drivers at the rate of £10 billion a year.[25]

And what about the lost opportunity to narrow downtown roads, widen sidewalks and lease out sidewalk space to retailers for stalls? At discount rates, retailers could get some space that lets them compete with the cheap land around super stores, accessible only by expensive highways. Downtown business is the urban road-kill of highway infrastructure, and car sickness is killing the city tax base. If this sounds a little flaky, recall that the Bank of America lined up with a group of transit reformers who argued that a continuing sprawl-freeway spiral "will make California economically uncompetitive and create social, environmental and political problems we may not be able to solve."[26]

A conservative bench-mark on the yearly public charges for roads comes from the comprehensive audit by the senior accounting firm of Peat, Marwick, Stevenson and Kellogg. Governments pay Vancouver car drivers $867 a year to drive about 12,000 miles, over and above the costs and taxes paid by the drivers. That will do as a proxy for real yearly carrying charges. What if we paid people that much not to drive?

Try to come up with something positive. Punitive measures, such as gas tax hikes, don't work unless coupled with positive measures.[27] Try to come up with something really different. Road taxes and high occupancy vehicle lanes are just Trojan horses for freeway expansion. Pay cab and car-pool drivers for every extra passenger they carry? Pick up the moving costs of people who move to within walking distance of work? Pay people to walk, bike or blade? Pay employers who introduce flex hours to cut prime time use of roads? Give mileage credits to grocery stores that deliver by bike? Pay a mileage bonus to bicycle rickshaws that carry people around downtown? Give a tax break to retailers and restaurants that pool their supply orders at a central depot so that delivery routes can be organized to reduce trips?[28] Provide free public concerts on Friday and Sunday evenings all summer, paid for with the interest saved by avoiding double-lane highways to cottage country that are needed less than 30 days a year?

Sound silly? In Portland, Oregon, they worked up an avoided-costs package to save the costs of a freeway. Instead of sprawling all over the place with freeways, they built a light-rail system that brought most people to within walking distance of work. They saved downtown jobs, kept traffic congestion at bay, and lowered carbon monoxide emissions, formerly in violation of federal health standards one day in three, to safer levels. A bike expressway and lower municipal debt sweetened the pot.[29]

Want to hear something silly? In St. John's, Newfoundland, they're spending $68 million to build a rush-hour bypass when $1 million on computers could clear up the problem by synchronizing lights.[30] Newfoundland was a runner-up for the coveted North American Road Builders Non-Starter Award. The winner was Prince Edward Island with its fixed link, a $738-million road over nine miles of ocean, that threatens the island's lobster and scallop fishery and leads to the layoff of 550 ferry workers. Though the awards ceremony was not publicized, there will be full TV coverage of the demolition derby during the winter, when ocean winds will pound against trucks at up to 40 miles an hour.[31]

Build It And They Won't Come

When the fast talkers of the global economy speak about opening doors for trade, they really mean opening roads. That's how they get taxpayers to pay for the just-in-time infrastructure of firms that de-pend on fast spenders, high turnover and quick turnaround. Catholic Workers at St. John's Kitchen in Waterloo, Ontario call this "the excessway."[32] Make the rich save, we say.

Public infrastructure that helps people save creates more jobs, a greater variety of jobs, and a higher ratio of local jobs than hard infrastructure that encourages spending. The idea, says Wally Seccombe, a historian who's followed the consuming patterns of isolated nuclear families,[33] is to create a network of organizations that "get more bang for the domestic buck, and increase the efficiency of domestic work, so you can have more without increasing your income." Or, as Anya Woestwin, Seattle's thriftiest environmentalist, puts it: "The basic goal is to use as few external resource inputs as possible, produce as much as possible, and have a really good time."[34]

Being a miser is a way to save without infrastructure of any kind. Driving from one discount mall to another cherry picking the sales is a way to save all by yourself, but at great expense for gas and highways. The smart and fun way to save is to pool information and time with your neighbors. The **Frugal Bugle** in Oshawa, Ontario, like the **Tightwad Gazette** in Maine, offers hot tips to subscribers on the best buys around town. **Gazette** editor Amy Acyzyn has turned two anthologies of ideas for "promoting thrift as a viable alternative lifestyle" into 250,000-plus sellers. **Bugle** editor, Joe Killoran, figures he can cover his costs and salary with 4,000 subscribers, a prospect that could put thousands of penny pincher aficionados in the publishing business.

Local tightwad clubs can cover the salary of an organizer who creates, as well as reports, good deals. Collecting dues from skinflints isn't a pleasant prospect, but an organizer can arrange discounts for members who use their own mugs for take-out coffee, bring their own bags to the grocery store, take their laundry without plastic wraps, shop in slow hours when stores are glad to have any customer, or who walk instead of using retailer-paid parking space. In Allentown, Pennsylvania, for instance, downtown restaurants offer a discount to customers who come by foot. The program is supported by the Coalition for Alternative Transportation and the mayor, who notes that the increase in walking reduces crime, boosts the downtown core and improves health.[35]

A pro-active organization of penny pinchers would also be able to restore discounts for those who pay cash, and end the discrimination against hard cash imposed by credit card companies that require everyone to pay rates that cover their inflationary surcharges. Talk about taking on box stores, the organizer could find funeral homes that offer voluntary simplicity in caskets and cut back the cost of dying. Maybe the local high school could be lobbied to cut back on the status trappings of proms, and make them accessible to people who can't hire a stretch, tux and hotel suite. At a rate of one staff organizer for every 10,000 tightwads, we're talking big job creation here. Cheapskate clubs can also publish inventories of used tools, children's clothing and skills for exchange, like Vinemount, Ontario's **Community Exchange Directory,** pitched to those "looking for something that money can't buy."

Buying co-ops also flourish in this area. The New York Public Interest Research Group finances much of its work by selling 80,000 memberships to people who sign on for big discounts on home heating oil that the organization gets in return for its high-volume purchase. In Quebec City, a car co-op, Autocom, sells shares for $500 to 54 members who can rent from among nine cars, depending on their need, for an hour or a day. There's a similar co-op in Eugene, Oregon. Throughout New England, where about 30 per cent of people heat with wood, wood cutting co-ops provide cut-rate prices to those who join in the work and split the costs of modern equipment.

Plenty Of Nothing

We can do a lot better than tuna helper to help stretch the limited incomes of the poor. Savings networks can double the real incomes of the poor, at a fraction of the cost to the public of doubling assistance rates, and with many other returns to the quality of low-income communities.

Being poor costs a lot of money. The poor don't have a car to drive out to the discount mall or U-Pick, on roads they pay for in taxes but can't use. They don't have a pantry or freezer to store bulk goods or specials. They don't have the utensils to cook from scratch. Low-income housing is flung together, with shoddy insulation and often with electric heating, cheap to install, but expensive to maintain. Poor areas get stuck with retailers who take advantage of their lack of mobility to charge monopoly prices. Banks charge customers with low balances higher service fees, and often require so much ID and security to cash a check that they force the poor into using rip-off check-cashing agencies.

Counter-institutions—updated versions of the Y, originally formed to offer city youth a recreational alternative to the saloon—will be major players in the welfare reform of the future. Community kitchens, perhaps allied with health clinics—Canada's world-famous medical reformer, Dr. Norman Bethune, advocated this back in the 1930s—can share equipment and information for thrifty, tasty and nutritious food preparation. Oddly enough, most of the foods that are best for health are almost dirt cheap in the vegetable bins and bulk barrels at supermarkets. Gleaners' clubs can contract with farmers in a win-win deal that cuts food costs and agricultural waste. Right now, a good 20 per cent of North America's food is left rotting in the fields,[36] a smorgasbord for insects that will later have to be sprayed. Gleaning, which is just U-Pick for latecomers, allows farmers to offer bargain basement prices for post-peak sales produce, along with produce that is perfectly good but doesn't meet the size or blemish-free standards of commercial graders.

In the new economy, saving and making money go together, a double win that's of strategic importance for economic development in low-income communities. The poor practice "trickle-up" economics. Their money doesn't stay in the neighborhood for long. It goes to absentee landlords, utilities, growers, manufacturers, social workers, educational specialists, and so on—anti-poverty programs do solve poverty problems for some people, after all—few of whom make their purchases locally and stimulate job creation. Anti-poverty programs that don't deal with this capital flight have little chance of success. Enough government money gets mailed to the welfare-dependent Native community in the James Bay region of northern Ontario, for instance, to keep its 7,000 residents, less than 1,500 families, in the lap of luxury. Counting welfare and bush food, there's about $110 million that goes through the region each year, says Rick MacLeod Farley, staffer with Mushkegowuk tribal council in Moose Factory. "But all the money leaves as soon as it comes in" to pay for imports of diesel fuel, food and consultants, Farley says. Close to 90 per cent of the local population is unemployed, he says, in an area with a living memory of being proudly self-reliant.

The point is to make poor peoples' money go further, not farther. To the extent that savings slow the drain of poor peoples' money, and keep it in the neighborhood for another go-round, they multiply job opportunities. Why not make that community kitchen double as an outlet for casseroles, offering nutritious takeouts in returnable containers, providing a way of making spare cash while baby-sitting is pooled? Who knows, maybe the future Casseroles R Us catering company will come out of a community kitchen? Or Bake My Day will rise out of a community oven like the one built in a Toronto neighborhood where mixed cultures share a common memory of baking bread in communal ovens?[37] ESCOs, based in and sensitive to low-income communities, can also use energy retrofits to spark community economic development. In the state of New York, taxpayers contribute up to $1 billion a year in supplements covering high fuel bills due to substandard construction, a bill that could be cut by 30 per cent, according to state energy planners, while employing residents to renovate their buildings.[38]

Workers Of The World, Relax

Everyone talks about the four-day work week as a solution to chronic unemployment and time-juggling. But half the people with jobs are putting in 50 hours a week. North Americans work a month more now than we did in the 1950's, when the 40-hour week became standard, a month more than most Europeans do today, a good month more than Europe's medieval serfs who took off for holy days and festivals at the slightest excuse, and a good two months more than those slackers in ancient Athens, according to Juliet Schor's **The Overworked Americans.**

Since we haven't been able to spend our way into the leisure society, maybe we could try saving. Some of the savings will come from changes in lifestyle that will be possible when we have more time. Many of them will come from juggling administrative budgets instead of our own personal time. That's because our way of arranging taxes and benefits hides the true costs of long work hours. Bruce O'Hara, author of **Working Harder Isn't Working,** estimates that these costs are so high that "each full-time worker now works 10 hours every week for free." Simply by updating budgeting systems and applying some new math, we can finance shorter hours and full employment out of savings. Here's our list of 16 ways to gain free time.

   1.   Local governments can issue town keys to honor those who take the plunge. The keys provide free or heavily discounted access for the whole family to public pools, museums, galleries, zoos and transit. This is virtually cost-free to municipalities, thanks to what economists call the "zero marginal cost" when high constant overhead costs create "excess capacity" in downtimes, the base of last-minute travel clubs or frequent flyer points. Public facilities have high overhead costs that don't go down by much in off-hours when they're barely used. It takes one bus, one driver, one tank of gas and one loan payment to transport 40 people in rush hour or four people an hour later, for example. A lifeguard can watch over two families or 10 for the same pay, as can a museum guide. The town keys help balance the budgets of four-day workers who have more time than money on their hands. Wherever the town card has been tried out in England, stores, restaurants and the-

atres jumped at the chance to be put on the discount list, since they also welcome off-hour customers.

2. Both private and public sector employers have access to cheaper credit than individuals do. They can issue discounted mortgages to four-day workers, who thereby recoup the losses of one day off a month with each one per cent drop in rates. This is a money-maker for public employers, who add one person to the tax base and take that same person off tax expenditures every time four workers take the four-day option. Private sector participants should get a rebate on payroll taxes for unemployment insurance to compensate them for any hassles.

3. Union pension funds can balance employment security for their members and a safe, ethical return on investments by offering discounted mortgages to four-day volunteers. This also encourages hiring of young workers who contribute to the pension plan.

4. Local governments can issue tax rebates to four-dayers who make highway expansion unnecessary by staying off rush-hour roads one day a week. By paving the way to a day off, rather than a traffic lane, the municipality can afford to forgive taxes at a rate of about $5 a week. This seems like nickel and diming four-day savings, until the car owner's personal expenditures for 50 days' saved commuting are calculated. Now we're racheting up the savings to cover at least two more of 50 extra days off a year.

5. Canada's unemployment insurance commission has a work-sharing program for companies on the brink of mass layoffs. Participants agree to spread a 20-per-cent layoff among themselves by going on a four-day workweek. They also share the unemployment insurance for the day a week on layoff. They all get 92 per cent of their regular pay for 80 per cent of their regular workweek. That's a good deal for workers. Employers also save because workers are at hand for a recall. Society saves because less people are at risk of losing heart and self-esteem and dropping into the underclass. And it costs no more to pay five people for a day's unemployment than one person five days' unemployment. "If the employer and government spend the same money and prevent 20 per cent of lay-offs, I'd say that's one hell of a program," says University of Toronto industrial relations professor Frank Reed, who can't figure out why the government keeps the program a virtual secret.

6.   Governments already let corporations and individuals deduct money donations to registered charities from their tax-able incomes. Canadian governments do the same for cash donations to political parties. If people power were placed on the same tax footing as guilt money, local and national gov-ernments could issue tax receipts to four-dayers who donate time to a specified range of community groups on their day off. Time could be valued at a set rate, perhaps the minimum wage for starters. It's a cost-free way for governments to boost local service organizations, because new workers who fill the vacu-um left by four-dayers will pay, rather than receive, taxes. Four-dayers get a break on their taxes, a change from the workaday grind, and a crack at new job skills.

7.   Jon Grant, chief executive officer of Quaker Oats in Canada and a strong environmentalist, wants workers to take one of every five years off so they can upgrade their education. In his plan, employers would provide half-pay for a year spent at an accredited learning institution, and would claim the out-lay for a tax deduction.[39] A boon for post-secondary schools, which have a high ratio of staff to students, the plan provides efficient delivery of training funds, which now have a bad habit of going to the upgraders rather than the upgraded. It's also an effective way for companies to downsize. No more early retirement buyouts that the best and brightest snap up on their way to a new career, while the clock watchers stay behind, clinging onto procedure manuals for dear life. For less than the cost of a decent severance package, organizations get up-skilled workers for their money.

8.   Senior Quebec tax official Paul Morin has laid out a painless tax incentive to create 135,000 new jobs in his province. In Morin's scheme, foregone income from a shorter workweek gets the same red carpet tax shelter treatment as any other job-creating investment. A worker who drops from a $40,000 to a $32,000 income by giving up a day's work each week is treated like an honor roll investor, and taxed at the rate of a $24,000-a-year income, cutting any loss in take-home pay to almost nil. In this instance, the province would lose taxes on a total of $32,000 for every new $32,000 job, fully taxable, created to fill the vacuum left by four, four-day volunteers. Job creation doesn't come any cheaper, especially in a province that was prepared to pay $200,000 for every job building the destructive Great Whale megaproject in James Bay.[40]

9.   Renowned pianist and Chopin interpreter, Anton Kuerti, suggests that workers volunteer for a three-day week, which really makes a pay cut worth the while. The volunteer will eat the loss of one day's pay. The government will make up the other.[41] For the price of making up two days' lost income for two workers, the government generates one new job for a four-day worker. When that new worker drops off social security benefits and starts paying taxes instead, the real cost to the government is almost nil.

10.   Worker compensation boards and health insurers could save money by giving rebates to employers who put their shift workers, now about one-fifth of the North American labor force, on 32-hour weeks. The graveyard shift got its name for good reasons. The body's circadian rhythms, an internal thermostat, evolved in the mists of time, before the 20th century's continuous operations. The rhythms are different for people and owls. That's why shift workers have a hard time eating and sleeping, are more vulnerable to chronic fatigue, depression, intestinal disorders, diabetes and degenerative heart disease. Shift work is likely more responsible for the spread of emotional isolation, blind frustration and anger across North America than the hate radio programs turned on during sleepless days.

Most shift work costs are borne by the general public or 9-to-5 employers. Accident rates are higher in the last hours of a night shift, and the consequences can be grave in a hospital, mine, transport truck, airplane or nuclear power plant. Thanks to long and irregular hours, most truckers suffer from sleeping disorders, Stanford University researchers found. "When 78 per cent of the people coming toward you on the road in 40-ton trucks have such a disorder, you have a problem," says Dr. William Dement.[42] One study suggests that night-shifts be limited to 4.5 hours where public safety is affected.

Shift work drives up personal health costs, another bill continuous operation employers pass on to the general public. The permanent jet lag, loneliness, chronic fatigue, heavy snacking, smoking and drinking associated with shift work can double personal sick-care bills. Women who work shifts are at higher risk for pre-term, low-birth-weight deliveries. How much does shift work contribute to the $2.3-billion-a-year tab picked up by North American employers for stress- and depression-related absenteeism?[43] Instead of the paltry wage premium for shift work, which doesn't cover the costs of tranquilizers and Rolaids, a time premium of one day per week is a paying proposition that will benefit health and injury insurers, employers, workers and their families.[44]

11. Employers who cap overtime at 100 hours a year should be eligible for rebates of unemployment insurance, health and worker compensation premiums. Overtime accounts for one-fifth of all hours worked in North America,[45] and is at higher levels now than during World War II, when factories ran short-staffed and flat out for the emergency.[46] Overtime is "the paradox of our times," a 1994 advisory report on welfare reform in Canada noted: some are working themselves to death, while others are dying for a job.[47]

Overtime is booming for a number of reasons. The frantic rush of just-in-time delivery keeps capital and storage costs low, but makes life cheap. Faxes and e-mail give law offices the leeway to miss the 6 o'clock mail deadline on briefs, time to cram in an extra case. Above all, high but fixed payroll taxes and fringe benefit packages—which average $7 an hour for full-time employees[48]—lower the time-and-a-half premium for overtime to virtually zero compared to the cost of hiring a new worker.

These savings are an illusion. When employers aren't suffering from absenteeism—which knocks out five per cent of payroll when productivity losses and extra costs of replacement workers are factored in,[49] much of it to cover stress and personal family obligations, not sickness[50]—they suffer from "presenteeism." Their asses dragging, overtime martyrs stumble along at half-peak efficiency. Overtime is also linked to higher than normal accident and injury rates, predictable enough given that most safety regulations for tolerance of noise, muscle strain and workplace pollutants are based on eight-hour days.[51] Chronic fatigue syndrome and repetitive strain injuries knock long-term disability insurance out of whack.[52]

Nor will workaholics get to keep checks fattened by overtime for long, because they're working themselves to an early grave, the follow-up punch to expensive divorce proceedings. Typical two-income couples spend 12 minutes of quality time together, and share 40 per cent less time with their kids than a generation ago, according to the 1994 PBS documentary **Running Out of Time**. We live in what Kristyna Hartse of the Sleep Disorders Center calls a "sleep-deprived culture" that gets by on two hours a night less beauty-rest than was standard a hundred years ago,[53] and a good 90 minutes less than health requires.[54] To make up for sleep, we take a caffeine jolt, the coffee break rating as a "Protestant siesta."[55] In **Conquering Insomnia**, Dr. Colin Shapiro links chronic sleep deficits to a high incidence of degenerative diseases, including cancer. Overtimers eat more junk, work it off less. Live fat, die young, with your suit on.

When employers cap overtime and use premium rebates from insurers to convert sick days to wellness days, we will move toward full employment with the savings.

12. The worst overtime offenders are already well paid.[56] Their hogging of jobs is a major factor in the last decade's widening of the equality gap across North America.[57] The hip but conservative **Economist** magazine suggests that decline of progressive tax schedules during the 1980s is to blame. By reducing the marginal tax rate on upper incomes, governments granted a tax break that squeezed young workers out of the good jobs and taxed them more on their bad jobs. Going back to the progressive tax levels of the 1970s, or at least isolating overtime for major tax penalties, will help jobs trickle down, and lead to a new competitive ethos, where, in **Chicago Tribune** writer Mark Hill's words, "spending time with the Joneses becomes more fashionable than keeping up with them."[58]

13. Moonlighters break for Sunday mall shopping. They're not out in the country long enough to brake for garage sales. John Fry, editor of **Snow Country,** argues that tourism operators should get behind the short hours movement, since they offer services that can't be wedged into one afternoon.[59] One way to create a win-win here is to earmark 10 per cent of entertainment taxes to boost deep discount tour packages pitched to four-dayers. All packages could feature train or shuttle bus transportation, cutting the costs and pollution of getting there. The fund could also finance development of infrastructure for visitors who aren't in such a rush to see everything before they leave. Walking trails and dedicated bike lanes and paths are a natural, as is training of local residents as nature and social history guides.

Overtime is a beach, where workaholics recover from exhaustion getting baked in the sun, somewhere faraway, mind and body numb. Their own energy drained by overwork, moonlighters drain energy from plane travel, spend their locally earned dollars far away, and come back as relaxed as when they left. The style of tourism associated with overwork costs many areas big. Canada, for instance, suffers an $8-billion-a-year tourism deficit, enough to stimulate 160,000 jobs if a home-visiting program were instituted. The logical customers for local tourism are four-dayers. If state and provincial governments wanted to get really adventurous promoting local tourist spots, they'd offer a sales tax rebate to those who holiday close to home and spend more of their vacation dollars where they earn them. It's a no-cost item, since out-of-area vacationers pay no local sales taxes anyway.

14. Payroll taxes—automatic deductions to cover unemployment insurance, workers compensation and the like, commonly costing in the range of $3,000 per employee—were supposed to be progressive, a way of making big employers pay their share of social costs. Ironically, the single fastest growing component of payroll taxes is unemployment insurance.[60] So, government payroll taxation policies encourage business to not hire, then impose the cost of unemployment on them, and then take a cut for administering programs to train and educate the unemployed. Put another way, payroll taxes reflect a decision to tax jobs rather than wealth or pollution.[61]

Payroll taxes encourage corporate dumping of social costs, easily done by moving to contracting-out or part-time staff. Payroll taxes discriminate against small and service companies, which are labor-intensive, and in favor of large capital-intensive manufacturing and resource corporations that have a much lower ratio of employees to net worth. Payroll taxes are also a culprit in overtime. Since the lump sum payments are fixed per employee, not per hour, they reduce the cost of overtime and increase the cost of new hires.[62] The same goes for fringe benefits, which add insult to injury with their low-tax status. If payroll taxes and fringe benefits tied to particular employers were phased out, and the costs levied on corporations on the basis of net worth, employers would no longer lose money when they hired new workers and allowed regulars to move toward shorter hours.

15. Contrary to the myth, there's no hollowing out of North American industry. There's just a job vacuum brought about by automation and increased productivity. In Canada, output per worker jumped 26 per cent between 1975 and 1990.[63] In the U.S., production shot up 5.4 per cent in 1994, as manufacturers shipped out more goods than they did in the mid-1980s boom, but with 450,000 fewer workers.[64]

Competitiveness means good times for machines, not workers, because our tax systems privilege machines over workers. There's no level playing field when employers get to write off rapid depreciation when they buy machines and get a payroll tax penalty when they hire workers. A study by the Bank of Canada found that a full one per cent of the workforce, or 130,000 workers, lost their jobs because of two trends: computer prices plummeted in the 90s while payroll tax costs shot up. This is affirmative action for machines. It forces humans to measure up head and shoulders over a machine to be considered for employment. This system of tax discrimination is a hold-over from second wave, Fordist days when mechanization boosted employment by expanding markets.

We've put ourselves in a Catch 22. The tax system favors machine- rather than human-based strategies to boost productivity, automated switchboards rather than friendly operators who can serve as a company's front-line, public relations staff, for instance. The benefits of machine-based productivity aren't spread among workers through shorter hours. If hours at work had been reduced in keeping with increased output per hour since the 1950s, for instance, we'd all be working 10-hour weeks. This didn't happen because workers had to compete with machines. If worker benefits increased, workers would have priced themselves out of the market, become less competitive with the artificially cheap machines they subsidized with their taxes. Putting machines in their place means a level playing field that makes them prove their value at tax time. By phasing out capital depreciation allowances, replacing them with human depreciation allowances, granted to employers who slow the depletion of human resources by instituting shorter hours, we can put the tax system behind a no-cost shift to shorter hours. Aside from making machines pay their fair share of taxes, governments could also take hi-tech off the welfare rolls. Investigators at the **Philadelphia Inquirer** identified $6 billion worth of questionable government grants, including $300,000 to help the Disney empire launch fireworks mechanically and $58 million to cover IBM's research—at a time when Big Blue was laying off 100,000 workers, cutting its own research budget by one-third and raking in $3 billion in profits.65

16. Life is short, and then you drive. But the money most people spend on cars goes faster than the car. An average car sputters along a little behind a bike, once the time breezing along freeways is factored in with the time crawling in traffic jams, and worked in with the time the car is parked, sucking up one week's take-home pay in three to pay off the bank, gas, insurance and taxes. There's a reason why car ads feature fantasies of gliding along mountain roads, the same reason booze companies feature cowpokes rustling up meat, not skid rowers begging for a dime.

Four-day workers don't have to drive themselves crazy. They save an hour a week commuting just by driving balls at the golf course on Wednesdays. They can afford to lose that hour by walking, biking or taking public transit the rest of the week. The time lost won't add up to much. The Washington State Energy Office estimates that a commuting bicyclist takes all of two minutes longer than a car driver to complete a 10-mile round trip, and saves $1,500 a year on car expenses.66 If they can suffer through that, they can bemoan their miserable carless life while hiking all July in the Rockies. They've bought themselves another month to play with, even if they just make their car last an extra five years.

Whip out a calculator and see if this math works for you. The average car owner pays $7,000 a year to cover payments, repairs, gas, parking and insurance. To afford $7,000 clear, most people have to work at least three months or 480 hours, or close to two hours a day. They do that so they can tool around in their own car for 500 hours. That's about how long it takes to drive the average 12,000 miles a year that we do, given that many of these miles are in stop-and-go traffic. We work that out to a total 980 hours to travel 12,000 miles, or a little less than 13 miles an hour. A biker can keep up with that and keep fit at the same time. What if we stopped spending that two hours a working day, going no miles an hour, and started spending that time biking? We could use unemploy-

ment insurance to give everyone a free, domestically
bike, since unemployment would disappear if the emp.
worked shorter days, weeks or months. That's a totally cr
idea, isn't it?

When Bob and Helen Hansen of North York, Ontario, gave
up their car, they used their driveway to park all-season gardening containers, soaking up the free heat given off by pavement. With their growing season extended, they can eat fresh-
picked food for almost half the year, and were able to give up
their refrigerator, a big item on any utility bill. The costs of residential land devoted to parking cars isn't often counted. One
estimate, which amortizes construction bills for a carport and
includes a costing on land made unavailable for other purposes, such as gardening, puts the figure at $746 a year.[67] So a car-
free home can do its bit in financing a four-day workweek.

Convenience foods, which are more properly called overtime
foods, represent another hidden opportunity cost of rushed
work schedules. Time is money, and it costs a fair amount of
money to buy time with intensively packaged near-foods.
With practice, "golden Wednesdays" can let people who enjoy
gardening and cooking from scratch save more than they make
working for a boss. Free time is very affordable.

Keeping Your Head Above Water

A spin-off of ESCOs, water saving companies or WASCOs, make
their money off what now goes down the drain. In return for free installation of conservation equipment, they keep the difference between what a business or resident would have paid for water, and
what they ended up paying, until the job has been paid off. Rich
Kerhovich, who runs a WASCO out of Oshawa, tells customers they
won't feel a thing for about two years. But after his costs are paid off,
all the savings go to the customer, who paid nothing for them. "Our
thing is that people don't even know they're saving," Kerhovich says.

Some municipal water utilities are learning that it's cheaper to conserve water that's already been treated and pumped than it is to clean
and pump more water. To keep pace with its rapid growth and in-

creased demand for water, Barrie, Ontario, looked at two mega-project options. It could build a $41-million addition to its waste-water treatment plant and get its water from a nearby lake by building a $27-million intake plant that would have to be upgraded later with a $20-million addition. Or, as it decided to do, it could get its extra water supply from customers, by helping them conserve. It costs households $460 in extra taxes to install low-flow toilets (which save almost four gallons a flush on the biggest water-user in the house), showerheads and aerator faucets in every residence. Seem like a lot of money to give away? It saved the city at least $9.3 million relative to the heavy construction option. Residents save another $18.4 million in energy costs, because they're now heating less water. The added bonus for the community is the creation of 2,400 local, mainly semi-skilled, jobs. The plant expansion option would have employed 1,600 workers, with hiring requirements that favored outside talent.

In the U.S., average rate increases jumped 10 per cent for water and 15 per cent for sewage from 1992 to 1994.[68] But in Morro Bay, California, city officials told developers they couldn't build any new projects that required an increase of the city's overall water supply, despite a growing population. Then the market worked its magic. To get credits from conserving enough water to float their new projects, contractors knocked on resident and business doors, clamoring to do water retrofits for free. The competition to save water was sometimes so intense that residents held out until they got a free drink or dinner in the bargain. Private builders retrofitted half the homes and businesses in Morro Bay at no cost to taxpayers or old-time residents. They also made sure their new buildings were water-efficient.

For cities looking to save for a rainy day, the next generation of water savings will come from seeing rain as more than what civil engineers call storm water. Rain barrels store rain that can be used later to water lawns, just like the water mother nature uses, without the chlorine additives that brown many lawns. Cisterns collect rain for later use in dish and clothes washers, which need less soap to get soft rain-water ready to clean. In either case, home eaves troughs can be disconnected from sewers, saving the city the costs of expanding sewage mains and treatment plants to handle rain. Cities that don't mind tilting the playing field in favor of conservation can also build a slight rise at the edge of city green space that stops rainwater from flowing onto the streets and into sewers, and keeps it on ground that can use the extra moisture. Waterscaping can also include more widespread use of "porous pavement," such as bricks instead of cement, which allow rain to seep into the ground through the cracks. Such measures can reduce sewage and water treatment bills in most areas by at least 10 per cent.

Old Growth

Inadequate government preparation for an aging population lies behind many environmental problems. One (of several) reasons why poor Third World parents have large families, for instance, is to ensure enough survivors to support them in their old age. "Universal pensions are the best birth control plan they could ever have," says Tony Mazzocchi, retired vice-president of the Oil, Chemical and Atomic Workers' Union.

In North America, we have the more fortunate problem of a bulging 1940s baby boom, with parents still spry at a ripe old age. But most seniors are house poor, their life savings tied up in their homes. Their kids, therefore, can only become beneficiaries of their inheritance when, life willing, "the kids" are themselves looking at retirement, their own kids having flown the coop and their most burdensome expenses over. While one set of parents sit on idle capital, another set is working their buns off to make ends meet, and the young set can't get a job because of people like their parents working overtime. What is wrong with this picture?

A simple twist on second mortgages puts past and future savings to work. A non-profit agency, Old Growth Reverse Mortgages Inc., could offer to issue advance payment for half the home value of retirees who volunteer for the program. The agency will be reimbursed for its investment and foregone interest at government rates 7of six per cent when the retirees go to happy saving grounds in the sky and the estate is settled. In a typical case, the agency would pay down $100,000 on a 65-year-old retiree's $200,000 home, collect $239,000 when the retiree dies at 80, by which time three per cent inflation has pushed the home's value up to $312,000.

The agency offer could be tied to a condition that the early windfall go immediately to a beneficiary who elects to a three-day week, to relocate in a smaller town that needs more people to sustain basic services, or some other option that creates job openings for the young. It's the new economics of eating your cake and having it, too.

Trading Up

Foreign aid has been described as a subsidy from the poor people of the developed world to the rich people of the developing world. This is too optimistic. Less than five per cent of foreign aid reaches the poor of the Third World. Almost all aid is tied to military purchases and energy megaprojects that benefit the donor country. These purchases contribute to such debt and dependency in the Third World that foreign aid actually works in reverse. Since 1960, about $1.4 trillion in debt payments have flowed from south to north, about 10 times what southern countries received in aid.[69] This financial hemorrhaging on bad debts, more often than not forced on subject populations by non-elected elites,[70] affects North Americans too. All that money flowing north goes to bankers, not workers making manufactured goods for export. Susan George, author of **The Debt Boomerang: How The Third World Debt Hurts Us All,** argues that one-fifth of U.S. unemployment can be blamed on this loss of poor nations' buying power.

Thanks to inappropriate imports of first world energy and transportation infrastructure, the World Bank says Third World countries lose $54 billion a year in waste, more than they receive in aid.[71] (As one example, the massive Aswan dam on the Nile River in Egypt now produces less power than is used in the manufacture of fertilizers for the soil that was once renewed by the annual flooding and silting of the Nile.) If foreign aid money were used to provide up-front financing of ESCOs, Third World countries would soon have $54 billion more jingling in their pockets. First world manufacturers of conservation or solar equipment made with materials or processes unavailable in the Third World would face major market opportunities, and a chance to jump start to mass production methods. And the whole world would breathe easier as Third World forests are spared from direct use as fuels, or indirect use for currency to import fossil fuels.

Leave It To Beavers

"I figure there's a thin line between efficiency and laziness," says Ed Burt, a 67-year-old farmer with looks, voice and innocence that could be mistaken for Jimmy Stewart. He's one of 200 farmers still making a living on Manitoulin Island in northern Lake Huron. He's watched 600 farmers give up and leave since he started in 1952. Burt won't admit any fond feelings for the beavers who have turned 15 of his 110 acres into swampland. "Beavers are Canada's national symbol," he says, "and whoever picked them didn't do too bad. They work all the time and most of it is pretty mindless. They eat themselves out of house and home, and then have to move on." He points at a canal they built to drag logs along. "Same mentality as Ontario Hydro. You'd almost think they went to college." Burt gets back for the pasture he's lost by using the beavers as cheap labor.

He gets enough firewood for three families from the trees they've gnawed down. He's building his retirement home with 45 cords of blocks cut from cedar they felled. He yanks out bulrush roots to fry in batter for a spring treat, a cross between leeks and asparagus. The cedar furniture and coffee table in the living room also come from the swamp.

Burt tramps through a woodlot he's let grow back after a clear-cut in 1948. "If I had my life to live over again, I'd thin this out for maple and oak and get a high price for the lumber," he says. He gets 80 gallons of maple syrup from the woods, about a third of its potential. The woodlot also provides him with a yearly supply of wild leeks, morel mushrooms and fiddleheads. He shows off his 100 wild pear and apple trees. They grow in gnarled clumps of three or four, so at least one shoot is protected from foraging rabbits and deer. Once they've got beyond the reach of deer, Burt grafts on branches of domesticated trees to get better yields. He takes 100 gallons of apple juice from the orchard, and feeds the rest to the pigs. Four of the 20 deer that freeload on his orchard in the summer end up on their dinner plates in the winter. The trick to survival is keeping cash outputs low by diversifying skills. "The local economy is like a pail with holes in it. The trick is to plug some of the holes, not pour in more water," he says.

Burt enters the house through the root cellar. He never gave up his wood stove for central heating, so he doesn't have to buy a freezer to store his vegetables over winter. Upstairs in the kitchen, Elda Burt makes most meals from scratch, including flour ground from grain in a device about twice the size of a coffee grinder. Self-reliance is a time-saver, not a burden, she says. "I feel all this modern stuff you buy is more work than what you did before. It's not that big a deal to make bread. With six kids, I couldn't just pack them in the car to go to town for a loaf of bread. You can make it in the time you're going to the store, and save the gas besides." Each spring, she makes rhubarb punch and bakes about 40 pies from rhubarb and wild strawberries. Fresh winter food comes from the greenhouse on the south wall. "It's 85 degrees during the winter, so I just lay out there instead of going to Florida," she says. Elda Burt also manages the pigs and barn, and still found spare time to write a local history, **Portraits of Manitoulin's Past**, as a fund-raiser for her church group, and to do most of the paintings in the living room.

Outside is the work shed, filled with oak door frames and bay windows cut from the woodlot. The doors are a mosaic of inlaid scraps, showing off the grains of different species. Burt also tinkers on a 1906 roadster, the oldest on the island. "I just like doing a lot of things," he says. "To become more expert is basically learning more about less, and being less able to adapt and express your talents. For some, it seems like a burden to do 15 things. For me, it's security and enjoyment. I always figured hoeing was therapy, not work," he says. "Unemployment's something I just can't figure. Do you ever see an unemployed squirrel? Everybody comes with a talent and curiosity. It's when people in the masses have mundane jobs that you get unemployment when a big factory closes."

The work shed is full of materials for their dream retirement home, built into a bluff, so that the ground can moderate temperatures in summer and winter, with six patio-size windows on the south side for heat and light. Walls, courtesy of the beavers, are made of cedar blocks, piled like bricks. "We've lived below the poverty line most of

The Far Side

Principle 3

Presents "elegant" design methods which outperform linear economies of scale with lateral "economies of scope" by meeting many goals through one action

"When faced with two seemingly insoluble problems, try tackling both at once."
International economic forecaster Linda Starke[1]

"To rationalize almost inevitably means to cut, to reduce, to eliminate—not to integrate or grow or create. Rationalizing is to the contemporary manager what bloodletting was to the medieval physician."

Management thinker Henry Mintzberg[2]

Elegance is economics with peripheral vision. A basic design principle of the new economy, elegance instills a commitment to what's called synergy, problem-solving strategies that develop multiple wins and positive side-effects from any one set of actions. It's the great equalizer for small organizations, because they can achieve optimal efficiency through economies of means or scope—making each action count several times—and outperform large organizations that sacrifice flexibility to achieve economies of scale. The elegant approach to winning friends and influencing people is providing common ground for community gardeners.

Companion planting is garden variety elegance. Long before Europeans colonized North America, Native farmers planted beans, corn and squash together. The climbing beans used corn stalks as support, and reciprocated by fixing nitrogen in the soil that corn depleted. Squash leaves provided ground cover against weeds, erosion and evaporation. Eaten together, they provided complementary nutrients.[3] This gardening strategy duplicates nature's methods, which economize on energy by endowing each plant and creature with several functions. Applied to an economy, the same approach optimizes returns on multi-purpose projects, which avoids the "complications" and "negative side effects" that so often come from maximizing returns on one project alone. Applied to a community, the strategy seeks win-win combinations across the board.

In the community gardening capital of North America, Anne Whiston Spirn, professor of landscape architecture at the University of Pennsylvania and author of **The Granite Garden**, co-designed Pittsburgh's expanding allotments with a strong sense of all the companionships they fostered. The community garden, a public area set aside for residents, "is a wedge into a neighborhood," she says, and "contains lessons for the design of larger neighborhoods."[4] This is unsettling stuff for orthodox planners, trained to use zoning to segregate urban functions—a paint-by-number way of keeping residential areas separate from areas of working, farming and shopping, or recreational separate from productive lands. This mechanistic application of the division of labor to space is an attempt to regulate urban order in the midst of chaos.

Zoning attempts to replicate the power relations of a single-industry town in a cosmopolitan city. Mining and logging companies like the focus of single industry towns. The lack of diversity minimizes competition for resources. Tourism operators get in the way when they complain about clear-cutting. Commercial fishers raise a fuss over the run-off from mine tailings. Reducing the range of interest groups reduces the need for win-win solutions that benefit all. In a single industry town, the people concerned about air, water and land quality are not producers, and their concerns are easily marginalized, treated as a luxury rather than a necessity. Urban zoning fulfills the same role. It squeezes out potential competitors, neighborhood businesses that might lobby against superstores, resident groups that might fight for pollution-free factories, for instance. It decreases the range of opportunities for self-employment or self-reliance—which is why unemployment is such a personal disaster in the city—and thereby increases the dependence of workers on a relatively small number of employers. Strict segregation of functions, in short, creates the death referred to in Jane Jacob's **Death and Life of Great American Cities**, the classic indictment of second-wave planning that undermined the economic and social vitality of urban villages.

In contrast to the dominant planning model, community gardens are about de-segregating cities. A small patch of land given over to community gardens packs more uses into a compact space than a Swiss army knife. At one and the same time, they:

1. allow people who own no land to produce fresh food, now valued at $23 million annually, at virtually no cost;

2.   provide healthy outdoor exercise, relaxation and even therapy, as with Montreal's award-winning gardens for seniors, who benefit from increased fine motor control, dexterity, pride and self-esteem;[5]

3.   offer recreation the whole family can take part in;

4.   extend the constituency for city parks to "passive" users, often excluded from parks built around "organized recreation" for jocks;

5.   act as a neighborhood crime watch, Jane Jacobs' "eyes on the street," over many hours of the day and evening;

6.   beautify derelict land on a pilot-project basis, without the deeds needed for permanent structures, thereby adding flexibility which increases the availability of land, even, as in North York, Ontario, in cemetery dead space not yet filled with permanent occupants;

7.   add biomass that converts excess carbon dioxide into oxygen;

8.   create space for a "new commons," public space for hanging out that was lost when streets were taken over by cars;

9.   provide a natural fire barrier between buildings;

10. add to green space that can absorb rainfall and divert it from sewers;

11. provide common ground for community development in low-income areas such as Walnut Terrace, North Carolina, where, supporters say, "the community garden is a deterrent to destructive or apathetic behavior because its very existence is an expression of peoples' togetherness, productivity, hope, responsibility and caring for the whole environment, from flowers to neighbors and families;"[6]

12. provide fertile ground for transplanting immigrant food traditions;

13. provide a job-training center for at-risk youth, as pioneered in Boston;

14. create spin-off jobs in commercial greenhouses and allied fields, as in San Francisco, where the homeless get top dollar for 26 varieties of salad greens sold to leading restaurants,[7] because, as urban critic Terry Fowler describes one such project in the Bronx, "in the course of organizing themselves to grow food, the people also organized a project to generate their own power;"[8]

15. offer a site for innovative partnerships with governments and charitable foundations, which can match grants to community "sweat equity;"

16. work out the bugs in sustainable agriculture, including organic growing and, in dry climates, low-water xeriscaping;[9]

17. encourage advances in intensive agriculture, since, in contrast to corporate farming, space is at more of a premium than time;

18. lower garbage disposal costs by providing nearby outlets for composting kitchen waste, the "twin sister" of community gardening;[10]

19. reduce the costly highway infrastructure for food transportation, and encourage "urban villages" where key services are within walking distance;

20. teach respect for nature, farming, natural cycles and future orientation, as in Boston's inner city where Dr. Arturo Cervantes, supported by Schweitzer Urban Fellows, finds the most important work he can do from his clinic is to teach children how to garden because it teaches them to gauge future results from actions taken today; that is, you plant now, you reap in six months.

Elegance is an economic version of judo that turns the weight of a problem to advantage by flipping it into a solution. "The poorest areas are rich in resources," says Ken Dunn, a leader of Seattle's gardening plot.

"It just shows what can be done by taking a little trouble," said Eyore. "Do you see, Pooh? Do you see, Piglet? Brains first and then hard work. Look at it! That's the way to build a house."

Children's writer A.A. Milne[11]

Elegance turns infrastructure into a sideshow. Once the habit of lateral thinking is formed, the side benefits of any decision start to multiply far beyond "killing two birds with one stone," or "two mints in one," the best that linear thinking offers. For engineer Greg Allen, this economy of means outperforms the economies of scale that rely on cheap resources.

Greg Allen's genius makes heads spin with the logic of elegance. His graduate degree in engineering and architectural training taught him that "getting good at this was not a good idea," so he's made a specialty of breaking the rules of both professions to extend energy savings across the economy.

In the heyday of government support for energy conservation following the oil price shocks of the 1970s, Allen worked on Canada's R-2000 building standards, still the international bench mark for saving energy through careful construction and insulation. Then he figured out "the dirty secret of R-2000," a formula that "institutionalized construction methods, and shut down real problem-solving." The challenge, he thought, was not to build tight to prevent energy loss, but to use mass and glass to gain energy, to turn windows and building materials into furnaces. "Mechanical systems and furnaces are the failure of architecture," he says.

Allen has won major award competitions over the past 15 years. One of his early inventions, Sol-Mate, a package that provides all the energy needs of a home with sunlight and a stick of wood a day, won him a **Popular Science** prize, still pinned up in his basement beside his invention while he searches for an investor to mass-produce it. He conceived the first experimental "advanced house" in Brampton, Ontario, another notch in his belt of passive-aggressive approaches to solar power—using the sun's rays to displace the need for, as well as create, high-grade energy. A stone fireplace decorates the back wall and stores heat from the adjoining greenhouse sunroom for release during the night. No use conserving home heating fuel, then burning it up transporting food that can be grown year-round, he reasons.

Another award winner was a "granny flat" that converts back-lane garages into in-fill housing for singles or single parents with one child. The conversion is elegant by itself, providing income for the owners, affordable housing for a group neglected by developers, increasing the density of urban areas so better libraries and public transit become viable. The flat features a soapstone wood stove that throws off heat long after the fire is out. The stove can burn clean with pellets made from waste sawdust, otherwise destined to give off methane gas, the most potent of the greenhouse gases, in a landfill. The stove not only cooks meals and heats rooms and water. A stove-top box developed for prospectors converts the heat into enough electricity for most household needs. The stove still conveys social warmth, unlike basement furnaces, where few lovers are invited to snuggle up and wait for the sparks to fly.

Allen is now working on two high-rises that turn landlords into electricity exporters. One features garburators that take kitchen waste to an enclosed composter, where the furnace burns off the methane produced by the compost. That knocks out methane and avoids burning natural gas, which Allen calls "the crack cocaine of the fossil fuel economy," for a double cut in greenhouse gases. Later, the compost is taken to the rooftop garden, where solar collectors and wind generators produce electricity for sale to the grid. A two-way connection that both imports from and exports to the grid is better than storing solar energy in batteries, the main cost barrier to stand-alone solar systems.

Allen has also engineered an environmental education center for the YMCA near Waterloo, Ontario. The central building has a lecture hall, meeting and exercise rooms. On the south side, windows draw heat and light. A stone, Finnish-style fireplace tops up the heat in winter, using deadfall from four acres of surrounding forest. In the winter, the fireplace supplements solar panels to heat shower water. Exercise bikes are hooked up to the lighting system. The toilets get their water from cisterns on the roof, and expel their waste to a living machine and polishing pond. A second building, a 32-unit residence set back in the forest, is built into a hill, so the deep earth moderates summer and winter temperatures. "The building will experience a mammalian approach to wintering," Allen says. The residences have wind generators and solar panels that avoid the expensive connection to a utility grid. Composter toilets turn yesterday's food into fertilizer. "Waste is a verb, not a noun," he notes. Capital costs for the entire energy and water system come out at $200,000, competitive with orthodox methods that stiff the owner with high operating costs for energy and site preparation.

Clever inventor that he is, Allen pooh-poohs clever inventions and technical fixes. "I have a fundamental problem with environmental management," he says. "Control over nature is not the objective. It's realignment, harmonization. Elegance is what makes the sustainable also affordable."

"Never make a single-issue decision."
Healthy homes builder and consultant Ed Lowans

Elegance will move public policy to the right—as in the right, intuitive, lateral side of the brain, not the formal, linear left side. That means taking on "the straights" and one-track minds who want to compartmentalize solutions so they fit in their departments. In the new economy, lobbyists will have to answer skill-testing questions ensuring that their projects meet the "It's a 10" standard—enabling realization of at least 10 goals—before they're adopted. Here are some projects that won't have trouble passing.

The Zen Of Housing

"To think of housing is a mistake," says Peter Burns, senior urban policy analyst with the Ontario government. Burns encourages co-housing developers to buy up low-cost inner city warehouses and factories for conversion to urban villages. Affordable housing is only one objective met in his scheme that:

1.   preserves and revitalizes architectural heritage;

2.   salvages and re-uses old building materials, which otherwise would go to landfill;

3.   facilitates energy-efficient renovations and adaptations, such as high-efficiency furnaces that co-generate electricity;

4.   is accessible to many family configurations, including single parent families, since child-care facilities can be incorporated;

5.   is open to many work arrangements, including home offices which can take advantage of the downtown location;

6.   provides community economic development opportunities by mixing income and family groups, allowing, for

instance, at-home mothers to cater food to busy couples, or teens to offer room service and baby-sitting;

7. is priced and mortgaged so that the poor can become home owners;

8. provides a low-risk, socially responsible investment for pension funds;

9. promotes intensification, increasing the efficiency of public services;

10. preserves the inner city's tax base.

Bargain Basement Cooling

Cities close to deep water can tap into renewable air conditioning that uses an inexhaustible supply of cold brew at their doorstep. When surface water warms in the summer, the colder and heavier water sinks to about the 80-yard line, where it's just above freezing, year-round. Tiny amounts of this water can be piped to downtown office towers, where air exchanges cool everyone off, without the need for air conditioners.

Toronto, with hot, muggy summers typical of the Great Lakes area, has already done the cost-benefit estimates. It would cost $50 million to lay pipes to bring cold water four miles to shore, a cost that might be split with the local water utility, since deep water is cleaner and free of the zebra mussels that clog most Great Lakes filtration pipes. It will cost $550 million to hook up major downtown office buildings, mainly because digging almost has to be done with teaspoons to get through the underground maze of wiring and pipes. Deep water cooling would eliminate the need for 200 megawatts of electrical supply, a saving of $400 million, and reduce global warming emissions by 170,000 tons if that displaced electricity had been produced with coal. Building owners would avoid the purchase of expensive new CFC-free air conditioners now required by law, and the ongoing need to buy electricity to power them. Costs can be recouped inside of two years, after which the plan lives up to its nickname—free cool. The solar megaproject would employ 10,000 workers for a year.

Here's how to add more layers of icing to the cake by using the opportunity of tunnel construction to mine construction aggregate and gravel, and by mining in such a way as to leave behind a functioning warehouse area. This is a pet project of Laurentian University geotechnical engineering professor, Dougal McCreath, keen on starting an underground economy that:

1.   stops the pillage of ecologically-sensitive areas for gravel, and reduces the transportation costs and road hazards of carting it to urban areas;

2.   provides stable ground for precision tooling industries and storage of heavy equipment and materials;

3.   provides year-round stable temperatures for cellar storage of wine and other goods, without the need for mechanical heating or cooling controls, and with enough thermal mass to forego expensive equipment for emergency backup cooling;

4.   keeps ugly facilities out of sight;

5.   reduces access points for thieves and vandals;

6.   eliminates runaway industrial fires and explosions, since the air supply can be cut off;

7.   offers opportunities for renewable "peaking" power, since generators can take advantage of a 1,000-foot free fall of water, pumped up at night when there's a power surplus and dropped in the morning when there's a shortage;

8.   frees up lakeshore for outdoor and recreational space by placing traditional port structures underground, just as people put unsightly furnaces and stored stuff in their basements, not their living rooms;

9.   slows the rate of suburban warehouse expansion by providing superior facilities near the heart of downtown;

10.   provides nearby job opportunities for inner city residents.

"No one factor is over-riding," McCreath says of his cave-age proposal, "but you have this plethora of benefits."

Smile, You're On Candid Camera

Photo radar devices tag freeway speeders by taking photographs of licenses whizzing by over the speed limit. Since automated photo radar dramatically increases the likelihood of getting caught speeding, it has an immediate impact on average driving speeds. Governments save so much money from reduced accidents, health and policing costs, they can afford to be generous with the revenues from speeding tickets. If these revenues were donated to community groups engaged in highway tree-planting, an elegant photo radar package would solve many problems, all at the same time. It would:

1.   free up police for more important duties than clocking speeders and waiting to testify against them in court;

2.   decrease police risks of getting testicular cancer from hand-held radar devices,[12] and lower the dietary risk of excessive donut consumption while sitting in staff cars;

3.   lower the highway accident rate by at least 14 per cent, saving over $50 billion a year in car and health insurance, since drivers who follow speed safety laws have more time and space to react;

4.   lower the death rate from freeway collisions by at least 27 per cent, saving an estimated $10 billion a year in lost earnings potential alone, since crash impacts come down by half with every 20-mile-an-hour decrease in speed;[13]

5.   provide stable funding for community groups engaged in highway beautification;

6.   consolidate a constituency for strict enforcement of speeding laws, needed to counter the yelps of right-to-bear-cars types, who believe they drive more safely than wimpy slowpokes;

7.   offer a wind and snow break for winter safety;

8. provide a future source of lumber, without the need for separate access roads, one of the more destructive elements of clear-cutting;

9. provide a psychological speed bump, since drivers automatically slow down when their range of vision is reduced by such factors as roadside tree plantings;

10. reduce gas used up by car air conditioners while riding over sun-drenched pavement and reduce the rate of overheated radiators, thanks to shading and evaporation by trees;

11. lower the burn from excessive fuel waste at high speeds—at 75 miles an hour, a car burns an extra quarter tank of gas to drive the same distance as the same model car going 60 miles an hour—with enough savings by this measure alone to meet stated government objectives on reducing global warming emissions;[14]

12. allow highways to be built with fewer and more narrow lanes, another multi-billion-dollar savings, since those driving at legal limits have more control than speeders, and do not need to keep as much distance from other cars;

13. allow public transit to compete with cars in terms of travel time, since drivers won't be able to make up for lost time in traffic jams by putting the pedal to the metal on freeways.

14. reduce traffic sounds carried to nearby residential areas by half, thanks to noise absorption by trees.[15]

School Bell Curve

Schools are where the most powerful groups in society are heard but not seen. Becoming invisible—that's the status of sugar, salt, cornstarch, animal fat, for instance, smuggled into more foods than most people realize—puts a product beyond debate, like the air we breathe. That's a habit monopolies strive to form during school years, when public taxes pay respected authorities to pass their message on to a captive and impressionable audience, with none of the controversy or expense of TV ads that target kids.

School meal programs in the U.S., supposedly for the poor, serve a square meal made from agricultural surplus, a backhanded way of siphoning $5 billion a year in federal subsidies to handle chronic waste problems of agribusiness at the expense of local farmers who could supply fresh produce.[16] Conventional cafeterias provide training wheels for the fat-food industry. Less than one per cent of U.S. school cafeterias offer meals with lower than 30 per cent fat content, and the norm is 39 per cent, a future heartbreaker of major proportions.[17] The salt content for lunches is about double what most kids should have in a day.[18] McDonalds and Pizza Hut compete for cafeteria contracts, while Pepsi and Coke fill the pop machines, usually leaving the school to pick up the electricity cost of the freezer. The nutrition curriculum is as good for nutrition as the forestry curriculum is for forests. It flogs the notion of four food groups, two of them animal fat, down from 12 food groups in 1930 and seven in 1954, thanks to the heart attack lobby.[19] Educational stations piped into schools carry twice the junk food ads of prime time TV, a breathtaking accomplishment in its own right.[20]

By contrast, the new wave of school nutrition programs go beyond serving poor meals to poor kids. They're designed to feature multiple benefits.

1. They boost school performance. The University of Montreal's Michelle Nadeau showed that kids who ate real breakfasts jumped ahead of kids loaded on sweets.[21] Nobel laureate Linus Pauling gathered research to show that vitamin C intake increased alertness and sharpness.[22]

2. They let teachers teach, by reducing behavior problems of kids from all income groups who are strung out on sugar jags or disorienting allergies from additives.[23]

3. They re-establish breakfast as a major meal of the day, overcoming the common habit in all income groups of skipping breakfast.[24] Proper breakfasts not only supply fuel for the morning, says **New York Times** columnist Jane Brody. They supply most of the day's vitamin C, calcium, iron and thiamin. Starting the day off right also leaves a whole day for the calories to burn off, making it the ideal meal for weight control, should schools ever get into the act of countering youth obesity.[25]

4. They introduce kids to a wide variety of foods, and the taste bud cosmopolitanism stays with them for life, says Cornell University nutrition professor Antonia Demas.[26] This provides a crucial cultural foundation for agricultural diversification.

5. They prevent degenerative diseases of later life, many of which can be traced to nutritional deficiencies in childhood, when the body is growing so quickly. Women, for instance, have lower rates of heart disease if they had low-salt, high-potassium diets as kids.[27] The Japanese estimate that $1 spent on school programs saves $6 in lifetime health-care costs.

6. They offer mouth-watering and hands-on learning opportunities. Ethnic foods are an entrée to social studies. Tending the school garden and greenhouse qualifies as manual education in its own right, as well as an introduction to biology and soil science. When senior students organize meals, they can be earning a credit in business training. At Walt Whitman High School in Bethesda, Maryland, the nutrition class perfected several vegetarian meals suitable for cafeterias, including spinach lasagna with béchamel sauce, vegetable frittata, Mexican pizza and Walt Whitman chili, which uses tempeh as a substitute for tofu, because tofu does not meet Department of Agriculture guidelines for school meals. Reading between the formal school lines is the invisible curriculum of respect for where food comes from.

7. They provide an opportunity to greenscape schools if rooftops are converted to greenhouses and parking lots to gardens. When teachers pay for parking like everyone else, space will be freed up, and parking lot revenues can finance the garden.

8. They provide an opportunity for local diversified farms to supply an assured market. If the food comes from a community garden, school funds help add new school rate payers to the tax rolls.

9.   They help establish the school as a neighborhood hub, a place where local parents and businesses can participate in the spirit of the African proverb: "It takes a whole village to raise a child." Such community partnerships are a necessary counterweight to those who use school to hook society's most vulnerable members on fat, says Dr. Walter Willett, director of nutrition at Harvard's School of Public Health.[28]

10.   Funded, in part at least, by a charge to parents, the programs can also encourage "sweat equity" as a valued and unstigmatized option to cash payments.

11.   Though free of dogma, the programs can help parents counter the effects of manipulative ads from the TV waist-land that apply more pressure than most parents can withstand. Once kids are involved in growing and cooking food, says California celebrity chef Alice Waters, author of the children's cookbook, **Fanny at Chez Panisse,** they "begin to make a relationship for themselves and take pride in the food and understand the value of it."[29]

12.   They might enlist students as adult educators who teach their parents about nutrition, as they've already done in the area of waste reduction and recycling.

13.   They reduce the school's bill for waste haulage, since foods with compostable and reusable packages can be featured. School juice bars provide a tasty and waste-free alternative to canned pop and tetrapak juice.

14.   School nutrition programs integrate holistic education in school guidelines. Once the principle of sound minds in sound bodies is affirmed, it can be extended to a host of factors affecting school performance, including inner city lead levels that have a devastating effect on brain development.[30] Schooling standards can't be raised on a strictly academic diet, University of British Columbia education professor Jane Gaskell concluded in her 1995 report on the 261 best high schools in Canada. "Any approach to school policy must recognize that the social and academic aspects are tightly intertwined," the report says.[31]

15. School nutrition programs provide an ideal pilot for a new style of voluntary but universal social programs that honor the commonalty in all people, the democratic foundation of public education. The surest way to keep social programs poor and second-rate is to designate them for the poor. Children of the well-to-do need nutrition programs as much as children of the poor. There's no reason to stigmatize nutrition more than any other aspect of the curriculum.

Re-Inventing Taxes

Green taxes are elegant sales taxes, taxes on bads instead of goods. They create a virtuous circle where traditional sales taxes, which only serve to raise revenue, are caught in a vicious one.

Pencil pushers like the one-size-fits-all uniformity of sales taxes, and the convenience of conscripting merchants as tax collectors. But uniform sales taxes have many faults. They are regressive, because they cost the poor as much as the rich. The public sees them as a sheer revenue grab, which ends up making them hard to collect. Black marketers offer to do the job for less "if there's no paperwork," which leaves consumers without a warranty and honest businesses without a customer. Most sales taxes discriminate against consumers of green products, who pay extra for environment-friendly goods, then have to pay the same tax rate as on products that pollute. Recycled products lower taxes by reducing the costs of landfill, for instance, but disposables pay no tax penalty for increasing the general tax rate to pay for their landfill. Some polluting products evade taxes on the grounds they sell necessities. Electricity and water are often tax-free, a boon to wasteful industries more than consumers, while energy conservation equipment is taxed. This discourages careful energy use and forces governments and utilities to offer cash incentives for conservation. Likewise, entertainment foods pay no entertainment tax, a tax break that drives up public medical and dental costs.

Green taxes are made for the tax revolt era. Set to recover the full life-cycle costs of a product, they make polluters, not innocent third parties, pay the tab for their decisions. A packaging tax, for instance, makes manufacturers and consumers carry the full cost of "convenience." The more people who evade this tax, the better. Landfill costs plummet. Government regulatory and public education programs that claim to promote waste reduction can be scaled down, because the price sticker is a very forceful educator and regulator. As more customers shift to recycled and reusable packages, local and labor-intensive businesses thrive, reducing government social expenditures.

Green taxes put market forces to work for the community and environment, and allow governments to be a little more light-handed as well as light-footed with regulations. That's because green taxes deliver accurate information about the true costs of a decision. Right now, taxes give false signals. Many people buy homes in suburbia, for instance, to avoid high city taxes. But each suburban home costs taxpayers about $40,000 in subsidies to cover the costs of roads, sewage, utilities, garbage pickup and social services to scattered populations.[32] Why don't governments give a $40,000 rebate to those who buy closer to the city core where the population is denser and cheaper to service?

Green taxes work best when revenues are earmarked for solutions. That's the big difference from "sin taxes" on tobacco, booze and gambling. They're as addictive to governments as to consumers because the money goes directly into the black hole of general revenues. By contrast, a green tax on cigarettes would be earmarked for a fund that covers the extra medical treatment smokers need. The more people who quit, the less draw on the fund, so it pays fund managers to offer free spa vacations to those who take the cure. Because they're earmarked for solutions, green taxes disappear when the problem is solved. Green gas taxes earmarked for alternative transit, for instance, will dwindle as fewer people make unnecessary use of their cars. The more successful a green tax is, the less revenue it raises. Government agencies that are big collectors will be subject to criticism, not praise. Green taxes, in sum, help government reinvent itself by aligning incentives, regulations and public education in tandem instead of, as now, at cross purposes.

Some governments may want to experiment with substituting green taxes for corporate taxes. Taxing corporations is a lost cause in a global economy, where multinationals simply move their central operations to a tax haven. The paltry take in corporate taxes costs governments a lot to collect, and as much for corporations to avoid. The rip-off knowledge economy employs 325,000 tax lawyers and accountants who deal in loopholes for the wealthy, not wealth creation. Giving up the mirage of collecting corporate taxes, and introducing flat-line, no-exception taxes on pollution—$150 a ton for sulphur dioxide or carbon dioxide, $100 a ton for garbage, basically the cost of repairing the damage—converts today's 325,000 jobs in tax evasion into 325,000 job openings for pollution evasion specialists. The first government to institute such a tax regime will be flooded with green and greening industries that want to take advantage of a genuine pollution haven.[33]

Golden Means

Principle 4

Uses "supply side management" to go with the flow of entropy, making the ends justify the means, thereby shedding resources, not jobs

"If we could increase the productivity of resources and energy in anything like the same way as we have increased the productivity of labor since the turn of the century—in other words twenty times—there would be a veritable revolution."
Tax expert Ernst Van Weizsacher[1]

"Until we have industrial systems that place value on natural resources, there is no way that human resources are going to be valued."

Green economist Paul Hawken

The only rules new entrepreneurs need to obey are the two laws of thermodynamics. The first law holds that energy is neither created nor destroyed, but can be changed from one form into another. This is a real downer for utilities that have to burn a lot of coal for a little electricity. The second law explains why so much energy from burned fuels is wasted and lost to pollution. It says that energy degrades toward disorganization, such that heat must move toward cold, until the energy is distributed evenly. This results in a high degree of disorder, or entropy. Conventional engineers curse the laws as you can't win and you can't break even. Far more than any government regulations, thermodynamic laws are the invisible killers of the current economy, which converts means into ends—or energy into useful products—at irredeemable rates of inefficiency. Jeremy Rifkin says a mouthful about living within the means of entropy.

Jeremy Rifkin has devoted his career to exposing the sacred cows of western economics, but he got to the meat of the matter with his 1992 book **Beyond Beef.** Meat is too hot for most economic critics to handle, maybe because it's seen as a purely personal preference, not an institutionally driven obsession. But pigging out on meat is a result of government, not personal choices. Living off the fat of the land is perfect for the agribusiness-petrochemical complex. It greases the wheels of a centralized, high-volume, capital-intensive system of food cartels. It's affordable at the scale it's consumed thanks to billions in subsidies that don't show up on the cash register, but only at tax time. That's when those who can't afford meat pay part of the grocery bill of those who can. The health consequences of the addiction to fat-marbled protein are also a metaphor, Rifkin shows, for an economy sick unto death with diseases of excess. Moving beyond meat is thus part of a larger menu of partnership with life forces. "Instead of using knowledge to increase our rule over," Rifkin wrote in his autobiography, **Declaration of a Heretic**, "we might just as easily use knowledge to become a partner with the rest of earthly creation."

To down their 65 pounds of beef a year, North Americans have saddled themselves with a food system at the wrong end of the law of diminishing returns. In traditional agriculture, domesticated animals are energy banks. They munch grasses, leaves and bugs that humans can't digest, and convert them to portable protein made available when edible plants aren't at hand. By contrast, animals in an agribusiness system are, in Rifkin's words, "energy guzzlers" that break the food chain bank. Cattle consume nine pounds of grain and corn, traditionally meant for humans, to yield one pound of marbled meat. Cattle trample on a land base that could produce five, 10 or 26 times more of higher quality protein, fiber and nutrients if it were devoted to grains, beans or spinach respectively. The rate of return on water is just as draining. A pound of beef takes seven times the amount of water needed to produce a pound of vegetables, rarely noticed thanks to $2 billion in irrigation subsidies to a small number of western ranchers. It's cheaper to put ranchers on social assistance than feed their water habit and put up with their beefs about welfare cheats among the poor.

The hidden costs of meat are also dispersed in rivers that carry six billion tons of fragile topsoil eroded by clumsy bulls, laced with feces that account for half the organic water pollution on the continent.2 The rest of that extra eight pounds of good food that doesn't end up as meat is farted out as methane to that great landfill in the sky, though there's no public flap over the cattle industry's responsibility for about a third of global warming gases generated on the continent. Another load of hot air that the politicians are responsible for. Poor converters of resources to the end, the fatty meat from corporate barns causes health problems that are hard for individuals and the economy to digest. North Americans, given false signals at the cash register, eat twice as much animal protein as they should. Given false signals on labels, we chose AAA cuts thinking it means high quality when, in fact, it means high-fat content. Then we stampede to diet clinics that cost well over $10 billion a year.

Meat over-consumption is implicated in many varieties of cancer and heart disease. The risk of prostate cancer, for instance, shoots up 80 per cent among big meat eaters, "more strong evidence that red meat should play a smaller role in our diet," says Harvard's Ed Giovanucci, whose research on the second-biggest cancer killer was reported in the **Journal of the National Cancer Institute** in October, 1993.[3] By contrast, the lowly and low-priced soybean supplies high quality protein, fiber, and a number of other nutrients that can lower cholesterol levels below the risk threshold, the **New England Journal of Medicine** reported in August, 1995. Soy enzymes are also recognized as cancer-fighters.

The personal is environmental, says best-selling health writer Harvey Diamond. If all North Americans went off saturated animal fats just one day a week, he argues in **Your Health, Your Planet,** they'd help preserve their tickers as well as 25 million acres of forest, 700 million tons of topsoil, plus one-and-a-half trillion gallons of clear water. The economy's arteries wouldn't be clogged by billions in subsidies to capital- and resource-intensive, rather than labor-intensive spending. And the world's circulation system wouldn't be clogged with 500 billion pounds of animal turd, and soot from 2.3 billion gallons of fossil fuel.

It's true that hamburger joints offer as close to a Zen experience many of us ever get: "Make me one with everything." Maybe that's why politicians have given up on kissing babies and pucker up to burger patties instead. After his inauguration, President Clinton chewed the fat with his chief advisors at the golden arches, a nice show of saving public money. Canada's Prime Minister Chrétien imitated the act when he bolted down a char-broiled in a highly publicized campaign pit stop. But there's no such thing as a free quarter-pounder. Green economist Alan During has shown how the costs keep repeating along with the burger, as he tracked the inputs of one quarter-pounder: 100 gallons of water, two pounds of feed, 1¼ pounds of topsoil and one cup of petroleum, all subsidized.[4] Their meal was on us.

If the economy can't take the energy loss, it should get out of the meat section. But meat is just one example of an economy that lives too high on the hog of squandered energy. This is an economy, says retired Cargill executive Richard Dawson, that "uses Persian rugs for indoor-outdoor carpet." Cattle are efficient compared to cars, which burn 98 per cent of their fuel just to propel the incredible weightiness of their own being. About 0.1 per cent of pesticides hit the target pest. The rest is for air and water. At best, 50 per cent of the nitrogen in fertilizers is taken up by the plants. The rest fouls up ground water. Only four per cent of the water that's treated with chlorine and fluoride is drunk. Most of the rest is flushed down the toilet. Less than one-third of the heat from coal, gas, oil and nuclear powered plants generates electricity—there's that dratted second law again. The waste heat goes to worse-than-useless pollution. Pioneer ecologist Howard Odum once calculated that it takes 16 years before a nuclear plant produces more energy than it took to build it, and to mine, refine and transport the uranium to it. After 16 years, most nuclear plants are beyond life support. Big sawmills think they're doing well if half the log ends up as lumber.

We could go on and on with this litany. Only one-third of the wood that goes through chemical pulping mills ends up as paper. The rest comes out as chlorine-laced pollution. Graduating the food system from an energy-loss clinic would also do something about fishing. Fishers waste a third of their annual catch. Enough is thrown overboard to provide China with its meat protein for a year.[5] As with beef, logs and electricity, poor conversion rates don't show up on the cash register. World fishing fleets pull in more from subsidies than fishing nets, $54 billion a year compared to $50 billion in sales.

Social distortions are also inevitable in an economy that lives on the wrong side of the laws of thermodynamics. Farmers, for instance, get a smaller share of the North American food dollar than packagers, and thus pay a heavy price for a food system that puts more energy into food transportation and distribution—an average food molecule on an average North American table has traveled 1,300 miles—than into food.[6] If farmers lived closer to their end-markets, they'd get enough of the food dollar to live on. Urban and industrial workers also pay a price. Artificially cheap resources remove the pressure from employers to manage resources wisely, to match inputs to outputs carefully. But when resources are subsidized and labor is not, the only pressure on management is to squeeze more productivity out of labor. Whence de-skilling, assembly lines, mechanization, automation and mass layoffs. This process would be slowed and reversed if resources and labor met on an even playing field. Then it would pay to have skilled workers who extracted maximum value from resources, and labor time would not be at such a premium. Contrary to the propaganda, expensive energy and resources make for more, not fewer, jobs.

Biting off what we can chew, moving our habits lower on the energy chain "represents a watershed event in the history of the human species," Rifkin argues.[7] "Moving beyond the beef culture is a revolutionary act," he says.

"Nature is the producer of real wealth, the economy a mere consumer."
University of British Columbia community planner William Rees

Economics is essentially a conversion experience, the rate at which energy and resources are converted into useful products. Waste is the ultimate in botched conversion, garbage that's useless, or, in the case of toxic waste, costs more to dispose than the original product was worth. Incineration burns the evidence, say Paul and Ellen Connett.

Burned out after crusading throughout the 1970s on behalf of victims of war and famine, Paul and Ellen Connett moved to Canton, New York, a picture-perfect college and dairy town near the Thousand Islands. They planned to raise their kids in a big home with a large yard on a quiet street, teach in a small university and host a radio show on classical music. It almost worked. But one day, the librarian at St. Lawrence University asked Paul Connett, a recent doctoral graduate in chemistry, to look over the scientific papers on the incinerator proposed for the area. Today, their basement is a publishing house where Ellen Connett puts out **Waste Wise,** the newsletter of record for the anti-incineration movement. Paul Connett crisscrosses the continent most weekends, giving the scientific lowdown on incineration to shocked community groups. They've helped put the kibosh to about 250 incineration projects since 1985, and to focus a grassroots protest movement, often put down as NIMBYism, on a positive program that turns the debate about garbage on its head.

Health was the big issue at first. As they learned about dioxins, the microscopic but deadly contaminants scattered in the air when chlorine-based products are burned, the Connetts raised the alarm among dairy farmers, worried that a hard rain of dioxin would destroy their product's reputation for purity. Dioxin is to chlorinated petrochemicals what radiation is to the nuclear industry. It doesn't look bad or stink. It isn't volatile, and doesn't attack body organs, like the skull and crossbones poisons. It isn't reactive, and doesn't assault cells, like cigarettes do. It's an insider. Dioxin confuses the body's message center and starts turning gene switches off and on, triggering chemical malfunctions that screw up reproductive systems. Instead of recovering energy from waste, as its supporters claim, incineration emissions convert healthful grass, the feed stock of dairy cows, into toxic carriers. This is about as bad as bad conversion gets.

The Connetts don't sleep easier knowing that the companies and technicians working to solve the problem are retreads from the nuclear industry after it went belly up in the 1970s. The technicians may be getting airborne emissions from incinerators down, but "that's a catch 22," says Ellen Connett. "What doesn't go up must come down." Any decrease in toxic fly ash becomes an increase in toxic bottom ash. Three tons of perfectly incinerated garbage become one ton of toxic ash, to be disposed of at a toxic waste site. That's why incineration creates, not solves, landfill problems. It doesn't upgrade garbage to energy. It downgrades it to toxic waste. Garbage in, poison out doesn't get high marks for conversion efficiency.

After a while, the Connetts figured out that the health debate itself was a waste of their energy. It's tiresome debating with what Paul Connett calls "consultitutes." Waiting for epidemiological results is waiting for a problem to become so big that even the Environmental Protection Agency can spot it. Epidemiologists, the saying goes, convert bullshit into airline tickets and overhead projectors—an upgrade of a sort, but not genuine conversion.

"To save time, let me summarize my view in two sentences," Paul Connett now says. "No risk is acceptable if it is avoidable. Even if they could make incineration safe, they could never make it sensible." Clever men solve problems, wise ones avoid them, he says, citing Einstein. "If the answer is incineration, then someone asked the wrong question," he says. "The question is not where do we put the waste, but how do we stop making it." The bottom line on thermodynamics, he says, is "we cannot run a throw-away society on a finite planet."

Tossing leftovers in the garbage is a ritual burial—on par with the pyramids of ancient Egypt—of enormous amounts of high-quality embodied energy that go into most plastic, metal and paper cotainers. Slowing the hemorrhage of precious high-grade energy puts a premium on re-use and recycling. This was once part of the collective mindset of the Canton area, not far from Potsdam, where the original reusable milk bottle first saw the light of day. Waste not, want not, was folk wisdom then. Reusables did a good job of preserving the energy that went into packaging. They hitched a free ride on a delivery truck that had to go back anyway. A douse in boiling water, and they were as good as new. But the big energy saving didn't come from preserving the container. It came from preserving a local economy with low transport costs.

Once companies started hauling juice, milk and preserves from distant facilities, the heavy glass containers that withstood many uses became dead weight on a transport truck and dead space on a superstore shelf. Carting them all the way back was out of the question. That's why reuse has gone the way of the dodo. Long distance haulers from centralized factories want compact, lightweight, un-breakable disposables. Aluminum and the tetrapak are for people who don't want jobs in their own backyard. For corporate central, the new packaging is very convenient. They save on trucking costs. They pass the cost of dealing with garbage onto the area that just lost its local bottling plant and production facility. The locals pick up the costs of welfare and garbage. There's a reason why big companies have the money to pay their top guys huge salaries.

Recyclers need to rethink how the agenda got moved away from reduce and reuse. Focusing on packaging misses the point that the medium is the message, the container is the content. The issue with tetrapak juice is the fake juice inside. Same with plastic creamers. Even more so with canned pop. The issue with cereal boxes is the sugar-loaded cereal killers. When people switch to real juice, real cream, refreshing beverages and genuine cereals, the packaging will look after itself. We should be worrying more about the use of our bodies as dumpsites for the content and mellow out about rescuing the package. Fat food joints make a big show about cutting back on their packaging waste, but this doesn't scratch the surface. Half the french fries sold in these chains make the trip from Washington and Oregon. Half the potatoes don't make the cut. The rest get the toss. Loaded with nitrogen fertilizers and pesticides, the rot contaminates the area's water supply, according to a report issued by the Columbia Basin Institute.[8] All this to turn a potentially nutrient-rich vegetable that can be grown anywhere into a heart attack in a box. The first watchword of waste management is good riddance to bad rubbish.

Recycling, as now practiced, services a long-distance, job take-out economy.[9] Whether the container is taken to landfill or recycled— and that's assuming that the mash of materials can be separated and turned into something worthwhile, a big if with any plastic that's been chlorinated—the municipality subsidizes the export of jobs. The conversion rate of tax dollars to jobs stinks.

So does the conservation of high quality energy. We need to subject the costs and benefits of recycling to some cycle analysis. Compare the fuel used in local versus long-haul delivery. Compare the resource input for glass, made from basic elements close to most areas, with the inputs for metal, plastic and multi-material packages, made from scarce, distant and energy-intensive resources. Aluminum, for instance, favored because it's light and easy to automate production lines, is sometimes called "canned electricity." The very production of these materials is littered with waste. John Hanson of the Recycling Council of Ontario estimates that we only see seven per cent of packaging waste in the garbage dump. The rest is in slag heaps beside mines and smelters, the slashed remains of a forest clear-cut, sludge spewing out of petrochemical pipes and stacks, toxic water from aluminum plants. It takes twice as much energy, usually fossil-based and polluting, to process food for a long-distance market than it does to grow it in the first place.[10] Tax dollars for recycling are being used to slow the backsliding of this spiral of energy abuse.

Don't solve problems at the back end, Connett tells the groups he speaks to. For an economy that takes out the garbage, go to the front of the line, and solve it there. "We've got to get back to the village, reinvent community," he says. We've got to stop talking about garbage, says Ellen Connett. "The issue is resources."

"Cultural capital is the only kind which is unlimited.... It is time man became less reckless with the earth's resources and more generous with his own."

Frank MacKinnon[11]

Economics for a small planet goes light on resources but heavy on jobs and skills. Workers and employers in new light industries are finding that the new opportunities take more broadening of horizons than tightening of belts.

Triple Duty

Co-generation technologies, promoted by fourth-wave companies over the last decade, work with the stern realities of the second law of thermodynamics to get the best bang for the energy buck. Co-generation is supply-side, as distinct from demand-side conservation, and it can cut in half the 25 per cent of energy burned across North America just to get energy.[12] A coal, oil, gas or nuclear power plant inevitably loses about 70 per cent of the energy input that fuels the burn for ultra-concentrated electrical energy. But that cast-off heat is plenty hot enough to provide scalding and lukewarm water for dishes and showers, or comfortable room temperatures. Sure, electricity can do that too, Larry Solomon writes in **The Conserver Solution**, "but then caviar could substitute for rock salt in de-icing your driveway."

Co-generators earn their keep by capturing and re-using heat before it's lost to pollution, gaining the highest possible conversion of energy to use. Some qualify as tri-generators, using the same heat from the same coal, gas, oil or uranium at the power plant to provide electricity, space and water heating, and air-conditioning.

One way of organizing delivery of co-generation is with district heating, which pipes waste heat from a power plant to local buildings. District heating is common, even mandatory, throughout Europe, but rare in North America, perhaps because of conformity to stand-alone individualism. But mittens are three times more efficient than gloves because they pool the heat from all fingers, so there are gains from sharing. District heating customers give up their right to switch from oil to gas whenever they feel like it, in return for a hook-up to pipes that transport waste heat, available for no additional energy, from the power plant. The jobs and savings, in other words, are in one-time local construction of tunnels and laying of pipe, not perpetually generating new power with imported fuels. "I used to head for the city engineer's office when I wanted to push conservation projects," says district heating promoter Michael Wiggins, a staffer with Canada's federal energy department. "Now I head to the economic development office."

Industrial, commercial and apartment building managers able to focus on two ways of making money at the same time can turn their chimneys into profit center generators that sell electricity to the grid or provide it to their own off-grid plant. The process heat used to boil ketchup or smelt steel can work up a head of steam that can be upgraded to electricity, getting one more use before it goes up in the air. This provides a cost-effective way of attracting new industries to an area: grant them the right to "wheel" their co-generated electricity to utility wires. Apartments and malls can work up their own version of co-generation. New, inexpensive and compact furnaces can turn the boiler room into an electrical plant, and let landlords either take their buildings off the grid or export electricity to it.[13] The more efficient tenants' appliances are, the more electricity the landlord can export. Why raise rents when the same income can be generated giving tenants efficient refrigerators?

Another trick of co-generators is to "cascade" energy, take advantage of each drop in temperature to perform a different task. This is end-use, as distinct from supply side, but it works on the same principle. The Air Watt, sold by Heatrade in Waterloo, Ontario, takes heat from air exhausted by air conditioners to pre-heat water, ideal for hotels or restaurants that wash a lot of dishes and towels. Just for fun, the two-way Air Watt also takes heat back from the water once it's scalding to boost the air conditioner.[14] Winston McKelvey, a retired shop teacher and backyard inventor in Knowlton, Quebec, has hopes of matching Bill Gates' fortune when sales of his Drain Gain take off. The hot water tank is the biggest energy user in most homes, and the heat goes into the sewers still piping hot after a shower or dish washing. McKelvey's device siphons the heat back to the outside of the hot water tank, where it transfers its warmth before proceeding to the sewer. The invention has been successfully piloted at a nearby nursing home, where it cut the water heating bill in half. "Instead of heating sewers" and putting the planet in hot water, says McKelvey, we can have money left over for local goods and services. When these kinds of end-use devices are matched to utility go-generation, new conversion ratios will cut energy use by three-quarters.

Perennial Optimists

Permaculture is a systematic approach to reducing our dependence on high-grade energy just to put food on the table. It opens up hundreds of thousands of new jobs with its version of green industrial parks, agro-forestry, and opens up a new site for growing the things we need, the woodlot.

Permaculturalists are best known for their opposition to tilling. Breaking up ground turns up the underground residences of "nature's ploughmen and recyclers," worms and other organisms that keep the earth aerated and nutrient-rich. It leaves the soil exposed without a roof over its head, uninsulated against evaporation, erosion and extremes of temperature. The Saskatchewan Research Council blames the loss of some 300 million tons of topsoil on excessive tilling.[15] Tilling is a yearly ritual with annuals, the staples of agri-culture for thousands of years. Annuals have some positives. They are relatively easy to manipulate genetically. Their energy goes into edible grains and seeds, not roots. Their high yield means surpluses that can be stored and transported. But annuals are at war with nature, which favors perennials and self-seeding annuals that look after themselves. That's why annuals require ongoing interference with the natural order. The arms race against the natural succession of hardy perennials—usually called weeds, despite their nutritional content—requires continual escalation of energy-intensive weapons, such as fertilizers, herbicides, pesticides, tractors, irrigation, and now biotechnology. Check out the labels on Killex, Attack, Ambush or Crossbow, if you have any doubts that chemical methods are about waging war on the planet.

Wes Jackson, a leading critic of agricultural militarism, estimates that two million barrels of oil are used each year for pesticides, and that 22 per cent of natural gas manufactured into other products goes to fertilizers. That's without counting the energy that goes into manufacturing, transporting and ploughing-in the materials. Jackson is researching ways to develop new perennials—raspberries, mint and asparagus are already standard—that can help farmers overcome chemical dependency. With no help from the petrochemical and pharmaceutical companies that now control most seed production and research—they know where their captive markets are—he's already come up with several species of high-yield perennials, including grains and corn, adapted to the prairies.[16]

The forest is an ideal site for perennial agriculture, a weird notion to those who can't see the forest for the lumber or who see wilderness and farming as sworn enemies. Permaculturalists favor "stacking" forests, much like gardeners juxtapose onions and carrots, which fend off each other's parasites, or lettuce and cabbage, which grow at different rates and so don't compete for space.[17] The idea is to orchestrate an ensemble of mutually beneficial or symbiotic relationships. Rich in minerals that have been brought to the surface by tree roots —one reason why medicinal herbs are often found in woodlands— the forest floor can sustain its own energy and nutrient balance, while sheltering at least six layers of plantings. Going thick with forests rather than heavy with machines pays off in yield per acre from increased productivity of both soil and space. Ecosystems function better the more species that are in them, researchers have now proven.[18]

In a model permaculture setting, onions, garlic and ginseng grow below ground. Mushrooms, herbs, lovage (a substitute for celery), sorrel (a member of the spinach family), fiddleheads and leeks form the carpet. Along the sunny forest edge are junipers, with berries that flavor sauerkraut and venison and can be made into gin.[19] Bushes of berries nestle beside edible flowers and low-growing fruit and nut trees. A vertical layer of beans and vines grow up the tree trunks in the orchard, along with nasturtiums, soapwort and sage to fend off the aphids. In the forest valley, billowing willows line the pond, where fish and aquatic plants, such as watercress, rich in protein and vitamin C, are grown. At the forest center, giant maples and oaks, today's syrup and acorn bread, tomorrow's lumber, form the canopy, crowning the lush life below, where branches are pruned for livestock feed and supplies for twig patio furniture and basket making.[20]

Foraging animals aren't enemies here. You scratch their backs, they'll scratch yours. Bees collect honey. Free-range chickens, biological pest controllers and fertilizers for the orchard, peck at grubs attracted by the woodlands, and expend less energy keeping warm because of the shelter offered by the trees.[21] Pigs escape from their pigpens and return to the forest, from which they were evicted by British aristocrats who wanted the way cleared for pheasant hunts.[22] Perhaps pigs can be used as hound dogs, as they are in France, where they're followed to the site of rare and costly truffles. The forest helps with other food functions. It's a shelter belt for adjoining fields, and helps raise the water table for field crops, minimizing the need for irrigation. Beside rivers, where permaculture should become standard, trees control the release of water run-off, preventing eroding silt and flash floods from mucking up the habitat for fish.

Taking off to the woods isn't for farmers who like working in barns or driving equipment back and forth on the field. In L'Isle D'Orléans, where the St. Lawrence widens near Quebec City, residents gain a perennial source of year-round income by keeping half the island in forest, and using agro-forestry as an income for all seasons. After maple syrup in the early spring comes asparagus, then strawberries, followed by corn, apples, and firewood in the fall. Produce is mostly sold to tourists, family-run inns and restaurants featuring traditional fare, digested with trademark eau de vie, fermented from aged maple syrup. In Oregon, the Rogue Institute for Ecology and Economy helps laid-off loggers bushwhack for wild mushrooms, Oregon grape (a substitute for ginseng) and beargrass, used in floral arrangements.[23] The $35-million-a-year wild mushroom crop "won't replace timber, but it will stand pretty tall," says Richard Zabel, director of the Western Forestry and Conservation Association. It's reckoned that the Oregon forest harvest, without much backing to stimulate new crops or markets, employs 2,000 people full-time and 1,600 part-time.[24]

Across Canada's east coast, it's estimated that renaturalization of softwood plantations back to hardwood—the pulp industry has downgraded native species stock to feed its mills—could eliminate chronic unemployment in the area if governments leased public lands in 300-acre parcels to woodlot operators. Most of the Carolinian forest there is rich in nuts and other food crops, and can be selectively harvested for furniture and firewood that replaces imported oil.[25] In agrarian areas that have been deforested, farmers who turn 25 per cent of their acreage over to shelter belts, sloughs and woodlots get a habitat that provides the family with wild food, and a chance to break into the farming market of the future. In Saskatchewan, a typical prairie area where overproduced wheat and canola glut their markets, Elizabeth Coxworth estimates that "energy plantations" of fast-growing trees could produce about 250 million tons of wood a year for fuel, lumber and furniture. Wood, she notes, requires one-eighth the energy of substitute materials such as plastic.[26]

A little historical research will help woodlot farmers identify starter crops. Self-sufficient pioneer farmers relied on mulberry bushes, osage orange trees and others for windbreaks, nitrogen fixers, feed for live-stock, and dyes for textiles, as well as lumber.[27] Permaculture cook-books will help develop new markets. "We have access to worldwide information," says Peter Bane, editor of the Tennessee-based **Permaculture Activist.** "We have a global painting palette, the perfect condition to empower local communities." Bane calls perma-culture the "how-to of the bioregional movement," which strives for regional self-reliance. More respect for the variety of edibles available in any one "foodshed" decreases the high-grade transportation energy used up by a conformist food system that goes to the end of the earth to find cheap but tasteless iceberg lettuce, when tastier sorrel is at hand.

Pulp Fiction

When you gotta go, you gotta go, but that doesn't mean you have to wipe your butt with old-growth forest. Every year, we trash thousands of square miles of multi-functional forests—otherwise capable of nur-turing recreation, tourism, agro-forestry or maintaining animal hab-itat, air and water quality[28]—into wood chips hauled to mills where a toxic chlorinated stew turns them into paper that's transported huge distances to be served up for one use as nose wipe, bum wad, diapers (250,000 trees a year),[29] burger wrapper, scratch pads, and pulp novels, as well as glossy stock that has to pass some test of time. Only give-away prices on stands of forest makes this papering over of means-ends differences possible. The same resource abuse happens with lumber. Almost one-fifth of the annual logging cut goes to produce 600 million pallets to carry all that bum wad and nose wipe.[30] Pallet recyclers think they're doing the world a favor when they recycle that lumber by chipping it into mulch, compost and manufactured wood. This is the pulp fiction of an economy that doesn't know which end is up. The tree, one of nature's most beautiful and useful pieces of bio-engineering is used to wipe and carry crap, while the chips from pallets gets doused in a dozen toxic chemicals to be used as a poor substitute for lumber in our homes.

REAP, Resource Efficient Agricultural Production, on the west end of Montreal Island, promotes a better match of means and ends. We need to end the era of hunting and gathering for lumber, and extend agriculture so it can supply routine fiber needs, says REAP director Roger Samson. In 1995, he hosted an open house for paper companies, and pulp and paper giant Domtar agreed to provide the services of its innovation center. Domtar is alert to the growing market for tree-free paper, which now accounts for nine per cent of world sales.[31] Holland is well-advanced in its effort to supply its own mills with hemp grown by its own farmers. Some Italian mills use seaweed, and mills in southern climates are working with kenaf and bamboo. Domtar also wants to avoid the transportation costs of hauling logs hundreds of miles, truckload at a time, to its mill. An experiment with wheat straw has been declared successful by Domtar vice-president Bob Eamer, who says the mix of wheat straw, chalk and recycled pulp makes high quality paper. This is getting closer to good materials management. Straw, now an agricultural waste that's often burned in the field, can become a second crop for farmers, with no additional energy requirements beyond those needed to harvest grain.

Switchgrass has yet to be tested in Domtar's mill, but Samson is crossing his fingers. If the experiment works, there's a major opening for sustainable agriculture and local economic self-reliance, he says. Switchgrass is a perennial weed that's native to North America. No tilling, no chemicals, no irrigation necessary. The birds like it, and farmers don't have to disturb their nests with harvesters until the energy-smart birds have gone south for the winter. The deep, thick roots are so good for the soil that Samson thinks switchgrass can be used to rehabilitate marginal land. The roots also mean lots of carbon storage to offset global warming. At the pulp mill, switchgrass doesn't need the chemical beating that trees get, because it's low in the glue-like lignin that chlorine breaks down. And switchgrass grows so fast, dense and high that a given area is 13 times more productive of biomass than trees.

Pulp companies are barking up the wrong species, Samson says. Trees should be saved for products where human labor and need add sufficient value to bring the annual cuts of timber down to size.[32]

The Grass Is Greener

Milk from contented grass beats the economics of milk from cows stressed out on bovine growth hormones (rBGH). The bio-tech drug keeps mother cows in a state of first flush nursing far longer than nature ever intended, and keeps farmers hooked on expensive chemical and veterinary services and crashing prices in an already engorged market. But dairy farmers who are looking to make money by controlling their own costs, rather than their cows' bodies, are looking at less energy-intensive ways of producing milk. Some have hit on the idea of putting their cows out to pasture, borrowing New Zealand paddocking methods. Irregularly-shaped paddocks, which conform to the lie of the land rather than the steering needs of tractors, hold a herd in a small area where they finish off the grass in about five days. Since the cows only trample and compact the soil for a short time, it springs back to life quickly, and earth organisms digest the manure for new growth. Pasture is cheap and nutritious food, says Dr. Ann Clark of the agricultural school at the University of Guelph in southern Ontario, and dairy farmers need to reinvent themselves as grass farmers.

These dairy methods help out nature at the same time. Managed grazing "could lead to 27 to 33 per cent less soil erosion and 23 to 26 per cent less fuel in crop production, and tie up 14 to 21 million tons of carbon dioxide and 5.2 to 7.8 million tons of nitrates in the organic matter of New York's pasture soils alone," says pasturing expert

Edward Rayburn, on staff with the extension service of West Virginia University.[33]

Wisconsin dairy farmer Paul Bickford swears managed grazing is the only way he can make money. "We don't measure by production, how many pounds of milk a single cow produces," he says. "We measure by income," how much money is left over after expenses. Like many dairy farmers, Bickford learned the hard way that high volume methods breed high production costs and big bank debts. He walked 550 cows away from his high-tech confinement barns and turned them loose, counting on nature to boost productivity.

"All my cows had babies last year. When was the last time you saw a tractor have a baby?" he asks, noting he needs the population increase to eat all the grass he's now growing. Letting cows roam doubles their productive life and reduces weight loss and vet bills from the stress of confinement in barn stalls. "Milking parlors" adapted to paddock pasturing—the cows come to the machine, rather than the other way around in barns—doubles the productivity of his machines and staff. Bickford's wife, Cyd, calculates that the low costs of paddock grazing increased her earnings per cow to $900, a big enough margin to let a modest operation survive. She started her herd of 20 Jerseys with $3,000. Her success led Bickford to encourage students to pay their way through college by managing small herds and offering to "mow the grass" for landowners with vacant land to rent.

With costs down, birth and survival rates way up and plenty of grass for feed, Bickford figures he's ready to move into share-milking, offering his employees part ownership of a herd. As the herd increases in size with new births, Bickford's total income would increase even as his share of the ownership and hands-on management go down. He figures the deal is a win-win for "self-sustainability."

Call Of The Wild

Since the dawn of civilization, tame food has been equated with progress, wild food with the barbarian stone age. That's because tame food yields a surplus that can be controlled by and fed to priests, professors and politicians who no longer have to spend their time grubbing for a living. But until the 1800s, domesticated agriculture just

centralized leisure, as distinct from expanding it. Free time for the
few came at the expense of constant toil by the many, mostly unhap-
py hoers, serfs and slaves who had a lot more time off in the old days.
Among the losers were women, matriarchs in many hunter and gath-
erer societies, and those who mastered wild medicines and religious
insights. People were tamed along with the cattle, John Livingstone
argues in **Rogue Primate**.

Domesticated food had costs as well as benefits. Inbred over the mil-
lennia, tame seeds and animals yielded greater surpluses, but often at
the expense of nutrients bred in the wild. The wonder grains featured
in today's health food stores—spelt, teff and quinoa, for example—
are those closest to nature, least manipulated genetically, with seeds
most able to survive on their own because they contain all the minerals and vitamins to survive unaided. And agricultural progress
required more human tending, not less, more energy inputs, not less,
with each genetic manipulation that screened for seed yield, at the
expense of hardiness and self-reliance.

Curiously, 20th century environmentalists have been as harsh on pre-
agrarian food systems as the sodbusters who broke and fenced frontier
ground, with no regrets for the decimated wild life that once sus-
tained Native populations. The turn-of-the-century leisure class
valued nature as a recreational escape from the stress and tear of
industrial life. Nature was pastoral, clean and pure, and "poachers"
and "pot shots" were put-downs of those who lived off the land,
threatening its value for amateurs, much like the despised wolves
that ate cute deer.[34] Modern environmentalists carried on this heritage with crusades against trapping for furs. Their market killed,
Native trappers in Canada's northern prairie now work on power
dams and uranium mines. Ironically, by decoupling nature from
livelihood, greens created a political landscape around environmentalism that pitted jobs against recreation, necessity against frivolity,
not sustainable against unsustainable jobs. When nature is only good
for recreation, wilderness is a dead duck.

But there's still truth to the old saying: give a man a fish, and you
feed him for a day; teach him to fish and you get rid of him every
weekend. Ontario, for instance, has 400,000 active hunters and
708,000 active anglers. An average of one meal a week comes from

wild game. "In a society where people are so dependent on the market economy, we have a situation where people are able to go out and put food on the table," says David Kraft, research co-ordinator for a Health Canada survey on fish and wild life nutrition. "This is a starting point for sustainability," he says. "What if governments treated lakes and forests as an agricultural resource, not a playground. Would we let companies dump toxic waste on farmland?" What about farmers poisoning the habitat of their competitors? A major toxin responsible for limits on eating Great Lakes' brown trout, for instance, is run-off from the pesticide Mirex.35 If the Great Lakes were restored to the liquid asset they once were, they could easily host a $10-billion-a-year fishery. Five million pounds of just one species, whitefish, came out of Lake Superior in 1950, for instance. Exotic zebra mussels, dumped from the bilge of foreign tankers during the 1980s, gorge on plankton that could provide for a $900-million-a-year catch of walleye.36 In west coast Louisiana, chlorine dumping qualifies fish caught along 35 miles of rich tidal water as rat poison, threatening the livelihood of some 7,000 full- and part-time fishers, says Willie Fontenot, a staffer in the state attorney general's office.

Redressing the balance in favor of wild resources—stay calm, we're not talking about going back to the stone age or out on militia target practice with AK47's—accomplishes two things. It lowers energy requirements for food, since wild plants don't need ploughing or spraying. It also allows those who want to protect nature to frame the issues in an everyday way. As with old-fashioned chivalry toward women, putting nature on a pedestal is part of putting down its potential. "Unless we weave little 'n' nature back into the everyday environment, big 'n' Nature will become an expendable abstraction," says Berkeley architecture professor Sim Van der Ryn. "Design with little 'n' nature should help reweave nature and culture, regenerating both."37

Here's a sample of wild resources that only take soft management to nurture and good recipes to enjoy. They can lay the basis for a low-energy food system stewarded by a new breed of wild-eyed farmers or by Natives who want to negotiate their integration into the mainstream economy.38 For instance, Salish Indian David Wolfman, gold medallist at the 1992 culinary olympics in Germany, has become a celebrity cook with recipes evolved from recollections of elders. He promotes "aboriginal nouvelle" through the First Nation Culinary Institute of Barrie, Ontario, the Native Canadian Chefs Association he heads, and his own company, Aboriginal Foods International. Blueberry bannock or wild rice pudding, anyone?[39]

1. Wild blueberries are a $200-million-a-year crop in New England, Quebec and Canada's maritime provinces, and a Wild Blueberry Association has been formed to promote the product and resist the incursion of chemical sprays—weed killers used in parts of Maine have been associated with cancer and put the industry's reputation at risk.[40] Cranberries, one of many agro-forestry crops introduced to the Pilgrims by Natives, are big in the juice market,[41] valued for their high vitamin C content and their ability to counter urinary tract infections among women.[42] A lush harvest sustains wetlands and Native co-ops in Ontario.[43] The prairies have berries galore; elderberries for wine and jam, lingonberries, high bush cranberries and wild grape. Plentiful wild roses—on the Atlantic coast they're called sea roses—have hips that are rich in vitamins A and C, iron and phosphorus, and can make teas and jams that are now imported. The petals can be used, as in the Middle East, in rosewater for glazing meat, a break from ketchup. In northern Alberta, 11 members of the Peace Country Fruit Producers Co-op market 28,000 pounds of Saskatoon berries a year.[44] In Ontario, the Indian Agricultural Program supports harvesting of evening primrose, formerly an imported staple in health-food stores.

2. Jane Brody calls wild rice "truly the top of the line." A self-seeding annual grass that grows without tilling or chemicals, it lends itself to Native control in the shallow lakes of Minnesota, Manitoba, Saskatchewan and Northern Ontario. Low in fat, rich in fiber, protein and B vitamins, it fetches a higher price per pound than uranium, the Saskatchewan government's choice for economic development in Métis and Cree communities. Wild rice receives a pittance of the marketing support doled out for western grains and minerals, and there has been no value-added product development of wild rice crackers, cakes or sake. Some wild rice harvesters get support from Ducks Unlimited, since the feeding grounds have no scarecrows to keep animals from snacking.

Louisiana's shallow waters and bayous, fast disappearing as oil companies bulldoze the back country, host exotic water hyacinths that resist poisoning but can be cleared for cattle feed. Spanish moss was once used to stuff furniture and the original Model T car seats, says swamp guide Marcus de la Houssaye, fighting to protect the wild marsh from roads.[45]

3. Nuts and seeds are quickly gaining status on par with fruit as a daily staple providing essential minerals and vitamins. Researchers with the European Seven Countries Study give part of the credit for low rates of heart disease in southern Europe to a diet loaded with vitamin E and "good cholesterol" from nuts. The **Harvard Heart Letter** devoted most of its June, 1994 issue to tree nuts. Citing rich contents of magnesium, zinc, selenium, copper, phosphorus, niacin and iron, the new medical wisdom holds that "the content list of nuts reads very much like that of a multiple-vitamin capsule."[46]

Wild seed harvesting can pull the chestnuts out of the fire of deforestation and pay for the restoration of traditional woodland species. The threatened black walnut bears a meaty nut that's used as a candy and medicine, with three times more protein per pound than beef. Imitators of the success of Rainforest Crunch can preserve Carolinian forests. And we need a food that honors John Muir, founder of the Sierra Club and a rugged hiker who tramped through the wilds with acorn cheese bread, a hiker's food he learned about from Natives. This could be the new economy version of campers' GORP— good old raisins and peanuts. It sounds nuts, but issuing licenses to seed harvesters may give governments a better return than licenses issued to loggers.

4. Licensed and trained harvesters can also roam the forests for wild mustard, rich in vitamins A, B and C, wild ginseng for healthy teas, sorrel for salads, May apples for marmalade, and groundnuts or "Indian potato," a member of the pea family with tubers that are excellent in soups and stir fries.[47]

5.   Wild meadows can become a beehive of activity for harvesters who build condominiums for bees, which pay the rent by gathering sweet nectars from trees and flowers they pollinate. Its concentration of wild nutrients makes honey the bees knees of traditional medicine. The bacteria held responsible for peptic ulcers, for instance, can be overcome by a certain type of New Zealand honey, as effectively as by antibiotics.[48]

Honey has traces of mineral salts, iron, calcium, potassium and phosphorus, but is a sticky issue with some, because its sugar is almost as bad for teeth and metabolism as refined sugar. But bees make more than honey. With 25 employees, Beehive Botanicals in Hayward, Wisconsin markets royal jelly, tooth paste, cosmetics and lip balm, all superior to petrochemical products. Bee pollen is a virtual mega-vitamin pill, with a full range of acids and vitamins.[49] Into their umpteenth rerun, beeswax candles can reclaim the market for romantic lighting from stock petrochemical brands, which took over a market that was none of their beeswax. Beeswax candles balance carbon dioxide burned with carbon stored, both in their hives and the biomass they pollinate. They don't give off other pollution, which is why they're recommended as petroleum candle substitutes in car survival kits for people needing warmth while stuck in a snowdrift.

For about $50,000, ideal for people looking at early retirement, beekeepers can be ready for business, augmenting their income by leasing their bees to farmers who need a pollination source.[50] Market share can only grow. Refined sugar from cane—under the gun for health disorders and environmental destruction, especially in the Florida everglades[51]—commands 90 per cent of the sweet tooth market. The U.S. government buys all surplus sugar to prevent a market glut,[52] but that's no doubt too hard to do with honey.

6.   Less than 10 per cent of maples are tapped for syrup, even though one backyard maple can supply a family's sweetness needs for the year. The syrup is rich in minerals, especially potassium. Governments can't figure out how to support the industry with the tariff protection and subsidies they give to refined sugar or logging. Quebec's strong co-ops of maple sugar producers were important allies in the battle for strong laws against acid rain, which threatens their livelihoods by killing off broadleaf trees.53 Micro-brewers can expand the forest syrup market to birch beer, a favorite drink of Queen Victoria.

7.   There's a lot more food in the ocean than fish. Sea vegetables such as dulce, kelp and Irish moss are rich in rare trace minerals such as iodine, and are sometimes referred to as superfoods,54 viable alternatives to heavily-packaged vitamin and mineral pills. Seaweed is a staple of scrumptious salads and soups throughout Asia, but in North America there's some marketing yet to be done before people will eat the food at their doorstep. In Mimigenash, Prince Edward Island, Irish moss capital of the world, the Seaside Co-op bakes seaweed delicacies such as Irish Moss Mousse at the Seaweed Pie cafe, and presses washed-up sea plants into postcards for tourists. Harvesters at Acadian Seaplants in Dartmouth, Nova Scotia, sell ocean greens to farmers for fertilizer and livestock feed. "Packed with upwards of seventy trace elements needed by plants," says Cape Cod gardening expert Jim Hildreth, "seaweed tops the list of local materials to dig directly into the soil and add to the compost pile."55

In Bella Bella, Washington, native fishers worked out a way to get product without killing the fish that lay the golden eggs. Their loose nets let herring escape after they've laid eggs on kelp, which improves their fertility. The herring swim free, and the fishers sell roe on kelp for twice the price of stand-alone roe squeezed from dead herring. Not far away, in Willapa Bay, workers remove chitin from shrimp and crab shells, and sell it to manufacturers of hair spray, stringed instruments and surgical thread. Then, says Allana Probst of Ecotrust, they mix the remains with sawdust from a nearby mill to produce high-quality soil conditioner. The world fishing fleet nets $54 billion in yearly subsidies, but no-one can figure out how to stimulate the transition from hunting to gathering by food beachcombers.

8. Wild plants and fruit-bearing trees are also a source of genetic material that can supply people in harsh climates with tender, fresh fruit. Quebec farmer and agriculture teacher Ken Taylor experiments with wild plum and pear trees that yield small but tasty fruit, hoping they can be bred to produce a bigger fruit while retaining their wild hardiness. He tries to culture trees that resist disease and cold temperatures and that fix nitrogen in the soil. "Anybody that is looking for more off-spring from Macintosh (apples) is tied into a life of spraying," he says. "That's not my idea of fruit growing."[56]

Where The Buffalo Roam

For those who wonder where's the beef in the new economy, the buffalo provides one answer. Deborah and Frank Popper of Rutgers University envision a "21st century frontier" in the west, where the buffalo is the centerpiece of a restoration economy that replaces extractive mining, logging and monoculture.[57]

Western farmers are already finding this isn't a bum steer. The Canadian Bison Association represents herders with 18,000 head of buffalo. They've found that nature did a better job of bio-engineering buffaloes as energy misers on the difficult prairie lands than agriscience has done with cattle. Three buffalo, bred to live off wild and unirrigated grasses, can live off the land required by one steer. The buffalo makes billion-dollar dam and irrigation schemes obsolete, and can help preserve the endangered Ogallala aquifer, now being drained for irrigation eight times faster than it replenishes itself.[58] Buffalo forage for their own food in all seasons, making heated barns and stored silage unnecessary. As a bonus for tree farmers, buffalo munch on broadleaf trees, and avoid the need to spray to protect softwoods. They give birth easily, without vets, and their reproductive life span is 25 years. They require little tending, and at any rate, "you can make a buffalo go anywhere it wants," says Len Ross, a rancher in Taber, Alberta.[59] Buffalo meat, 25 per cent higher in protein and 20 per cent lower in cholesterol than beef, gets twice the price of steer flesh. The meat can be marketed for steaks, roasts, sausage, burgers and jerky. Buffalo skins can be sold for coats, heavy duty gloves and riding gear. The skulls alone go for $325 in tourist traps. One novice Alberta operator nets $10,000 a month on his buffalo ranch.[60]

U.S. buffalo ranchers gain publicity from CNN owner Ted Turner's 2,400-head, 120,000-acre spread. Robert Scott of the Institute of the Rockies in Missoula, Montana, figures buffalo ranchers can make $48,000 a year off a restored 16 square mile grassland, by issuing licenses to trophy hunters. The game farms would stimulate local butchering and taxidermy operations, he says.

About 28 Native bands in the U.S. are dancing with buffalo, a trend spearheaded by Sioux leader Fred Dubray, who wants to restore Native self-reliance as well as western scrublands. His company, Tote Hea Ka, "the whole buffalo," gets value-extending sales from hides, bones for utensils and skulls for jewelry.[61] Many Métis of northern Saskatchewan, heirs of the most respected buffalo hunters of the wild west, hope to gain access to ranch lands now monopolized by logging companies.

Buffalo don't go against the grain of prairie conditions or market realities the way wheat does. As breadbasket for the world, North American wheat lands export as much topsoil to the wind as they do grain to the world. The value of production lost to erosion on the Canadian prairies is estimated at $380 million a year.[62] In the American West, the figure is 15 tons per acre per year.[63] World grain markets are glutted, and the multi-billion-dollar subsidies from both governments instigate more trade wars than trade. In fact, grain subsidies—in Canada, they average out at about $16,000 a year per farm, and in the U.S. they top $4 billion[64]—have done little but depopulate the west. Growers farm the subsidies rather than diversify into crops that are easier on the land, get higher prices, and create more processing opportunities. Travel subsidies discourage processing in the west, says Winnipeg consultant Richard Dawson—a retired vice-president from the food production, distribution and manufacturing world-giant Cargill—who thinks farmers should diversify into ethanol crops and buffalo grazing, as well as hemp. Cereal grains are best grown near where they're consumed, a trend that also favors rye and buckwheat, more adaptable and nutritious, less needful of chemicals and irrigation, than wheat. Wheat's reputation as king of the grains comes from processors, who like the elastic dough that water and air can be added to for a fluffed-up look on the shelf, according to Guelph University expert on food policy, Tony Winson. With its wheat germ milled out and chlorine bleaching added in, it's best suited for play dough, not food. Wheat, not buffalo, belongs in the west's past.

As a variant on buffalo herding for those who fancy lean pork, some game ranchers are succeeding with wild boar. The Western Canadian Wild Boar Association has 50 members.[65] In Crabtree, Quebec, Louis Joseph Froment and Louise Beaulieu raise 250 wild boar on their ecological farm, a fenced forest. They charge an admission fee to visitors, who receive a tasting of boar delicacies as part of their tour.[66]

Soul Food

Meat and potato Anglo-Americans have always been able to live high on the hog, their food too rich for their own good and too energy-intensive for the planet's health. Ketchup and salt add zest, pepper adds a dash of daring, cornstarch and air add bulk—which is why cereals and ice cream are sold by the carton, not the pound, and why there's lots of space left inside for free booby prizes—grease adds taste, sugar adds aftertaste, microwaved Cheez Whiz adds variety, and packaging and freezing add cost.

Ironically, most high cuisine and holiday delicacies started off disguising what lowlifes had to eat. The French mastered sauces to smother cheap cuts, and when that was too costly, they didn't turn their noses up at frogs' legs or snails. Gefilte fish is mashed carp. Upper class stomachs turned at chicken wings, grape leaves, johnnycakes, sushi and, above all, lobster, forced on the poor until the 1950s. If only welfare reform could make the poor swallow their pride scarfing lobster instead of macaroni, which has fallen on bad times since Yankee doodle days, when yuppies of the 1770s gathered at macaroni clubs.[67]

Denied the right to hunt wild game, the poor hunted bargains and rescued ham hocks and tongue from the garbage. They also had to figure out how to preserve and present food with the least amount of energy, a key difference between yesterday's food from waste and today's junk from food. Asian spices, pheasant under glass (tenderized by flies), smoked fish, jams and pickles substituted for refrigerators, while al dente cooking saved on heat. Yogurt, sour cream and blue cheese worked in harmony with the reality that milk is a live food with bacteria, and used that knowledge to create value-added, not energy-added, treats—a little smarter than boiling the life out of milk with pasteurization to produce a low-cost drink with a longer transport and shelf life.

The next generation of soul food, without the humble pie of poverty, will be based on methods that make the most of food energy and take the least energy for transportation, storage and packaging. Low on the food chain, high on the talent chain. Though a high conversion book of recipes is about the only cookbook that hasn't been written yet, some opportunities are obvious. Full use comes before re-use. Throwaway beet tops are now featured in salads. Carrot and celery tops can be boiled for soup stock. Apricot pits can be cracked for vitamin B17, thought by some to be an anti-carcinogen.[68] Pumpkin innards can be rescued from the composter after Halloween for seeds that stave off prostrate cancer. Reuse comes before recycling. Rotted fruit can be placed on wire mesh over aquaculture tanks, attracting bugs that fish convert to protein. Vegetable tops can be fed to rabbits for another meat source. Watermelon rinds make great pickles and citrus peels make marmalade, allowing fresh juice vendors and restaurants to branch into new sidelines that make organic packaging pay its way. In Seattle, the family-owned Spent Grain Baking company collects, for free, the high-nutrient grains left after a batch of beer has been made to bake flavorful bread.[69]

Greenhouses extend growing seasons, but at an energy cost. Tasty winter greens can also be sprouted on the windowsill from beans and seeds, a nice break from lettuce, and packed with nutrients that stand on their own merits. Dried fruit beats the winter blahs and helps farmers out of the squeeze of monopoly processors. Right now, farmers with perishable crops are at the mercy of high-energy canneries and freezers, who buy at peak season when supply is high and prices low. But drying out in the sun provides low-cost, low-energy storage that's more nutritious than canning and can be done by farmers themselves.[70] Dehydration reduces the bulk carried in transport trucks by orders of magnitude, and doesn't require refrigeration. Jane Brody warns that dried fruit is as heavy on the calories as the minerals, but recommends it for cereals and cakes instead of sugar.[71] The intense flavor lets them beat the caloric competition in many desserts, chutneys and sauces, as three top Calgary chefs make a habit of doing.[72]

As for food preparation, some authorities venture the claim that vegetables can be eaten raw, saving energy and preserving enzymes and vitamins destroyed by heat.[73] Cooking pots and steamers that conserve heat and water are widely available. The Japanese have pot lids that work like thermoses, allowing heaters to be turned off sooner and taking a big swath out of the dinnertime peak in energy demand.

Cold Warriors

When unions do it, it's called featherbedding. When doctors do it, it's called professionalism. Job monopolies that control the health system are case studies in the poor conversion of talent. The medical monopoly forces people to pay for salaries of those high on the pecking order, with training that often under-qualifies them for the task at hand. The American Medical Association "is definitely fighting for their 'in' group much more than a labor union ever fought automation," says Herbert Bailey, who championed vitamin E's role in curing heart disease at a time when it was ridiculed by the medical establishment.[74]

Supply-side health reform will grow a host of paramedical specialties with skills honed for the job at hand. Pharmacy technicians trained at a community college can read labels on big bottles before pouring pills into small bottles as well as university-trained pharmacists, and for half the fee, for example. Nurse practitioners, or advance-practice nurses, suggest the potential for combining supply-side with demand-side management. Nurse practitioners can advise rest, plenty of liquids and chicken soup, just as well as doctors, and they can spot symptoms that require a doctor's attention. Better than that, they have the training and aptitude to pass on nutritional and lifestyle advice that doctors don't have the time for. Doctors, after all, receive most of their training in acute care hospitals, where they'll be making most of their referrals, but not where they'll be caring for patients.

One **Business Week** report cited several studies indicating that advance-practice nurses could deliver over 60 per cent of primary care, without lowering the quality of service.[75] Canada's internationally recognized health-care reform advocate, Dr. Michael Rachlis, cites evidence showing service is improved when nurse practitioners fill in for doctors.[76] In Quebec, nurses trained to take calls on 24-hour coldlines reduce the demand on expensive emergency services to check temperatures and chest congestion. The common cold costs an uncommon portion of medical bills, and gives an example of how paying attention to the conversion of energy, whether human or natural, can bring down costs substantially.

Atlas Shrunked

All that's needed to make the North American economy energy wise is to turn off the welfare tap. Executives will be the first to agree that government handouts sap initiative, reward slackers, help deadbeats avoid their responsibility, demoralize honest workers, degrade the work ethic, and create a ghetto where fast buck artists set the example for others. There is ample proof of this in the business underclass created by government subsidies, that sorry lot of tobacco lords, junk food dealers, ad purveyors and financial con artists at the commanding heights of North American business, the people behind the new right that Marc Reisner calls Banana Republicanism.[77]

It's easy to get sidetracked in the subsidy debate, now framed by efforts to expose neo-conservative double standards when it comes to welfare spending for the rich and poor. From the standpoint of fourth-wave economics, resolving the debate doesn't turn on exposing corruption in high places. It doesn't turn on different philosophies about the divine right of governments or markets to rule over human affairs. Nor can the debate be resolved by balancing out cross-addictions, maintaining two sets of incentives that work at cross purposes: one set to subsidize environmentally unsustainable corporate practices, and one set to slow the slide of socially unsustainable corporate practices.

From the standpoint of fourth-wave economics, subsidies are a box of herbicides. They thwart the natural succession of new companies aligned with the laws of thermodynamics. Old guard companies have handled competition for space and resources among themselves by merging into sprawling conglomerates and laying off staff. But that only intensifies their dependence on state aid to block new competitors, because each step toward economic concentration gets them further out of whack with the laws governing natural productivity. Subsidies have to compensate for the energy overhead of centralization and long-distance trade, for instance, and if the rich won't cough up the taxes to cover the subsidies, then the money has to come from somewhere else—this is the physics of neo-conservatism. From this perspective, canceling subsidies is the easiest and surest way to take the economy to the detox center.

Lots of nice things will happen when we cut out what Ralph Nader calls "Aid to Dependent Corporations." First, this is where the big money is, $167 billion a year in the U.S.[78]—$440 billion if tax breaks no one else gets are counted[79]—and about $20 billion in Canada, where the larger subsidies per capita suggest that climate alone separates the country from banana republics.

Shaking down the poor with welfare reform yields at most $50 billion a year, proof again that the poor are not good people to go after for money. Second, wealthfare reform gets rid of the high class underclass—the upper crust counterparts to the slum's pimps, dealers and hustlers—which neither business nor government have yet been able to do. Third, when government stops scratching the back of big business, it will lift a burden off the backs of emerging companies that only need a level playing field to crack the big time. Fourth, as these new companies thrive and expand, their labor-intensive methods will assure jobs for all able-bodied and available workers now on social assistance. Welfare as we know it will be reformed with full employment.

A full-blown subsidy debate has to deal with transition problems for the simple reason that few of today's corporate giants will survive the transition. Their very strategy and structure, to borrow business historian Alfred Chandler's phrase, mean they can't stand on their own two feet. When taxpayers stop paying their overhead and out-of-pocket expenses, they'll be right-sized out of existence. The stock market will be merciless enough. There's no need for a "three strikes and you're out" policy—forcing bankruptcy on all companies guilty of violating environment or health and safety laws three times. A two-year cap on welfare pay-outs to corporations just prolongs the agony. That's why the subsidy debate needs to shift toward creating a Sunrise Fund that pools and disperses today's most harmful subsidies to help employees of obsolete companies retrain and prepare for a post-subsidy era. There's no need to look for new money. But the money that now goes to back losers and entrench inefficiencies can buy time for adjustment. Just to practice bending our minds around this, we could think in terms of a box of chocolates with $35 billion a year in it, the conservative Cato Institute's estimate of subsidies that now finance the most obvious polluters.[80] Since new service, farming and light industrial enterprises hire at the rate of 20 workers per million dollars, that's 700,000 job-years worth of start-up assistance.

Here is a sample of what tough love could do for government pay-outs that sponsor pollution and ill health, followed by a few thoughts on how a Sunrise Fund could be put to good use during a brief transition period. After that, all good business noses will be at the grindstone, not stuck in the government till.

1.   Help California corporate farmers dry out by canceling the average per-farm irrigation subsidy of $500,000 a year.[81] This will discourage farmers from growing rice and other water-intensive crops in an area that receives no rainfall for half the year. They do it now only because one acre of water one foot deep costs them $10.

Other subsidies that make this one work won't be needed. No reason for Michigan and Ontario taxpayers to shell out $7 billion for freeway development[82] when the freeloaders have nothing to ship. No need for U.S. taxpayers to make up the $5 billion a year difference between what truckers pay in taxes and fees and what it costs to maintain heavy transport routes.[83] That subsidy only made sense when water-intensive crops from a dryland area were being rushed past bankrupted farms in areas where water is plentiful. And no need for a prolonged subsidy to get farmers in those areas back into production now that they can serve their local market.

2. Cancel the approximately $2.5 billion in export enhancement subsidies that go to three global grain corporations, and the $110 million in grants covering the advertising costs of moving the likes of Chicken McNuggets, Pillsbury canned and frozen corn, M&Ms, Gallo wines, and Dole fruit in overseas markets.[84]

3. Cancel the $9 billion in direct grants and taxpayer-subsidized insurance schemes that now go to 15 per cent of U.S. farms, feeding their monoculture habit and encouraging them to stay in glutted markets. Ditto for the $2 billion in price support schemes that feed monoculture in Canada.

4. Cancel the $400 million a year in subsidies to haul western Canadian wheat, food aid to countries where the poor don't eat wheat, via Hudson Bay in the polar north.[85]

5. Cancel the $150 million a year worth of grants and tax deductions on fertilizers, pesticides and fuel that Canadian farmers receive, and which subsidize unsustainable farming techniques.

6. Cancel the $1.4 billion in yearly price supports for U.S. sugar farms, 40 per cent of which goes to the largest one per cent of firms, according to Chuck Collins of the Tax Equity Alliance of Massachusetts.[86] This money underwrites destruction of the Florida everglades, and undercuts competition from companies in the legitimate food industry that offer local and healthful sweeteners.

7. Cancel unemployment insurance boondoggles that reward primary industries for poor planning. Canada's unemployment insurance gives seasonal and boom-bust workers in primary industries $4.93 for every dollar they pay in.[87] That means other workers and companies pay logging and mining conglomerates to keep workers at their beck and call. If primary industries were grouped together for purposes of financing unemployment insurance, they would have an incentive to provide value-added jobs that could carry workers through off-seasons or downtimes. According to B.C. forestry economist Michael Mascall, the total value of lumber subsidies pays the first $15,000 earned by a logger each year.[88] But then, as Nanaimo, B.C. economist David Weston argues, "if God had meant us to think, He wouldn't have given us all those forests, would He?"

8. Bring U.S. mine royalties into the 20th century. Royalty levels set in 1872 let mine companies live in the past. In 1993, Toronto-based Barrick Resources bought up U.S. land with $10 billion of gold in it for $8,965.00. The federal interior secretary called it "the biggest gold heist since the days of Butch Cassidy," but let the robbers get away with it.[89] A budget prepared by Friends of the Earth estimated that the U.S. treasury loses $500 million a year with this giveaway, $32 million of which pays the yearly salary of Barrick's founder.[90] That's a $500-million head start on highly taxed recycling companies that conserve resources.

9. Cancel all the local subsidies and tax dodges to companies that foul up the earth. Since 1961, the New York State Power Administration has sold electricity, the crucial ingredient needed to turn salt into the poison gas, chlorine, for one cent a kilowatt hour. That seven cent an hour subsidy amounted to $2 billion over the 1970s and '80s. One chlorine firm got the equivalent of $125,000 per worker per year. All firms benefiting from the scheme get an average $23,000 per worker per year.[91]

Greg Leroy's review of candy store offerings notes Alabama's $255 million grant to Mercedes-Benz, $177,000 per job, Kentucky's $140 million to Dofasco, $350,000 per job and a host of others that would make good reading for welfare moms who receive $67 a month in extra support for their third child. Corporate lust and promiscuity pay much better than that.[92]

10. Cancel the tax shelter write-off for corporate spending on misleading advertising. This is an incentive to pollute the public airwaves with ad nauseam about booze, pop, potato chips, candy, cereals and burgers that violate healthy food guidelines adopted by governments.[93] It also fosters monopoly in the food sector,[94] at the expense of mom and pop operations that can't afford ads themselves but have to make up the taxes avoided by their competitors. Promotional methods of small companies rely on word of mouth, which comes from quality, which comes from labor, which is taxed to the hilt. Taxing advertising at the same rate as other capital expenditures would give spending on productivity improvements a boost, even out the playing field for small local businesses, or bring in about $4 billion a year in revenues to North American governments.

Tax favoritism for junk food is matched by U.S. department of agriculture rules that prevent most health food stores from accepting food stamps. To qualify, stores have to sell goods from all four food groups, including meat and dairy products. "A gas station that sells frozen beef burritos, apples, milk and cereal is eligible for the food stamp program," **Vegetarian Times** notes, "but a small health food store that carries a variety of soy products, legumes and fresh vegetables isn't."[95]

11. Cancel the tax-free status of gambling on currencies and derivatives. Speculators get to play on slot machines that turn world financial markets upside down without paying any of the gambling taxes charged at casinos. There isn't even a simple sales tax like there is on real goods. Little wonder that the economy loses its Barings.

Nobel laureate James Tobin has proposed a tiny sales tax on this trillion-dollar-a-year anti-industry. At 0.1 per cent, it's estimated that the so-called Tobin tax could finance the elimination of payroll taxes, encouraging companies to hire more workers.[96] The great economist John Maynard Keynes favored such a tax to encourage enterprise over speculation,[97] a view endorsed by the U.N.'s Commission on Global Governance in 1994.

How to put all the money we save from canceling welfare programs for the wealthy to good use?

In agriculture, one option would be to offer $25,000-a-year contracts to family farmers who perform certain restoration activities, such as planting shelter belts, or who experiment with new production and distribution methods in keeping with their region.

Former tobacco farmers in the American south are already doing this on their own initiative, with help from groups such as the Community Farm Alliance in Kentucky. But they have none of the baseline support enjoyed by farmers who stick with a toxic product, tobacco, which kills half-a-million North Americans a year. Governments let tobacco farmers operate in a closed market that gives them a higher rate of return than on useful farm products. As soon as they break the tobacco habit, they face cutthroat competition, at prices that drive them under. Nevertheless, many are now experimenting with direct sales to restaurants and with non-food crops such as wood for crafts and furniture.[98] Once paper production goes tree-free, they'll have ample markets for hemp and kenaf, which grow well on the same soils as tobacco, and perhaps for ramie, a fibrous nettle that makes ultra-strong paper and cloth.[99] But while the economy climbs the learning curve, farmers will need a hand up.

Likewise, increased tax revenues from mining could be spent hiring any miners who lose their jobs to reclaim lands destroyed by mining. Plant and bug engineers with Boojum Research Ltd. in Toronto are now capable of re-engineering tailings ponds, usually loaded with multiple toxins, into bogs that provide food for critters that neutralize acids and other poisons.[100]

Unlike farmers, workers in many industries have no future in an unsubsidized world. Nuclear workers only have reruns of Homer Simpson to look forward to the moment the trough is closed. Other than a few openings at the history museum of bad ideas, chlorine workers are out of luck. Tony Mazzocchi, recently-retired vice-president of the Oil, Chemical and Atomic Workers Union, spent the last half of his career looking for ways to help workers out of toxic industries. His idea, recalled from his youthful days after World War II, is to give veterans of toxic industries the same fresh start on a new life that war veterans got. The proposal is backed by Professor Barry Commoner, author of the brilliant **Poverty of Power,** which links declining productivity to power subsidies gone mad. "We have gotten ourselves into this crazy situation," he told a 1992 Greenpeace conference on chlorine, "of spending enough money on the failed attempt to deal with the petrochemical industry that we could afford to close it down and pay the workers and give them a chance for a new life."

It's not very expensive to finance. Companies that account for 80 per cent of toxic releases only employ 17 per cent of the workforce.[101] Moreover, when the chlorine industry goes down for the count after it starts paying its own way, there's a job bonus for any workers who have the training. Chlorine depletes the job layer faster than it depletes the ozone layer. Every tax dollar given away to the industry goes to a product that displaces skilled labor—pesticides take the skill out of farming, dry-cleaning solvents substitute for the knowledge of wet cleaners, and so on—which is why more subsidies are currently needed to create fewer jobs.

Governments and businesses can't have it both ways. Governments can't beg off regulating the market while distorting it with subsidies. Businesses can't talk legal deregulation when industry survival is in fact regulated by subsidies. The new entrepreneurs don't need to talk out of both sides of their mouths. Their methods can stand the test of the economic marketplace easier than they can meet the competition of the political marketplace.

The only fly in the ointment is the mass of workers and managers caught in the middle through no fault of their own, because of wrongheaded political decisions to finance industries voted most likely to pollute. That's why a Sunrise Fund is needed, which can be financed over its short life by transferring pollution grants to emerging alternatives.

An Ounce of Prevention

Principle 5

Aims for management by results, and shows how investing in " avoided costs" and "demand-side management" can finance social and economic renewal

"How to move from a least-price to a least-cost system is the industrial question of this and the coming century. It costs less...and it takes more people to do it."
Green economist Paul Hawken[1]

"Anybody who would invest $40,000 to $60,000 a year to lock somebody up, rather than $6,000 to $8,000 a year to lift them up, is not using conservative economics."
Jesse Jackson[2]

As many old wise tales attest, a stitch in time saves nine. Prevention costs less than damage control. That's why the futures market of the new economy will rest on prevention. Community agencies serving expectant moms have found the savings opportunity of a lifetime, and are proving that whatsoever you do for the little children, you do for the economy.

The Montreal Diet Dispensary provides food, vitamin pills and counseling to 2,500 mothers-to-be each year. "We have proven that better nutrition during pregnancy can make a difference in a baby's birth weight and health," says executive director Marie-Paule Duquette. Since 1980, the volunteer agency has reduced the incidence of low birth weight babies by 50 per cent. Every time the agency succeeds, it saves the health, educational and social services system up to $1 million in the lifetime costs of administering to people who weigh less than 5½ pounds at birth.[3]

A nine-month head start at getting things right the first time starts with simple precautions at the time of conception.[4] Cutting out coffee reduces risks of miscarriage by one-third.[5] Getting off booze, tobacco and hard drugs cuts premature births in half.[6] Ensuring expectant moms have adequate folic acid from dark green vegetables reduces the risks of spina bifida and neural-tube defects by half.[7] Warning moms-to-be off additives in hot dogs and keeping them free of electro-magnetic radiation significantly lowers the chances of their kids contracting childhood cancers.[8] It's even likely that crime fighting starts this early. A study of Danish statistics, the only ones comprehensive enough to plot the line between individual birthing difficulties and later crime records, suggests violent crimes among teens can be brought down by 18 per cent with higher standards of pre-natal care.[9]

Quality health care doesn't come any cheaper. The Harvard School of Public Health conducted a tough-minded study of "secondary prevention" measures for prolonging life. A year of life bought with a heart transplant cost $104,000. A year bought by removing asbestos from walls cost about $2 million. A year of life from pre-natal care was costed at "less than zero." The Harvard researchers argue that $31-billion-a-year worth of health spending could be redirected to productive channels such as this.[10] The same proportions hold for Canada. "We could probably cut health-care costs by one-third by spending more in those other critical areas," says British Columbia's chief medical officer, Dr. John Millar.[11] By getting medical and health care right side up, we can jack up the productivity of the North American economy. The proportion of North America's GNP that goes to sick care—nine per cent in Canada and 14 per cent in the U.S.—is well above what other advanced nations spend for the same or better health outcomes.

Yet the North American health and social services system suffers from chronic child neglect. The U.S. has the worst low birth weight rate in the industrial world[12] and ranks 19th in the world for infant mortality. If Harlem was counted on its own, it would rank 44th in the world.[13] The U.S. is the only country in the developed world not to ratify the 1989 Convention on the Rights of the Child, and has the second worst record for child deaths from abuse.[14] In 1995, Canada experienced its first increase in infant mortality since the 1940s.[15] Both Canada and the U.S. hold up the rear in industrial world rankings for measures to counter child poverty.[16] The medical system in both countries is geared to the near-dead. As much as 30 per cent of medical resources go into dragging out the last 12 months of life, and half of that goes for the last 90 days. Whenever money is spent on pregnant mothers, it goes to repeated pre-natal ultrasound and fetal heart monitoring, both costly measures with little evidence to support their value. "We doctors tend to work on the basis of experience and experience has been defined as making the same mistakes year after year," Dr. Richard Goldbloom said, releasing the comprehensive **Canadian Guide to Clinical Preventive Care**, which documented these abuses.

This suggests what the major barriers are to child-proofing the economy. With medical costs ballooning—in the U.S., they went from $57 billion in 1980 to $311 billion in 1995, and the Congressional Budget Office is predicting they will break the $2 trillion mark by the turn of the century[17]—there must be a powerful neurosis that keeps the system from confronting the source of such financial pain. One problem is that the political muscle is gathered at the acute care spectrum of the economy. That's where the well-paid professionals and experts huddle and award professional glory to breakthroughs in tube and orifice medicine. That's where the headlines are when something runs amok and hands are wrung about medical ethics and the sacredness of life.

Low-cost methods don't stand a chance. There's no Nobel prize for the best exercises to ease natural child delivery. Powerless groups get the shaft. Canada spends five per cent of its government research funds on the needs of women, and the U.S. spends 14 per cent, for instance.[18] The U.S. government hands over $77 billion a year to those who doctor the poor, giving physicians and drug companies $21 billion more than the poor receive in allowances and food stamps.[19] Sick care robs resources from health care, and poverty programs work in reverse as long as prevention is an afterthought. A raft of studies document the impact of poverty and unemployment on physical and mental health. Babies born to poor families are twice as likely to die in infancy as babies with the foresight to be born in rich families, definitive Statistics Canada figures show.[20] Unemployment is a leading killer, a team of researchers found in a landmark study for the **Canadian Medical Association Journal**.[21] Yet few ask the question posed by Sharon Kirsch in her 1992 report, **Unemployment: Its Impact on Body and Soul**. It's not a question of whether our economy can afford our health system, Kirsch says, but whether the health system can afford the economy.

If we had a free market in health care, instead of a medical monopoly over sick care, community agencies could enter competitive bids on at least the $31 billion a year identified by Harvard researchers to finance projects that improve or prolong more life at better cost. This would give a running start to clinics that treat community development, personal empowerment and responsibility as part of their mandates. In inner-city ghettoes across the U.S., outreach agencies associated with Lessons Without Borders are using community cures learned from development workers in the Third World.[22] The new model of family-centered care clinics, says Jean-Victor Wittenberg of Toronto's Sick Kids Hospital, is at odds with medical traditions of treating parents as a nuisance and a source of infection. Street-based tuberculosis clinics should be able to get their hands on some of the $700 million a year in cures shot in the arms of the homeless, and work that down to 1988 levels of $2 million.[23] By grabbing the right end of the problem, they can also slow the spread of new TB strains that render standard TB antibiotics obsolete.[24]

TB, once thought to be a disease of the shameful past, brings us back to the great wave of social and health reform at the turn of the century, when fear of contagion sparked holistic efforts toward raising community standards. That successful example of a safety-first, medical-social partnership was splintered by a new medical orthodoxy, says York University's Dr. Trevor Hancock, who helped develop the World Health Organization's healthy city projects. "In the industrial model, you just do what Henry Ford did, break things into smaller pieces of specialization," he says. "That's what led to the shift in medical thinking from a concern for cities in the 19th century to a concern for molecules today."

"The environment is in trouble, and the more it suffers, the harder it is on your skin."

Seventeen Magazine

Economies need to be end-tested as well as means-tested. Results-oriented "life-cycle accounting" helps identify the cost-effectiveness of prevention. The procedure is reminiscent of early tests for insanity, when psychiatrists placed a mop and pail beside a running tap. Those who went for the mop and pail, instead of turning off the tap, were put away.[25] Michael Perley puts politicians to the same test on air pollution.

Michael Perley was a senior lobbyist for the coalition that won 1990 clean air regulations designed to cut North American acid rain pollution in half. In **Poisoned Skies: Who'll Stop Acid Rain**, co-authored with award-winning journalist Ross Howard, he goes after the "one-eyed accountants" who stalled action for a decade, claiming it cost too much to get rid of pollution.

"What goes around, comes around" does not begin to describe the web we unravel when first we practice to pollute. Acid rain, invisible and odorless but vinegary with about 10 times the natural pH level[26] of good-old-days rain, falls from skies overdosed with sulfuric and nitric acid from smelters, coal plants and cars. Mined materials that find their way into smelters and fuels should be declared "unnatural resources," says Stan Rowe, author of **Home Place.** Only when they were buried deep in earth's basement, after billions of years of geological history, did life on the planet become possible. "Mining and the modern use of mining products are turning the geological clock backwards," Rowe says, "recreating the Precambrian environment when acid rain, laced with radionuclides and heavy metals, washed the rocks of a world hostile to life." They've come back with a vengeance, and work on nature like Murphy's Law on speed.

The hard rain showed up first in lakes. In eastern Canada, 15,000 lakes were pronounced dead. Even in Florida, far from the big smelters, 54 per cent of lakes suffered a bad acid trip. The toxicity problem was compounded when acid broke down the protective soil cover that locked in lead, cadmium and aluminum, specks of which found their way into lakes. Forests showed up on the sick list next. Leaves etched by acid, their seeds sterilized, trees couldn't reproduce. Then came declines in farm output, as the soil was demineralized by acid leaching. Then building owners took a financial acid bath, their paint, stonework and metal claddings corroded by acid. When the medical statistics came in, acid rain was the third major culprit in lung and heart disease, responsible for 55,000 deaths a year, just behind direct and second-hand cigarette smoke. It's hard to isolate acid rain, but it's not very hard to track the direct impacts of air pollution on health. Researchers with the American Lung Association watched what happened on days when smog levels in Ontario went beyond the province's legal limit of 0.08 parts per million and hit legal U.S. limits of 0.12 ppm. Hospital admissions for respiratory problems jumped up anywhere from 24 to 50 per cent.[27]

The economic body count looks something like this: losses to sport-fish tourist economies, about $1 billion a year; damage to the forestry industry, $11 billion a year; crop losses, over $2.1 billion a year; corrosion damage to buildings, at least $5 billion a year, including $66 million to restore the Statue of Liberty. That's $19 billion a year before we get to medical costs. Polluters took the rest of the economy to the toxic cleaners. Seeing through the smoke and mirrors of pollution politics means seeing pollution as a take-away. It off-loads one company's waste costs onto other companies and the general public, and forces them to pay the clean-up bill.

Polluters, in documents they used to justify delays of legislation, claimed it would cost them $4 billion a year over 20 years to clean up their act. Politicians were slow to do the math and see that as a $15-billion-a-year saving. And, surprise, the studies were way off in their estimates. Once INCO, the Sudbury-based nickel producer that spewed out 20 per cent of Canada's acid rain, set its mind on correcting the problem, it saved buckets of money. It cost the company $600 million to cut back on its smoking, an investment that will pay off in seven years, because the new system extracts more minerals from ore, captures sulfuric acid for industrial sales, and reduces smelter fuel bills. When permits for sulphur dioxide emissions were first listed at the Chicago board of trade, it was expected that companies would have to buy them for between $1,000 and $1,500 a ton. They now list at $132. "The price shows that companies were inflating the costs to avoid complying with the regulations," says University of Maryland environmental law professor Robert Percival, who encourages groups to buy up shares and take them off the market.[28] There are still 176,400 available, which, for some reason, never get mentioned in media reports on the stock market: "The power to take away clean air with 176,400 tons of sulphur dioxide is holding steady at $132."

Perley now heads the Ontario Campaign for Action on Tobacco, which, like similar movements mushrooming across the continent, treats tobacco as an air pollution issue. A definitive 1993 study by the U.S. Environmental Protection Agency classified second-hand, passive, or side-stream, smoke as a Class A carcinogen, which causes more harm to non-smokers than smokers in terms of inhaled benzene, cadmium and nickel. It's estimated that U.S. workplace health and safety measures protecting non-smokers on the job will save 40,000 lives a year and $39 billion in medical costs. "Environmental issues are increasingly oriented to public health, personal health, rather than trees and lakes," Perley says, "and this is where environmentalists are really going to make headway."

"How the construction today of great and glorious works can impoverish the future, no man can see until his mind is beset by false analogies from an irrelevant accountancy. The nation as a whole will assuredly be richer if unemployed men and machines are used to build much-needed houses than if they are supported in idleness."

Keynesian economist J.M. Keynes, 1933[29]

Implementing preventive economics is essentially a balancing act—there's that accounting barrier again. Business accountants now count despoiling of resources as income and restoration as a cost. But if the multi-billion-dollar costs of financing electricity from nuclear reactors or finding a toilet for the nuclear industry can be postponed to the indefinite future, some whiz kid should be able to figure out how to finance prevention out of future savings. While we're waiting for "Green 1-2-3" accounting software, here are some trends to watch for.

Protection Money

Only mad scientists and the mainstream media cast doubt on the urgency of dealing with global warming. The $180-billion North American re-insurance industry certainly knows what's cooking. It's inherited the wind from an outbreak of floods and hurricanes over the last decade.

The carbon dioxide let loose in the atmosphere has reached 355 parts per million, up from 280 in 1800 when it was relatively balanced. That was before the mass burn-off of fossil fuels, coupled with the destruction of forests that once stored carbon. No one factored in climate damage when the costs of clear-cutting were estimated, notes Greenpeace founder Robert Hunter, now a leading environment writer.[30] The 10 hottest years since 1860 have all taken place since 1980,[31] causing oceans to warm and rise. If forests don't equilibrate

the system, hurricanes and floods will, nature's way of letting off
steam when it gets hot under the collar. Through the 1960s and '70s,
there were 14 major hurricanes. In the 1980s, there were 70.[32] In
1995, there were 15 tropical storms, half of them hurricanes, and at
least one of them, Opal, came on two months after the usual peak
season for such storms.[33] Sixteen out of 20 of the worst insurance
catastrophes in U.S. history have happened since 1989, a blame to be
laid partially at the feet of the insurance industry itself for insuring
people who chose to live in flood plains and on mountain cliffs made
accessible by roads. In 1992, storm losses hit $20 billion, up from $1
billion in the early 1960s. Lloyds of London lost £6.7 billion between
1988 and 1991, and had to go after its investors for their last cuf-
flinks.[34] If the trend continues, the insurance industry will be flat-
tened by floods, since half the world's insured risks lie within a yard
of sea level.[35]

It's an ill wind that blows no good. The age-old re-insurance strategy
of spreading the risk, "the law of large numbers," won't weather the
storms when freaks of nature are freaks of carbon overload. The law
of large numbers is a reactive, not preventive, strategy. "We're not
the dog," says Franklin Nutter, head of the Reinsurance Association
of America.[36] "We're the tail of the dog."

Insurers have begun to identify their business interest in preventing
further global warming. In Europe, some farsighted insurers have
even joined forces with Greenpeace. The reinsurance industry, together with lowland areas of the world that have an equally vested
interest, can finance a carbon exchange on the futures market. The
exchange can fund restoration of forests and grasses that lock up carbon dioxide, or invest in forest- and grass-based ethanol fuels that
equalize emissions with new growth. Health insurance companies
might even want to chip in, since they face Lloyds-level bleeding as
temperatures change and exotic insects and bacteria move beyond
their old stomping grounds.[37]

New companies can bid for carbon storage contracts let out by the
carbon exchange. They might, for instance, use carbon exchange
funds to buy up forests from clear-cut loggers, then thin them out
over long rotations so the forest biomass actually increases faster than
in nature. The threatened old growth forests of the Pacific northwest

are prime candidates for a set-aside purchase, since they are the most productive hosts of new carbon-storing biomass in the world, outperforming tropical forests by a five-to-one ratio, according to senior Vancouver environment reporter Ian Gill.[38] Prairies grasses are another carbon exchange natural. Switchgrass, considered ideal for ethanol by the U.S. Department of Energy, locks more carbon in its roots than is burned off from the grass.

If the carbon exchange were launched with one per cent of the North American reinsurance industry's worth, it would generate over 40,000 jobs a year bringing down the future liabilities of the reinsurance industry. If lowland areas and health insurance companies bought a stake, if governments kicked in something to compensate the exchange for hiring the unemployed, if Canadian logging companies—recognizing that they've been losing 2.2 million hectares a year to forest fires since the 1980s, twice the average annual loss before then and twice what they cut[39]—threw in their two cents worth, the carbon exchange would soon be the biggest employer on the continent.

Jobs Unlimited

Floods haven't been this bad since the days of Noah's Ark. In 1995, the European lowlands had their worst in 40 years.[40] California rivers overflowed in Los Angeles. Fast snow-melts unleashed spring floods in Alberta, later also the scene of raging fires that took more forests out of production in one season than in any one year over the past decade. Not many years earlier, U.S. midwestern floods caused $30-billion-worth of damage, setting hundred-year records for many areas, despite the fact that rainfall levels had often been much higher in non-flood years.

Wagging the finger at global warming isn't enough. Flooding is also on the rise because we've removed the sponges nature uses to mop up after a rain—wetlands, flood plains and forests that store moisture and release it slowly. Snow on a forest floor, for instance, melts about a month later than open snow, a little time-delay thermostat that nature worked out long ago. The Great Lakes lost their biological sump pumps when wetlands were paved over, destroying a resource valued by Michigan's Department of Resources at $490 an acre for its storage capacity.[41] Riverbed flood plains used to store both water and silt, but about 50 million acres have been drained along the Mississippi over the last 200 years. There's not much give left. Dikes compound the problem by forcing the water into narrow channels that, in some places, means the surface of the water is higher than that of the surrounding land.[42] "Ironically, the result has been more flooding, not less," says dike critic Andrew Glass.[43] The International Joint Commission responsible for the bi-national management of the Great Lakes recommends "planting trees and shrubs to anchor the soil" instead of putting fingers in dikes.[44]

With an instinctive grasp of the new economy, some Mississippi basin residents have started to package a solution. In North Dakota, the Nature Conservancy raised funds from bake sales and Scout collections of beer cans to buy 5,000 acres of flood plains. The group will restore river banks to prevent future flash floods.[45] In one Missouri county, farmers turned down an offer from the Army Corps of Engineers to cover 80 per cent of the costs for new cement embankments, and sold their flood plain lands to the National Fish and Wildlife Foundation.[46] Bruce Smith, the "beaver evangelist" of the U.S. Forest Service works with volunteer groups in the northwest that give an assist to beavers. The beavers build dams that slow flash floods in creeks and gullies, revive water tables in drylands, and restore areas overgrazed by cattle. The silt that builds up in beaver ponds is rich in nutrients which feed new growth after the beavers move on.[47]

There are many ways to gift wrap naturalization projects that prevent expensive disasters by restoring the productivity of nature. Australia has a Landcare and Environmental Action Program that pools funds from unemployment insurance, welfare and training to pay unemployed youth a decent wage to rehabilitate riverbanks and historic sites. This is not chain gang stuff. The youth work four days a week and study the theory of what they're doing on the fifth day. They move on after 26 weeks with a job reference on their resumé and a new career idea in mind.

President FDR's New Deal is the granddaddy of depression-buster initiatives. The Civilian Conservation Corps employed 500,000 youth at its peak during the 1930s, and the Works Progress Administration hired eight million. They planted 11 million acres of shelter belts in the west, preventing the erosion that caused the dust bowl, and built botanical gardens, zoos, state parks and playgrounds that still pay dividends today.[48] Though many of these projects are outdated by today's standards, the New Deal leaves a bench mark of how many people can be put to work restoring infrastructure, on which expenditures have fallen by half across North America since the 1970s.[49]

Greenfare can be piloted on flood control projects. It can pay workers out of a fund that pools unemployment insurance, welfare, and training funds, topped up by a down payment covering government and insurance company savings in avoided damage from faulty infrastructure. This is the new economy's answer to workfare and welfare reform. There's no reason to sweat the drop in funding for school-based training for the unemployed. The "great training robbery" costs $3.7 billion a year in Canada and is slagged by both unions and managers for dead-end courses.[50] U.S. trainers reportedly blew $1 billion training unemployed west coast loggers without graduating one person into a new job. "They're sticking a lollipop in the mouths of rural communities so they won't scream so loudly," Don Golden, former senior state planner for Washington, says.[51] A 1990 evaluation of New York welfare trainees showed eight per cent of Blacks and five per cent of whites went on to a job.[52]

Greenfare restores jobs to their rightful place as the keystone of anti-poverty programs. Without them, welfare money does an economic freefall. After 10 years of improvements to welfare rates, Canada's poor had $27 billion less income in 1991 than they did in 1981 due to the disappearance of traditional jobs, says David Ross of the Canadian Council on Social Development.[53]

Give Peace A Chance

Central governments take about $1,023 from each Canadian and $1,097 from each American every year for military spending. Despite media reports to the contrary, the cold war is still on, and is seen as a graver threat to national security than global warming. Just one-quarter of the $1 trillion a year squandered on death industries, Hazel

Henderson has shown, could fund enough preventive programs to meet the food, water, housing, medical and energy needs of the world, while stabilizing population and pollution and retiring the Third World's debt.[54]

But this is getting us off track. We promised to stick to ideas that could be acted on, even with today's standards of political leadership.

Fat Is A Feminist Issue

Animal fat is the leading killer and crippler of North American women. Excessive fat consumption increases risks of heart disease, cancer, osteoporosis and menopausal complications. When it comes to fat food, "no means no" puts the power of prevention in women's hands.

Needless to say, diet can't undo damage from carcinogenic chemicals that do proportionately more harm to women than men. "The breast unfortunately functions as the body's hazardous waste dump," says Debra Lee Lewis of the U.S. Department of Health and Human Services in Washington.[55] Fatty tissues needed for reproduction store persistent chlorinated compounds such as DDT, involuntary exposure to which increases breast cancer risks fourfold.[56] A chlorine-free cookbook hasn't been written for the simple reason that the idea of a blank book has already been patented by the publisher of **What Men Know About Women.** There is no individual choice in these matters. From this perspective, Sandra Steingraber, who contracted breast cancer at 20 and has since dedicated her career as a professional biologist to combating industrial toxins, correctly calls cancer a "human rights violation."[57] Pollution is "invisible violence against women, says San Francisco-based health worker Judith Brady, herself a breast cancer survivor. "We have to stop being nice girls, and start fighting as if our lives depended on it, because they do."[58]

But some personal musts dovetail with a comprehensive anti-cancer strategy. Vigorous exercise can reduce cancer rates among pre-menopausal women by as much as 60 per cent, reports Leslie Bernstein, professor of preventive medicine at the University of Southern California. "This is the kind of prevention we need," responded Dr. Susan Love, director of the breast center at the University of California at Los Angeles, the leading authority in the field. "This is lifestyle changes, instead of drugs."[59] Diet can reduce the intake of toxins from food, since poisons are more highly concentrated in animal fat than in vegetables and grains lower down on the food chain. Ovarian cancer, which affects two per cent of North American women, is linked almost directly to fat consumption, according to a 1994 study published in the **Journal of the National Cancer Institute.** Cutting out a little less than two hamburgers' worth of animal fat a day lowers risk by 20 per cent. Consuming the same weight in vegetable fiber lowers risk rates by 37 per cent.[60] North American breast cancer rates are the highest in the world. Low breast cancer incidence in China correlates with a diet that has one-tenth our level of animal fat, says Colin Campbell of Cornell University, a senior cancer researcher and director of the classic study of plant-based diets. "The closer one approaches a total plant food diet, the greater the benefit," he says.[61]

"You can talk about an anti-carcinogenic diet," says Dr. Anthony Miller, director of a breast screening study of 7,000 Canadian women which confirmed that diets high in fiber protected against cancer.[62] Soy protein alters women's hormones and mimics the anti-cancer drug, tomoxifin, it's now believed.[63] A phytochemical, isoflavin, seems to account for soy's ability to reduce breast and prostate cancer levels by a third in Asia. The phytoestrogens in soy, as well as in flax seeds, are the likely candidates for preventing cancers affected by hormones, including breast, colon and prostate cancers, says Dr. David Jenkins, Director of the Risk Factor Centre at St. Michael's Hospital in Toronto.[64] As well, animal studies show the lignin in flax seed could reduce breast cancer tumors by 50 per cent, the University of Toronto's Lilian Thompson told the American Association for Cancer Research.[65]

There's an opportunity here for neighborhood food processors to come out with a range of tasty soy products, from custards, smoothies and shakes to casseroles, spaghetti sauces and stir-fries, all tastier when the tofu is fresh made, using simple processing technology.[66] Olive oil is as good for reducing breast cancer as it is for heart disease, Harvard School of Public Health epidemiologist Dr. Dimitrios Trichopoulos found. Mediterranean women, who consume large quantities of olive oil, have less than half the North American breast cancer rate. "Rather than feeling helpless against these cancers," says

Trichopoulos, we know that "vegetables prepared in olive oil may actually provide an easy and rather pleasant way of reducing risk."[67]

The death sentence from heart disease doesn't get the attention that cancer does, but about five times more American women die of heart attacks than breast cancer. In Canada, heart conditions are responsible for 40 per cent of female deaths a year, but male-practice medicine has been slow to diagnose the disease or treat its unique female dimensions.[68] Diabetes, for instance, is almost twice as likely to lead to heart disease among women than men.[69] Increasing vitamin E intake is a proven preventative, as is diet that slashes fat intake.[70] Hold your fat intake to 30 per cent or less of your daily calories, recommends Canada's leading women's magazine, **Chatelaine,** advice which might sit well with fat-food advertisers who buy space in the magazine, but which is at least twice the level recommended by leading experts.[71]

North American women also suffer from abnormally high rates of osteoporosis, weakened bones that limit free movement by seniors and require more than $10-billion-worth of medical treatment each year.[72] High consumption of dairy products, commonly marketed as a calcium-rich bone-builder, may actually be the culprit, since the high protein content of milk seems to leach the body's store of calcium.[73] Just as overly protein-rich diets are responsible for early onset of menses among North American women, they are likely responsible for the relatively late onset and strong force of menopause. Estrogen, a popular menopause prescription among doctors, is implicated in increases in the breast cancer rates of older women.[74]

Harping on diet is often denounced as "blaming the victim." This view confuses onus of responsibility for onus for action. Harping on diet is about liberating the victims from wanton disrespect for women on the part of government and the health and food industries.

The Sky's The Limit
Seven years after she and her husband bought a lake-side retirement home the grandkids love to visit, Billie Elmore learned "out of the clear blue sky" that the North Carolina government planned to site an incinerator four miles away. She'd heard about the protest by

15,000 citizens against an incinerator in a nearby county six months earlier, in November, 1987. The meeting made the **Guinness Book of World Records** as the largest public hearing ever. It started with a rousing chorus of **America the Beautiful** and ended when police provided a safe escort for state officials to the county line. Other than that, psychotherapist Elmore says, "I knew nothing from nothing about the environment or garbage or toxic substances." Five years later, senior state officials canceled all incineration plans after constant public debates and protests by citizens, spearheaded by the 60-groups Waste Awareness and Reduction Network coalition. By that time, state officials had been put through their own ordeal by fire, suffering over 20 siting defeats at the hands of "the Methodist ladies from Lee County," as Elmore's co-workers were first known, and of NC WARN.

Elmore has her own version of the seven habits of highly effective incineration fighters. "I want people to know what happened in North Carolina," she says, "because we won, we won, we won."

1. Go for it. Have passion and bulldog determination. Never back down or compromise.

2. Form coalitions of grassroots groups that can help out.

3. Find alternatives. "That's absolutely indispensable, otherwise what you get hit with at every turn is 'what would you do with it?'"

4. Never be accused of fighting fair. Don't ever lie or use violence. But after that, always stress that "the sky's the limit." In 1990, leaders of one of the NC WARN groups purchased a 48-acre holding in the midst of the land parcel set aside for the incinerator, sold $5 shares to 10,000 people, including touring Russian dancers and Asians bidding on the tobacco crop. Since land can't be confiscated in North Carolina without paying owners, the move killed that incinerator siting. The shared land is now used as a demonstration site for organic gardening and farm restoration.

5. Involve ordinary people. The proposed Lee County incinerator was defeated when organizers distributed orange ribbons which were then hung on the front lawns of all residents opposed to the facility.

6.   Be innovative with tactics to attract attention. "The more creative your strategy, the fewer people you need to carry it out."

7.   Pass on your legacy. In return for helping jump-start one group, insist that they help out the next.

The incinerator threat over, Elmore has taken up full-time painting as her art association's 1996 Artist of the Year. NC WARN remains a powerful force influencing the state's waste agenda. It's trying to overturn the economic development strategy of offering southern hospitality to toxic industries. North Carolina is the number two state in recruiting new industries, and number seven for toxic releases, says NC WARN's new director, Jim Warren. "We need to challenge industrial recruiters to bring in clean industries," he says. "Alternative waste and alternative development strategies tie together so closely," he says.

Born Free

Principle 6

Explores new ways of increasing the common wealth,
making sure the best things in life are free

*"You gotta say this for the white race—its self-confidence knows
no bounds. Who else could go to a small island in the South
Pacific where there is no poverty, no crime, no unemployment,
no war and no worry—and call it a 'primitive society'?"*
Activist Dick Gregory[1]

"Exploitation, manipulation and destruction of the life in nature can be a source of money and profits but neither can ever become a source of nature's life and its life-supporting capacity. It is this asymmetry that accounts for a deepening of the ecological crises."
Third World development critic Vandana Shiva[2]

Economic freedom increases access to goods provided free by nature and community. The real "tragedy of the commons" happens when goods and services that were once free and public are taken over by corporations and put up for sale. That's why Trish Horton had to buck the system to give her newborn a free and easy start.

Seven months pregnant, 19-year old Trish Horton of Morrow, Georgia, picked up a copy of La Leche League's **The Womanly Art of Breastfeeding** in her local library, and made the decision to breast-feed her newborn. Without any support from nurses or doctors, she's kept at it for the two years recommended by the World Health Organization. "It's a sad commentary on the entire medical community when a woman has to find out what is best for her baby in a library," she says. "Doctors have got to get educated."

Hundreds of generations of newborns drank self-reliance with their mothers' milk before food and drug conglomerates started flogging formula bottle feeding during the 1950s. In 1973, British nutritionist Derek Jeliffe sounded the medical alarm with an article on "commerciogenic malnutrition," and the scientific evidence has been piling up ever since. UNICEF blames complications from formula feeding for 1,500,000 infant deaths a year.[3] Canadian, Australian, British and Japanese research confirms that North American formulas lack the omega-3 fatty acids needed for eye and brain development.[4] As well, breast milk offers an "antibody cocktail" that boosts babies' immune systems. Breast-feeding can reduce ear and respiratory infections by at least half[5] and does about the same for acute diarrhea, iron deficiency, and child-onset diabetes. It has also been found to lower the incidence of multiple sclerosis.[6]

Breast-feeding is as good for moms as it is for babies, over and above the pride and bonding they enjoy. Long-term breast-feeding helps prevent uterine cancer, and can cut post-menopausal breast cancer rates by 20 per cent.[7] It also lowers susceptibility to osteoporosis.[8]

"Affordable health care begins with breast-feeding," says the New Mexico Breast-feeding Task Force. The savings cup floweth over when babies get off the bottle. Just by supporting mothers who want to breast-feed—about 65 per cent of Canadian moms start off with good intentions, but only 36 per cent keep it up past one month[9]—creates enough medical savings to finance a wide range of pro-infant reforms. Aside from the $8 billion spent each year on formulas, the energy costs of sterilizing bottles, and the expense of junking or recycling half-a-million formula packages a week, Dr. Jack Newman of Toronto's Hospital for Sick Kids estimates there are $15-billion worth of yearly hospital savings to be had across North America if 60 per cent of moms stick with their breast-feeding intentions for at least a year. There's no need to find new money to hire maternity-ward nurses who specialize in helping newborns and moms gain the skills and confidence they need in those first anxious days. In the U.S., funding could just be reallocated from the $500 million a year spent on social assistance subsidies for formula.[10] In a bid to reduce the costs of treating poor children for deficiency diseases, the Quebec government gives a $50 monthly bonus to breast-feeding moms on social assistance, hoping the incentive will double their breast-feeding rate and bring it up to the provincial average. The breast-beating politicians who like to talk about cutting the costs of welfare might look at this way of cutting the costs of poverty.

Mothers' groups that champion breast-feeding are in the forefront of reclaiming economies from the almighty dollar, weaning the next generation from cradle-to-grave chemical dependency. The low level of institutional support for natural feeding methods is consistent with the way government statisticians leave women's unpaid work out of national accounts. Home-making and raising the next generation, family values as it were, don't rate a mention in the Gross National Product tables. They are, like all nature, not ranked as a contribution in GNP accounts, and are thereby rendered, like nature, "an invisible factor in the economic universe," says Marilyn Waring, author of **If Women Counted: A New Feminist Economics**. Only when a forest is destroyed and turned into lumber does it rate in national accounts, Waring argues. And only when mothers turn to the bottle, and start the cash registers ringing, do they make it into the economics books.

"The GDP works like a calculating machine that adds but cannot subtract," says Jonathan Rowe of the San Francisco-based group Redefining Progress and his colleagues in a lead article in **Atlantic Monthly.** "By the curious standard of the GDP, the nation's economic hero is a terminal cancer patient who is going through a costly divorce," they say, since money changes hands. "It is as if a business kept a balance sheet by merely adding up all 'transactions,' without distinguishing between income and expenses, or between assets and liabilities." That's how social and environmental health get pushed out of planners' equations for a sound economy. "Free market economics" belongs right up there with media ethics, business think tanks, industrial parks, hospital food, conventional wisdom and military intelligence in the hall of fame for mutual contradictions. The market, like Oscar Wilde's cynic, knows the price of everything and the value of nothing.

Waring has been joined by other harbingers of new economics, who want to see a value attached to the "love economy" and natural systems. The group includes science broadcaster David Suzuki, Barbara Brandt, author of **Whole Life Economics: Revaluing Daily Life,** and Rowe. "As long as Gross Domestic Product is the standard measurement, people who care about social cohesion and habitat are going to lose every time," Rowe says.[11] This thinking is beginning to have an impact on such institutions as the World Bank which has introduced a new system for determining a country's worth that incorporates natural, social and human capital. It puts Australia at the top of the list, followed by Canada, with Japan, fifth and the U.S., 12th.[12] "This new system challenges conventional thinking by looking at wealth and not just income, says World Bank Vice President Ismail Serageldin. "It also expands the concept of wealth beyond money and investments."[13]

In 1995, the British Columbia Women's Hospital became the first
hospital in North America to refuse free samples and come-ons from
formula companies, and will be monitoring the results to see if their
own good example helps new moms understand that health is not for
sale. As for Trish Horton, she's out to "spread the word" to other
moms. "I am determined to make a difference, even if it's just keeping one other Medicaid mom from becoming a victim of marketing,"
she says. "But right now, I need to go nurse my baby."[14] The longest
journey starts with the first suck.

"The fresh air will do you good."
Newspaper ad for GEO Jeep

Human energy is better than renewable and cheaper than free, because it improves with use. A low-cost, environment-friendly, health-promoting transportation policy gets off on the right foot with walking, the ultimate in public transit. "It's the slow and steady tortoise who wins the race," say fitness experts Drs. James Rippe and Ann Ward.

James Rippe and Ann Ward promote a small step for health and a huge step for urban design at the University of Massachusetts Cardiovascular Rehabilitation Program. When they saw heart patients recover after walking regularly and briskly, they got down to research. The result is the Rockport Walking Program, a daily diet and exercise planner that burns calories off the body, not the gas tank.

Nothing beats walking for long-lasting weight control, they found. They started with a study of 80 at-risk people, mostly overweight veterans of crash diets. The control group that mixed low-fat meals with brisk walking lost an average of 17 pounds over four months, while improving their cholesterol and blood pressure counts. Even those who stuck to eating greasy foods trimmed off 10 to 15 pounds of weight over a year when they did four, 45-minute walks a week.

Stepping out is also a miracle cure for medical, fitness and diet bills. Don't accept expensive substitutes, advises leading aerobic walker Casey Myers in **Walking**. "Fitness consumers" spend $2 billion a year cocooning with various torture racks and treadmills, when "usable fitness" is as free as the great outdoors, he says. The same goes for the $6 billion a year now lost on various diet powders, appetite suppressants and virtual foods.[15] We foot big medical bills when we don't walk enough. A definitive Harvard study confirms that inactivity is as hard on health as a pack of smokes a day.[16] The U.S. Center for Disease Control says five, 30-minute walks a week is enough to ward off heart disease. Getting back in touch with the body's need for exercise is also the high road to mental health, since endorphins released by the body when it's put through its paces give a mental boost, sometimes called "runners' high." One expert says the 12.6 per cent rate of severe depression suffered by Americans—up 10 to 20 times since the turn of the century—is the result of a caged-in sedentary lifestyle. The University of California at Berkeley's **Wellness Letter** blames chronic overweight suffered by a third of Americans for half the health problems of people between 30 and 70. Walking that off before doctors put the knife to the problem could save in the order of $100 billion a year.

For those who want upper body strength, or just blissful peace and quiet, there's always paddling and rowing. Power trippers on motor boats are among the worst polluters on the continent, André Mele shows in **Polluting for Pleasure.** One hour of pleasure boating burns as much fuel as a car does over 700 miles. North America's 12 million power boats create as much hydrocarbon air pollution as cars. And inefficient outboard motors dump the equivalent of 40 Exxon Valdez sinkings worth of oil in waterways each year. Apart from making free time very expensive—the two happiest days in a power boater's life, it's said, are the day he bought his boat and the day he sold it—motor boats are running at dead slow 17 per cent of the time they're in use. Kayaks and canoes can match that, and the paddlers have no need to hurry to pay off their bank loan anyway. We need to start telling boaters to live free or die, or word and finger motions to that effect.

But losing beer bellies and thunder thighs is a piece of cake compared to shedding ugly fat from city transportation budgets given over to cars. "The paradox of transportation in the late 20th century," says Toronto planner Joell Vanderwagen, "is that while it became possible to travel to the moon, it became impossible in many cases to walk across the street." Though planners are obsessed with rationalizing commutes to work, the great majority of car use is for short trips. The first step in remedying that is making cities walkable. Sidewalks are for roads dominated by cars. We need more side roads, not more sidewalks. Human-scale street and traffic planning—designed with health in mind—save billions of dollars on highway construction and maintenance, as well as unnecessary car use. There's a community payoff too, when transportation policy doesn't rush people off their feet. "There is more to walking than pure fitness," says James Rippe's star patient, Robert Sweetgall, who marathoned his way across the United States twice to get the word out on walking away from heart disease. "We can discover who our neighbors are," he says.[17]

But Rippe and Ward are very strict about one thing: no starvation diets or punishing exercises. "Deprivation is a dirty word," they say. The aim is self-control, not self-denial. "When a walking program is combined with a moderate low-fat diet, people will lose weight, keep it off, feel better, and gain control of their lives—some for the very first time," they say. Being physically correct isn't about "health fascism," but laughter as the best medicine. Rippe has proposed a Sesame Street style of street design that's made to flex funny bones as well as muscles, with hopscotching, jumping and climbing replacing the obstacle course of cars. "As individuals and as a society," he says, "we are perilously close to forgetting how to play."[18] Having fun is a pedestrian idea, an example of the free play that can happen when we open our minds as well as our hearts to planning around our own means, resources and free energy. Change is afoot.

"Nature's bounty belongs to the people"
Original, but long dead, motto of Ontario Hydro.

Freeing up the economy isn't as quick as swiping an apple from a tree, as convenient as sticking a plastic nipple in an infant's mouth, or as easy as hopping in a car. Open access to free and public goods requires a rich mix of personal and community skills. Here are some trends to watch for.

Virtual Free

If Rockefeller owned the sun, it's often been said, we'd have solar power. Actually, the conspiracy against free is more perverse and pervasive than that. It's got so bad that even solar power advocates concentrate on "active", not "passive" solar, on photovoltaics that use the sun's rays to generate expensive electricity, rather than devices that simply store the sun's heat. Thus, solar hot water systems, which capture the solar radiation pelting the roof and which are ready to be marketed on a mass basis with today's technology, are orphans of the Rockefeller syndrome.

The installed cost of a top-of-the-line, maintenance-free, low-pollution, solar water pre-heater is less than $2,500 retail, $1,800 wholesale. They can be leased by a utility or ESCO for "virtual free," that is, for less than what people now pay for electric or gas heating. Leased at nine per cent interest for $300 a year, they're paid off in less than a decade, with 15 years of absolutely free hot water yet to come. For every thousand leases, over 25 high-paying industrial and installation jobs are created. In year 10, when the full fuel savings click in, new consumer spending by every 1,000 happy solar customers creates eight service jobs. Multiply that out for a city of 10,000 residences, and ask your politicians, utilities and pension fund managers why some 300 workers are needlessly drawing $3 million from unemployment insurance and social assistance, money that could pay everyone's first-year installment on the solar water heater.

Suit Yourself

There are positive ways for bosses to dress down their workers. In the equivalent to the fall of the Berlin Wall of dress codes, IBM dropped its paramilitary big blue suit when it found that clients wanted service personnel to roll up their sleeves and get creatively down and dirty. "The dress issue was a barrier between us and our customers," says IBM Canada President Bill Etherington, wearing a sports jacket and casual slacks.[19] Xerox has followed suit. Suit sales have taken a plunge across North America as men opt for clothes that suit their personality.[20] There's also some relaxation of expectations that women dress two job levels up from their current occupation.[21]

For those who can bear up to the humiliation of ring around the collar, slacking off is a nice way to give at the office. Many companies charge $2 a day for the right to dress in civvies, and donate the money workers save on dressing up to a charity. Casual clothes make a statement. T-shirts and sandals are really solar outfits, since they let people hang loose and get by with less air-conditioning in summer than those who wear suits designed with Britain's cold and damp offices in mind. The average office would save $2,500 a summer in air-conditioning if it relaxed dress codes, the Rocky Mountain Institute estimates.[22] Sweaters are proper green attire for winter. Hanging loose with clothing also helps preserve a company's brain power, since the 150,000 tons of perchlorethylene released into the water supply by dry cleaners each year is known to cause brain damage. Giving up the dressed-to-kill mindset lets us counter pollution casually, without having to put scientists and regulators on the payroll to come up with ways of adjusting the brain so that it adapts better to PERC.

Too Cheap To Meter

Some conservation measures are so cheap, so idiot-proof, and so rich in paybacks to the general public that it's best to give them away. This strategy flows from an adaptation of the answer to that age-old philosophical query: "how many economists does it take to change an incandescent to a compact fluorescent light bulb?" The answer: "None. The market will look after it."[23]

Here's how the free-for-all could work with water-saving equipment. The scenario is based on calculations from an Ontario Ministry of Natural Resources study of about five million residential units. Bought in bulk, a water conservation package that includes a low-flow toilet and showerhead, and aerator faucets costs about $300 to manufacture and install in one unit. Average households could pay off that investment with one year's savings on reduced water rates and energy savings, given that less water has to be heated. The payback to the municipality is just as fast, because all that wasted water had to be filtrated, chlorinated, fluoridated, and pumped uphill in needlessly wide water mains. So municipal governments can come out ahead even if they give the equipment away.

Ironically, the costs of marketing the equipment can easily equal the manufacturing and installation costs. That's the case with many sales-intensive products, including cars that people are already pre-sold on. So why not give the packages away, and create 2,000 industrial and retrofit jobs for a decade? Rather than going through the bother of setting up complex bookkeeping systems, Amory Lovins suggests, it might be easier to spread around boxed packages marked "Government Property. Do Not Take." This is how potatoes first became a hit in France. A brilliant marketer persuaded the king to keep potato fields under armed guard during the day, luring peasants to sneak in at night and steal the prized possessions, henceforth dubbed "apples of the earth" in French, with the prized taste of forbidden fruit.[24]

With energy savings, the best job creation is always yet to come, because most people spend their new disposable income on labor-intensive services, such as restaurants. If Ontario's five million families were typical, and spent their $300 in savings available as of year two, they would create about 30,000 service jobs in perpetuity. If those new jobholders all came off unemployment insurance or social assistance, taxpayers would have $320 million a year in found money to spend on the next conservation project, enough to finance 6,400 new jobs, which is enough to cut another $80 million from public assistance, and on and on, all at no cost.

Splendor In The Grass

For all our efforts to stretch food dollars, we leave a free source of tasty and nutritious food to grow like weeds in the wayside. The irrational hatred of weeds, part of a cultural obsession with conquering wild ecological balance with neat geometrical order, leads us to scorn an important resource that's bred to survive on marginal soils without cultivation or poisonous herbicides. We'd be a lot better off if we ate weeds more and sprayed them less.

When the truth on dandelions gets out, we'll save millions on food bills, toxic herbicides and cleaning up polluted waters. Dandelions are a nutritional powerhouse. Richer in vitamin A than carrots[25] and not bad for vitamin C, they're one of five bitter herbs listed in the Old Testament, the bitterness indicating strong mineral content of potassium, calcium, silicon, and magnesium. The dandelion is a critical ingredient in herbal medicine kits, and many regard it as superior to antacids.[26] Leaves are tastiest in spring, when other crops are just poking their heads above ground. They serve well in salads, with a few flowers tossed in for color, sautéed with garlic for Dandelions Italian, or mixed in the juicer with carrots. Flowers boiled with lemon juice and a little sugar make dandelion honey, says Cayuga, Ontario self-sufficiency buff Jackie Mockrie. The roots make a coffee substitute, the flowers, wine. "The interesting thing about dandelions is that if they weren't weeds, they would probably be cultivated in massive greenhouses," says herbalist Nicholas Morcinek. Right now, they only make the petrochemical companies rich, keeping the money flowing from all directions for dandelion sprays, fertilizers and fuels for substitute crops that aren't self-starters, and chemical pills to make up for food deficiencies.

Many other detested weeds—rarely praised as "pioneer species" that bore through and aerate compacted land as they sink deep roots for hard-to-get nutrients[27]—have what it takes for food that's good and cheap. Chickweed, slipped into soups and chowders, provide vitamin C and rutin.[28] Burdock root from troublesome burrs is sold as gobo in China, where it's recognized as a blood purifier and kidney cleanser.[29] Chicory, sometimes called curly endive, brightens up coffee. The Roman poet Horace sang its praises as a pick-me-up before it was known that chicory roots are rich in calcium, potassium, phosphorus, iron and magnesium as well as vitamins A and C.[30] Spritzed with lemon and served as a side dish with fish, the stems are standard in traditional Greek eateries. Red clover makes a tea that U.S. agriculture scientist Dr. Jones Duke claims has anti-cancer properties.[31] Stinging nettle, a hit with butterflies, is sometimes called Indian spinach. Spring leaves (picked with gloves) have been used in soups, teas and beer since the Middle Ages. Real men eat quiche with nettle stems. A nettle compost tea is considered top-rate fertilizer, natural enough given the rich store of mineral salts, zinc, B vitamins and carotene.[32] Nettles are richer in nitrogen than many commercial fertilizers. Their high protein content also makes dried nettle leaves ideal as animal fodder.[33]

Weeds are already chic in upscale markets. Bulk sections of health food stores sell dried weeds for a higher cost than most vegetables. Dandelion leaves, lamb's quarter and beet tops are staples of designer salad mixes. Field mix has a better ring than weeds. Quebec food writer and photographer Anne Gordon has done weeds justice in **La Cuisine des Champs** (field food)—cattails with Gruyère cheese and mustard, or dandelion salad with daisy petals and wild sorrel say something about the futility of weedwhackers. One famous Quebec chef featured basic backyard chickweed on his menu, renamed as exotic Chinese watercress.[34] Very de rigueur.

We've got a job to do with weeds. Why not a Weed Free or Pioneer Species co-op, a novelty detox center for those buzzed out on coffeehouses, serving up wild delicacies from an overgrown field? Or a dual profit center lawn-care company that does hand weeding, then turns around and sells the home owner fresh field mix? Or a meadow run on community garden lines to provide fresh greens to people on low income? Weed this and reap.

The Public Teat

North American families have the least public support in the western industrial world. **Mothering** magazine is campaigning for a parental bill of rights modeled on the G.I. program offered to World War II vets. Promoted by economists Richard and Grandon Gill, the proposal would provide an at-home parent of pre-schoolers an education grant valued at $15,000 a year.[35]

The grant, which compensates parents for extended breast-feeding and extensive reading to their kids, is self-financing from health and educational savings. It's widely recognized, for instance, that parents are best at giving kids a love of reading that lasts a lifetime, something no elementary teacher can make up for.[36] The Gills' proposal simply gives parents the time to turn their advantage to an educational skill, instead of coming home from work exhausted and plunking the kids in front of the idiot box until parents are ready for their half-hour of quality time.

As a job-creation program, the grant is hard to beat. Parents who volunteer reduce over-crowding in the labor market, a factor identified as critical to sustainable wage levels by Berkeley professor Harold Wilenski. His multi-nation survey of employment policies showed that Europe's generous paid parental leave programs helped to "balance the demands of family and work, and to avoid child neglect." Paid parental leave had a bigger impact on the job market than any other job-creation policy, he found.[37] In Denmark, where a center-right government introduced extended sabbaticals funded by unemployment insurance, the program cost nothing. Since the people who replaced those on sabbaticals came off unemployment insurance, the two groups just switched incomes for the year. Yet the economy benefited even in the short term from the boost in self-esteem and training among the formerly unemployed, and the boost in energy from those returning after their sabbatical.[38]

Walk Of Ages

Popping pills causes old age in seniors. Despite all we've learned about Alzheimer's, osteoporosis, high blood pressure and failing sight—that they're preventable and even reversible diseases, not the inevitable suffering of aging—most doctors remain committed to high-cost surgery and pills.

American seniors are about twice as likely to be put under the knife as seniors in Canada's non-profit hospitals.[39] The biggest increase in prostatectomies is for men over 75, beyond the age when it's help-ful.[40] In both countries, prescriptions are doled out at a rate of 16 per person per year[41] without much quality control. "The fastest way to end a physician-patient consultation is by writing a prescription," says Dr. Warren Davidson, who studied the problem for the **Canadian Medical Association Journal,** and concluded that "seniors are being drugged silly," mainly by doctors who speed through visits.[42] Canadian seniors, on the public tab, spend $200 million a year for drugs that respond to what Dr. John Spence of the University of Western Ontario calls "white coat syndrome," high blood pressure caused by nervousness about being tested.[43] The inattentiveness of doctors is highlighted by the fact that three out of four American seniors who commit suicide visited a doctor within a week of their deaths. It's estimated that six million of America's 32 million retirees suffer from clinical levels of depression which goes undiagnosed, according to Dr. Barry Liebowitz of the U.S. National Institute of Health. Apart from its impact on the mind, depression triples the risk of strokes and slows recovery from other illnesses.[44]

The biggest health risks seniors face may come from eating alone. More than two-thirds of seniors eat alone most of the time and almost half eat alone all the time, a Toronto Department of Public Health survey found. The lonely, old person's diet of tea and toast is three times more likely to put our elders in hospital for long stays than a healthy diet will. Closing hospitals to save money won't help the 59 per cent of seniors who are at risk for malnutrition and illness and the 25 per cent who are at high risk. But, providing organized "congregate meals" for seniors would save money by keeping them out of hospital. The savings would pay for the meals, the deparment's figures show.[45]

Complications from over-prescription—including an increased chance of falling and breaking bones while over-sedated[46]—account for more than 20 per cent of hospital admissions among the elderly.[47] In the U.S., 650,000 seniors a year are hospitalized as a result of adverse drug reactions.[48] Once in the hospital, the food causes mal-nutrition that's often as serious as the original problem.[49] "Unfortun-ately, we seem to have better quality assurance for cleaning floors in a hospital than we do for clinical practices," says leading health reform advocate Dr. Michael Rachlis.[50] And with drug companies in a merger frenzy that positions them to control medical corporations[51] —which makes as much sense as merging Neighborhood Watch with the Mafia—the $300-billion-a-year market in drugs and medical devices will continue to soar.

Fortunately, good things still come in free and near-free packages. Multivitamins boost elderly immune systems and help fight infections, according to a **Journal of Clinical Nutrition** study.[52] Anti-oxidants counter cataracts and age-related masculopathy, research at Boston's Schepens Eye Research Institute shows.[53] Leafy greens reduce the risk of age-related macular degeneration by half, says Johanna Seddon of the Harvard Medical School.[54] Potassium, read-ily available in potatoes and bananas, slows the onset of osteoporosis and kidney stones.[55] A glass of cranberry juice a day treats urinary infections among older women, according to Harvard's Dr. Jerry Acorn.[56] The smell of lavender oil helps cure the insomnia rife among seniors better than drugs, Dr. David Stretch of Britain's University of Leicester found.[57] None of this comes as a surprise to Dr. Mathias Rath, recently retired from the Linus Pauling Institute of Science and Medicine, who claims the bias against such cures comes from drug companies that can't patent them.[58]

Regular exercise and social interaction keep seniors young at heart and stabilize degenerative conditions wrongly blamed on aging. "I have two doctors, my left leg and my right," the famous historian George Macaulay Trevelyan said at 86. Exercise reduces seniors' suffering from internal bleeding by as much as 30 per cent, according to a 1994 study by the National Institute on Aging.[59] "Strenuous exercise is not something you can purchase and not something an expert does to you, for you, or with you. It is your own virtually cost-free, self-administered, guaranteed intervention," says exercise specialist Keith Johnsgard.[60] Weight training increases bone density, and reduces muscle loss and hip fractures among older men.[61] The same goes for mental exercise. Joan Lindsay, a specialist in aging with Canada's Centre for Disease Control, says mentally active seniors have a better chance of resisting Alzheimer's.[62] Poetry reading is better than pills as an upper for seniors. "It's therapeutic," says Dr. Alexander Macara, head of the British Medical Association. "The pharmaceutical industry might not like it, of course."[63]

Walkers Of The World, Unite

Traffic engineers build a transportation system for cars, then wonder why so few people walk anymore. When they're having a bad trip, pedestrian advocates imagine what it would be like if affirmative action for cars were ended and cars were denied their special privileges. Sometimes they have sick thoughts of sending traffic engineers back to school, where they would have to bone up for Lame Excuses 101. Their course of study would include how to pay city staff to clean sidewalks after a snowstorm, but encourage drivers to shovel off roads voluntarily since the city can no longer afford that service; how to slope roads down toward the middle, not the sidewalk, so that slush and rain splash cars, not walkers; how to leave road space for drivers after cyclists and walkers have been provided for and their needs anticipated for the next 20 years; how to buy street lights that are sized, like the antique gaslights in many tourist areas, to illuminate sidewalks, not roads; and how to provide advance green lights for pedestrians, not cars, at intersections, so walkers can take a direct diagonal to where they're going. For their flaky arts course, Blacktop Nightmares 201, they will learn dialogue and peer support techniques while they debate explanations for the decline in driving, and bemoan the passing away of old insults such as street- and jay-walker. They'll head over to the pub after class, thinking they can listen in secret to **Life is a Highway** and golden oldies by the Beach Boys, only to find them removed from the juke box and replaced by **These Boots Were Meant for Walking.**

Re-inventing the foot forces city politicians to walk the talk about livable cities. It requires a new sense of streets as public space, not drive-throughs, a new aesthetic, and a host of human-scale planning gimmicks. But once the infrastructure is in place, free transportation will start to become the norm. Here are some ideas for putting the world at our feet, brainstormed with Chris Bradshaw, a regional planner and idea hopper in Ottawa and editor of **Ottawalk News.**

1.   Revise city plans that prohibit "mixed use." Allow small convenience stores and quiet drop-in cafés to locate in the middle of streets so people don't have to drive to the corner for a quart of milk. Create urban villages, as in Seattle, with main streets featuring low-cost, low-volume, shops that thrive on

repeat business. These changes work on the demand side of transportation by eliminating the need to travel long distances for basic supplies and services.

2. Eliminate compulsory parking requirements for new housing and office developments. Tax parking lots for frontage, not the value of buildings on them. Parking should compete for space at the same market rates as other uses. If buskers will put more than a dollar an hour in the meter for a 40-square-foot space in prime retail territory, they should have the same dibs on it as a car. The less dead space for heavy metal, the more streets thrive as living places.

3. Institute planning criteria that take walkers' safety and comfort into account. Office towers that block sunlight, create wind tunnels and leave long stretches of dark, lonely space at night aren't for walkers. Diagonal rather than purely rectangular street grids allow walkers to take advantage of the laws of geometry and take the hypotenuse, commonly known as the shortcut. Organizing urban layout for the shortest distance between two points increases the range of a one-mile walk by up to 30 per cent. This may necessitate walk-through parks and squares throughout the city center, with space made available once cars and parking lots no longer consume over one-third of the downtown area.

4. Redesign busy intersections, perhaps by raising the roadbed to the sidewalk, as they do in several European cities. This makes crossing easier for seniors and the disabled, reduces splashing, and provides a nice speed bump—"automated police," as they're sometimes called—for an extra margin of safety. Advance greens for pedestrians allow them to cross diagonally instead of waiting for two lights. Keep street corners rectangular instead of rounded for fast car turns, forcing drivers to give pedestrians wider berth. "The more you wield, the more you yield" should apply to streets as well as waterways.

5. Arrange street furniture for "eyeability." A walk should be a chance to stretch the mind as well as the legs. Postered kiosks add color. Pocket parks offer a place to rest. Sidewalk vendors offer refreshment. Busking gives entertainers their first public appearances and helps keep a marching beat. Garbage receptacles can have planters on top.

6.   Organize public transit around the needs of walkers, not drivers. Subways turn people doing the right thing into moles, leaving the good views for drivers. Subways drive up the cost of public transit, because tunneling is so expensive. The cost of subway stations, commonly in the area of $100 million each, means stops are infrequent and beyond walking distance. That's why they have to be driven to. By contrast, street rail is made for walkers. Stops cost next to nothing. Local businesses congregate all along the line, not just at nodal points. Speed is fast because the train has a dedicated lane. In Calgary, Alberta, the driver can control intersection lighting to avoid waits.

7.   Reserve the right of way from old canals and rail lines for greenbelts and foot-propelled users. This has been done with central Connecticut's Farmington canal, as well as in Seattle and Washington. "I'm amazed at the ability of trails to connect communities and encourage people to meet each other at a slow speed and human scale," says Dave Burwell of Washington-based Rails to Trails Conservancy. "It's America's new front porch." Ottawa's canal is a haven for footloose and fancy-free walkers, bikers, skaters, tourists and lovers. According to **Psychology Today**, walking beats the competition for intimacy, chosen over kissing, candle-lit dinners and cuddling by both men and women.[64]

If car companies had more political savvy, they'd do an end-walk around the persistent demand to reform cars by taking up the campaign to reform streets. Reforming streets is cheaper and easier than reforming cars to make them pollute less, take less space and cause fewer accidents. The car companies have to invest billions of dollars in these innovations, few of which add to the efficiency of the car's transportation function, and few of which solve the problem they're supposed to solve. If more people drive when cars become more fuel-efficient, for instance, nothing is gained. It makes more all-round sense to scale back the use of cars and to reduce pollution and improve street safety that way. Cars should not be used for short trips, which is mostly what they're used for now. Just turning the car on and off causes 70 per cent of the exhaust emissions of a two-mile round drive, according to Randy Neufeld of the Chicagoland Bicycle Federation, because the clean air devices aren't operative then. On the basis of that finding, Chicago nixed a $6-million proposal to synchronize street lights for business commuters, and put the money instead into short-commute bike trails.

And if city politicians turned their road departments into transportation and access departments, they'd also save a bundle on infrastructure. With costs down, and jobs staying within local business districts up, neighborhoods that design around human energy and walkability should be rewarded with lower tax assessments levels, Bradshaw argues.

Fad Free

A waist is a terrible thing to mind. About a third of the population spends over $100 billion a year on diet and exercise programs that get them nowhere. Most "lite" and low-fat products are bogus. They make up for lard with sugar, salt and trans-fatty acids, just as hard on the body and the calorie count. And crash diets always bounce back. This stuff is for losers, not dieters.

When one person in three is wolfing food down, and one person in 10 is bulimic or anorexic and woofing it up, we should know that we're suffering from compulsive life disorders, not eating disorders. "We have yet to understand that obesity and anorexia are simply opposite poles of the same problem—disordered eating, disowned self, disowned power," psychologist Judi Hollis argues in **Fat and Furious: Women and Food Obsession.** Hollis recommends an "empowerment diet" to "open up with a nurturance other than food." It starts with self-respect—"when our voices are not invited or honored, we take them out to lunch," she says—and with the first rule of recovering alcoholics, to "absolutely insist on enjoying life."

Here's some free advice. Turn off, tune out, drop in. Strengthen your pitching arm by tossing the channel flicker. Lunge toward the TV and flick it to off. The only thing they don't show on TV is people watching TV because it's too boring. Get full to busting with veggies, fruit and grain. McGill cardiologist Colin Rose and nutritionist

Sandra Cohen-Rose estimate that a low-fat diet would save $300 billion a year in food bills and health costs.[65] Spend your share of the $100 billion you don't spend on junk food on a biking or hiking holiday each year. Spend your share of the $100 billion you don't spend on diet cults on a second biking or hiking holiday each year. Spend your share of the $100 billion you don't spend on heart disease on a third biking or hiking holiday each year. What part of Get a Life don't you want?

Support Your Local Police

To have the same ratio of police to violent crime incidents today as in the 1960s, the U.S. needs to hire one million more police officers. With wages, headquarters and equipment, that comes to a cool $70 billion a year. That could come out of the $261 billion spent policing imaginary foreign enemies, says **Atlantic Monthly** writer Adam Wilinsky.[66] Alternatively, both budgets could be cut, and police could be told to take a walk, and go back to their old street beats.

Just as more highways don't reduce traffic congestion, more cops in cars don't reduce crime. To the extent crime is based on neighborhood disintegration, and the loss of free crime-watch services such as eyes on the street that neighbors once provided, it's neighborhood forces that need to be beefed up. Cops in cars aren't good at that. Constables on patrol are.

Community-based policing, which puts the constable on patrol back into COP, is proving effective. Like other forms of renewable energy, it displaces the need for new supply. In Montreal, a constructive relationship between police and anti-racism leaders following a racial shooting led to an experiment in walking the beat in the troubled Côtes des Neiges neighborhood. The crime rate dropped 78 per cent the first year, while crime in the rest of the city increased. "When you're walking the beat, you have to explain little things," says Constable John Parker, who does a 10-mile walk each day. A police car separates police from the people, he says. Before, police "used to drive by in their car and didn't get out unless there was an incident," says a local merchant. Now, "they're talking to people, and that's the key," he says. "The police have come down from their high horse, to our level."[67] Good reports are also coming in from local cops riding bikes. "We seem to get to know people better when we're on the bikes," says constable Luc St. Jean. They also find that two wheels are better than four in chasing suspects across parks and alleys, and in getting to the scene of the crime fast. "It's not at all unusual for us to arrive at the site of a call before the car patrols," says officer Alain Rioux.[68] Police now use bike patrols in 600 cities across North America.[69]

Community policing dovetails with increasing public space for city walkability, says transportation planner Joell Vanderwagen. "You can't have public transit without public space," Vanderwagen says. "But public space has been designed out of cities by malls and condos. It's like going back to the dark ages of fortresses, and everything in between controlled by highwaymen." With the growth of walled suburban communities, four million Americans now seek safety by living behind bars of their own making. This is not what the land of the free is about.

Steal This Bike

The easiest way to stop bike theft and contribute to the business cycle is to leave unlocked bikes lying around. Amsterdam's urban guerrillas, the Provos, started the practice in the 1960s, painting bikes white and leaving them around for commuters. Cambridge, England, has picked up the idea. Police donate unclaimed bikes to the city, which paints them green and places them in 26 "bike parks," leaving bikers to take the idea from there. Copenhagen plans to put 500 bikes in coin-op machines that require a deposit, refunded when the bike is returned to any coin-op in the city. A volunteer group in Portland, Oregon, leaves 100 yellow bikes scattered around the city, with a notice asking lenders to leave them on a major street for others to use. In Toronto, Ontario, the Cabbagetown Bike Club and Street Co-op use unclaimed and donated bikes to teach repair skills and provide bikes to low-income youth and street people, a nice way to link free bikes with community economic development.

Kissing off the little bit of revenue taken in from selling unclaimed bikes at police auctions is better than kiss-and-drive drop-offs at rapid transit stations, which end up reinforcing the centrality of the car. Most urban North Americans live just a few miles from a rapid transit line. With good lock-up services there, people can drive their own bikes to the stop nearest home, hop rapid transit, then take a joy ride to work.70

Shining Examples

Principle 7

Casts solar power in a new light with biological
processes that meet energy and chemical needs
through a thousand points of light

*"We think too narrowly about solar power. After all, fossil fuels
are just dead solar power. We need to tap into living solar, that's
complementary with the planet."*
Solar Energy Society of Canada Vice-President Greg Allen

"The race is on to develop methods, to draw more income from the wild lands without killing them, and so give the invisible hand of the free market a green thumb... it is within the power of industry to increase productivity while protecting biological diversity, and to proceed in a way that one leads to the other."
Pulitzer Prize-winning biologist, Edward Wilson

As soon as we think in terms of flicking imaginations, not switches, solar power is ready to go. The sun already powers agriculture, and farmers can find their place in the sun growing fuel, fiber and agro-chemicals as well as food. Joe Strobel plans to use the oldest cash crop ever tilled to deliver power to the people.

Joe Strobel is the first farmer in North America to grow hemp legally since the 1940s, when the ban against the herb was temporarily lifted as an emergency war measure—Hemp For Victory was a government slogan back then—to secure domestic supplies of rope for the military. In 1994, Strobel and his partner, engineer Geof Kime, harvested 30 tons off 10 acres of the sandy soil of Tillsonburg, Ontario that is normally reserved for a perfectly legal crop, tobacco. Canada's bureau of dangerous drugs issued Strobel a license to grow "low THC" hemp, which has to be inhaled by the ton to produce a moderate marijuana buzz, so he could experiment with an alternative crop to tobacco. What he found was an alternative crop to forest-based lumber and paper, to pesticide-laden cotton, and to petroleum-based energy and chemicals.

The Johnny Appleseed of hemp, Strobel is as much a pothead as Thomas Jefferson or George Washington, both champions of industrial hemp in their day, or pioneers in Canada, who were required to grow "not less than 10 acres" of hemp for the British navy as a condition of their land grants. A physical education teacher who introduced the "healthy hustle" into morning exercises in Ontario schools during the 1970s, Strobel took over the family farm when he retired,

and started looking for options to tobacco. Jeff Shurie, a local advocate of legalized marijuana, introduced him to Jack Herer's underground classic, **The Emperor Wears No Clothes**, an expose of
"Hempgate," the forces behind the 1930s law that outlawed hemp.
Until then, hemp was as American as apple pie, Herer shows, and
was used for a score of industrial purposes. The American Declaration of Independence was written on hemp paper and Betsy Ross
sewed the first U.S. flag with hemp fiber. But pulp and paper and
chemical monopolies whipped up a drug scare to suppress agricultural
competitors, Herer charges.

The book rang true for Strobel, who learned about hemp at his
mother's knees. A Hungarian emigrant, she was wed in a hemp dress
and grew hemp on her new world farmstead for "black butter," a
nutritious peanut butter substitute for kids and a standard feed for
livestock. Before the reefer madness scare of the 1930s, few thought
of growing hemp for purposes less high-minded than industry.
Traditional hemp farmers planted the crop densely to force tall
growth on the cellulose-rich stalks, at the expense of THC-bearing
buds which need a lot of space. The stalks were also harvested a
month before the buds matured. If the law was only intended to
stamp out marijuana, anti-drug squads would never have had any
trouble distinguishing industrial from recreational producers.

Turned on by hemp's industrial possibilities, Strobel offered his harvest to innovators across the continent. A firm in Minnesota that
compresses waste straw into hockey puck sizes to fuel school wood
stoves is checking out the energy content of the hemp's bark. The
hemp core, or hurd, goes to Trois Rivières, Quebec, where a pulp and
paper training center is experimenting with various mixes for paper.
C and S Builders in Oregon uses the hemp hurd to make fibreboard
and panels, and owner David Cedar pronounces it "as good, if not
better than" tree-based board.[1] Strobel estimates that 50,000 carbon-
and cellulose-based products now made of non-renewable resources
can be made from hemp. "The market seems endless," he says.

Though the harvest is high-energy, the plant is not. It actually
reduces the embodied energy content of most products. Grown in
good soil with the right pH balance, hemp has a low need for petrochemical pesticides and herbicides; when native North American

seeds were used before the 1930s, hemp had a reputation for being self-reliant, requiring no fertilizers, pesticides or irrigation. As hemp starts to supplement pesticide-laden cotton,[2] it will reduce the energy content of fabrics. It will also save port cities in the south. Some rivers are so polluted by cotton pesticides that the future of downstream ports is jeopardized. The harbors can't be dredged for fear of unsettling the toxic sediment, distressed harbor masters have realized, and are threatening the shipping industry. Hemp pulp, unlike tree pulp, is also low in lignin and thus doesn't have to be chlorine bleached, knocking out another high-energy toxic effortlessly. In short, hemp is a solar product that both creates and conserves energy.

Though originally championed by the counter-culture, hemp is now poised to go mainstream. Farm equipment manufacturer John Deere gave hemp a rave review in the February, 1995 issue of the company publication, **The Furrow**. Gordon Reichert, a marketing specialist with Agri-Food Canada, gave hemp the thumbs up in a special bulletin his government department printed on hemp paper. "It is extraordinarily productive of biomass and has been shown to have excellent potential for textile and cordage, paper, building materials, cellulose plastics and resins and the seeds are used for food and oil," Reichert wrote.

Reichert's paper was presented at a 1995 hemp conference in Germany, a roll call of experiments going on across Europe. Thirty Dutch scientists have been working with a $40-million research budget to breed specialty hemps for the pulp and paper industry, to be grown by a co-op of 1,000 farmers, who will make the country self-sufficient in paper production. In France, hemp is being used for health-conscious construction, since it is strong, acts as a fire retardant, breathes well, and contains no pesticide or herbicide residue. Kimberly-Clark uses hemp in its two French paper plants. In Germany, hemp is being used as a substitute for asbestos in car brake and clutch linings, and one prominent auto maker plans to use hemp to produce a compostable car, reminiscent of the car Henry Ford built entirely out of vegetable plastics, including hemp, in 1941. To stimulate hemp production, the European Economic Community subsidizes farmers who grow it at a rate of $400 an acre. When it's up and growing, hemp is expected to eliminate imports of fuel and fiber, and release the EEC from the burden of subsidizing food crops, all of which face glutted markets.

Meanwhile, back in North America, Adidas is releasing two new shoes with hemp canvas. "It's a sturdy material, and the shoe meets all our engineering requirements," says Adidas Canada's John Kawaga. "The weave on the hemp is going to stand up. It can be washed. There are pretty practical reasons for buying it." In New York, the Fashion Institute of Technology is working on dies and processing methods preparatory to full-scale commercialization of hemp garments. The U.S. Hemp Industries Association has hired the former director of the Cotton Association, Jim Hangeley, a heavy hitter with good connections in New York's fashion industry, where hemp is expected to displace 20 per cent of cotton fibers in blended fabrics within 20 years. Even the polyester textile people are excited about hemp since blending it with their petroleum product will allow it to breath, and lower their demand for fossil fuels. One-hundred-per-cent hemp fabric will become more commonplace since it's long and stable fiber is well suited to people with environmental sensitivities.

The train is leaving the station, but North American farmers aren't yet allowed on it, due to an obsolete law. That, too, may change in short order. In the U.S., the cultivation of hemp may well enter into negotiations between governments and farm leaders as the quid pro quo for giving up farm subsidies. And in Canada, the Canadian Auto Workers Windsor Regional Environment Council is leading a petition drive to transfer the main responsibility for hemp cultivation from the Federal Bureau of Dangerous Drugs, which granted less than a dozen experimentation licenses in 1995, to the Ministry of Agriculture, which would make hemp's cultivation legal, though licensed. Licensing, if applied fairly, could spread the wealth of hemp among farmers and help to keep it out of the hands of corporate farms focused on hemp monoculture.

Hemp will save the family farm, Strobel says, because its many uses will assure farmers a decent price for a crop that's in high demand. He'd like to see growing permits issued to diversified family farms that use hemp as part of their rotational system. That way, the hemp market won't be supplied by monoculture and won't be subjected to price collapses. And, as more farmers move to supplement their income with non-food crops, prices for food crops will edge up so that farmers can make a living from them too. "We've got to cut back on every food crop that's bunging up the marketplace and promote other crops that have more beneficial uses," he says. Hemp is also a lifeline for manufacturing in farm-area towns, since its bulk discourages long-haul transportation to centralized processors.[3]

Some pretty spectacular claims have been made on behalf of hemp, and two points need to be made to put them in perspective. First, hemp will be a case study of a farm-based knowledge industry. Because of its illegality since the 1930s, knowledge about the plant and the technology needed to harvest and process it is 60 years behind the times. Most of the seeds bred over at least 200 years in North America have been lost. It will take a co-ordinated effort across many sectors to overcome this backwardness, stresses Craig Crawford, leading promoter of hemp industries in Canada and a member of a North American panel, financed by the pulp and paper industry, which is evaluating the use of hemp. Second, hemp is only one, albeit a very promising one, of a series of agricultural crops that can cross the line between food and chemicals, food and energy, and food and building materials. As we wean ourselves from toxic petrochemicals, there will be a renaissance of agro-chemicals, or bio-chemicals, what David Morris of the Minneapolis-based Institute for Local Self-Reliance calls the "carbohydrate economy." Many of the biochemicals are already price competitive—in the case of solvents they are often cheaper—and all of them result in qualitatively lower levels of pollution.[4]

Hemp will be the flagship of the carbohydrate economy and the giant killer of the fourth wave. It makes food, fuel and fiber accessible almost everywhere on the continent, undermining monopolistic control over scarce resources more effectively than any anti-combines act. It spares forests from unnecessary logging, renders imports and transportation of bulky commodities unnecessary, and converts diffuse, low-level solar energy into high-energy products. But it is not the only boat in the green armada. Straw for instance, which is now burnt off as waste, will likely come to predominate in paper and manufactured wood, because it can be picked up for prices that will likely undercut hemp as the dominant material. Hemp fans do the wonder plant a disservice if they fixate on it, and not the broader challenge of finding crops that improve farm incomes, increase regional self-reliance and replace toxic petrochemicals. When farmers are allowed to make agri-chemicals while the sun shines, solar power will come into its own.

"We do not need another 'world view' but a new 'view of the world,' an outside perspective that reveals the Earth in a way that is truer and brighter, more vivid and more accurate than we formerly possessed."

Leading western naturalist Stan Rowe[5]

Solar power works in mysterious ways, its wonders to perform. Landscape architect Michael Hough has found there's nothing new under the sun, and is researching ways to integrate two of the oldest solar technologies—trees and water tables—into modern urban design.

It's time landscape architects get physical, says Michael Hough, leading theoretician for a profession destined to replace civil engineering in the new economy. An environmental studies professor with international consulting experience, Hough is best known for his book **City Form and Natural Process,** a plea to go beyond the tradition of decorative parks that segregate recreation and beauty from the ongoing rush of life. He favors designing cities around "working landscapes." Natural ways of heating and cooling buildings, or cleaning air and water, leave engineering solutions in the dust, he says. Sticking solar power where the sun don't shine, Hough's imaginative approaches extend the reach of solar methods far beyond what's available through photovoltaic panels for electricity.

The sun doesn't shine all the time. It can't always be turned into high-grade energy at competitive rates. But natural processes responding to the sun's energy are always at work, ready to be tapped. Thus, Hough argues, solar power is often found where it's least expected—underground in water tables or above ground in trees.

Savings grow on trees, the workhorses of the new urban infrastructure. They are organic air conditioners. One tree cuts summer heat as much as five degrees by shading solar radiation and by giving off 100 gallons of water that snatch up 2,300 calories of heat energy from the air in the course of evaporation. Studies by the Lawrence Livermore labs in California indicate that tree-planting reduces peak-load energy demands at a cost of one cent a kilowatt hour, half the relative costs of many energy-efficient appliances and about one-tenth the cost of new power.[6] A tree is a giant carbon filter and retention tank. It sucks up rainfall, then cleanses and releases it slowly so it doesn't flood sewage mains and filtration plants. A tree is an oxygen mask. It takes the carbon dioxide we and our fire-breathing technologies give off, stores the carbon and puts back oxygen. The pores in leaves store about half the particulate matter loose in the air, protecting our lungs again. Over a season, one 12-year-old maple removes about two-thirds of an ounce of the pollution from heavy metals, such as cadmium, chromium, lead and nickel, all damaging to humans in very small amounts.[7]

A tree is insulation. Precision landscaping with deciduous trees can reduce solar radiation stored in roofs by two-thirds and in walls by half, University of Arizona horticulturists William Miller and Charles Saccamano have documented.[8] In winter, evergreens in the yard operate like an outer wall, breaking northern winds that blow away one-third of a home's heat, Friends of the Earth researchers promoting Global ReLeaf have shown. One study shows that a single urban tree performs $57,151 worth of work controlling temperatures, rainfall and air pollution over 50 years.[9] A U.S. Forest Service report estimates that 95,000 green-ash trees in a city like Chicago cost $21 million to plant, and net $38 million in savings over their lifetime.[10]

The lowly ditch—the politically correct word is swales—is another object worthy of landscape designers, says Hough. If cities let rain water along with bath and sink water travel along ditches to retention ponds, the water table would save the moisture for a dry day and save the city expanding sewage mains and filtration plants. Ditches and ponds can also give cities a beauty bath, providing water and habitat for birds and other small animals. Winnipeg, Manitoba uses storm water ponds to create free recreation space for boaters and birders. "This is a way of making land and water precious resources pay," says Hough.

Solar infrastructure also turns the handling of humdrum functions into opportunities for community art and expression. The cement fetishists miss this potential, as suggested by their technobabble term

for rain, "storm water." Toronto architects James Brown and Kim
Storey have prepared plans to substitute a necklace of parks, creeks
and ponds for part of an $80-million sewage and storm water main
slated for the western downtown area. They envision re-exposing the
city's multitude of small rivers and creeks, which still flow but were
enclosed and turned into underground storm water runoff passage-
ways, so that rain from streets is cleansed through engineered gravel
moraines, marshes, trees and planted ponds in city parks—a strategy
sometimes known as "daylighting". The reform would deliver swim-
mable water to a now unswimmable beach. Bike and walking paths
would braid the ponds, providing a pleasant transit route. In winter,
the ponds would be skating rinks. "Storm water is a cultural resource," says Brown. "Architecture has never dealt with the low, like
sewage. We have to find ways to bring them up." In a similar vein,
Patricia Johanson, author of **Art and Survival: Creative Solutions
to Environmental Problems**, urges artists to treat public works as a
gallery, not just a site for technical achievement. That way, artists
can "affect survival by making a world that is both beautiful and nur-
turing." If a sewage main or parking lot has to be built, "then put a
few more layers on top of it so that the landscape becomes available
to birds and animals, so that joggers can run on it, and children can
play or have classes there," she writes. "What I try to do in my projects is to give back 200 per cent. It almost becomes a game for me to
see how many layers of public benefit I can load on top of what I've
been hired to do."

Hough's hope is that cities will use the savings from bio-engineering
to go ivy league and finance set-asides of at least five per cent of
urban land for working landscape. That's enough room for about 50
million trees per city, with a capacity to absorb global warming gases,
trap about 455,000 tons worth of carbon dioxide, and offset the
"urban heat island effect"—the term for heat captured, stored and
intensified by cement and asphalt. Even an acre of straight grass,
which provides no shading, gives off 2,400 gallons of water, enough
to suck up as much heat as a 70-ton air conditioner.[11] Extensive
planting, especially around parking lots, lowered summer temperatures in Davis, California by 10 per cent, and cut air conditioning
bills in half.

Speaking of which, can anyone explain why asphalt is given a color that attracts heat? That's the question posed by Art Rosenfeld, the leading particle physicist of his day before he was lured into the study of conservation in 1974, when he published **Energy Efficiency: A Physics Perspective**. Physicists, he says, "are a bunch of soreheads who question systems. Engineers will make it two per cent better, but physicists will say the whole system can be improved." He's since worked at the University of California's Center for Building Science, developing "super windows" capable of retaining or blocking enough heat to make the entire output of the Alaska gas pipeline unnecessary. Now, he's intrigued by simpler measures such as tree planting and painting asphalt white. Both cut down on the urban heat island effect of paved city cores that can add three degrees to a summer heat wave, and could save a city such as Los Angeles $100,000 an hour in air-conditioning bills. "The profits from this kind of conservation are obscene," Rosenfeld says. "I don't even bother with changes that can't knock out at least 10 power plants."

The new landscape architecture is coming out of nowhere, Hough is happy to say. "Nowhere" is the English translation for utopia, and dreamers who think on these lines do not have a record of sensitivity to the frailties or peculiarities of individuals, time or place. In politics, the legacy of utopianism is dictatorships. In architecture and engineering, the utopian legacy is in monuments to the ability of science to overcome limitations of place. What Hough calls "pedigree" architecture, usually sponsored by the wealthy and powerful, also descends from this utopian tradition. So does the true-grid mentality of road and sewer engineers, who have used pavement and pipes to triumph over unique regional characteristics and create nowheresvilles across the continent. In **Out of Place: Restoring Identity to the Regional Landscape**, Hough argues that respect for lowly and local adaptations to geography are at the heart of solar engineering, and the diversity of solutions it promotes. The cookie cutter, standard fixture in any big landscape or engineering firm, is not designed for working with the sun. Hough prefers the methods of Arctic Inuit soapstone carvers, who claim their art is in releasing the forces that were always there.

"Let nature do the dirty work."
Safe Sewage editor, Karey Shinn

To make a scene, solar entrepreneurs and energy land-scapers have to work with local materials and conditions to minimize fuel needs. That's what people did for eons, before artificially cheap fuels caused us to forget about "passive" solar strategies that made full use of the energy potential in the interactions of the shapes, contours and materials in buildings and landscapes themselves. As in the distant past, so, too, in the immediate future, the sun will really shine in practical adaptations that displace the need for high-grade energy. Here are some trends to watch for.

Sunny Disposition

The sun is lousy for night lighting, but during the day it works better than light bulbs. For about $500 installed, a 13-inch by four-foot light pipe carries reflected sunlight down from the roof, and spreads it over a space of about 24 square feet in the room below. Sought after by people with environmental sensitivities, who can't take the flickering and narrow spectrum of artificial light or the chemicals in light bulb ballasts, the pipe is also economical for a wide range of office, warehouse and home uses. It's ideal in garage workshops and stairwells, for instance. Aside from distributing free sunshine, the pipe reduces air conditioning bills in office buildings, where 80 per cent of the electricity used by light bulbs is discharged as waste heat, creating the necessity for air conditioning, even in winter. The warm and natural feel of sunlight also beats the office blahs. Some retail-ers—Wal-Mart is one example—find their sales soar when customers check out goods in broad daylight. When these benefits are com-bined, they pay for the light pipe in a year, after which they light up your life for free.

Savings On A Hot Tin Roof

While the winter sun might not be up to heating huge and drafty factories, warehouses or garages, it can certainly cut energy bills by preheating air used for ventilation. Conserval in Downsview, Ontario, invented and markets a "solar wall," made of blackened and perforated aluminum. The wall preheats a large volume of fresh air before it's pumped into the workplace for ventilation. Clients include GM, Ford and Bombardier. A performance review by Natural Resources Canada indicates that the wall pays for itself with one season's fuel savings.

Conserval founder John Hollick, winner of several international awards for his inventions, is now working on an all-season home adaptation, an extra "skin" of aluminum on the roof. In the winter, the elevated level of aluminum attracts and stores heat from the sun's rays under itself which slows the escape of heat from inside the house. In the summer, the extra layer of roofing blocks the sun's direct radiation from getting stored in the roof proper, thereby limiting the sun's impact to convection alone, which is only one-quarter as powerful as radiation. Pushing the building envelope one step further, Hollick's solar roof will also act as an air conditioner. An adapter will allow the foil to function like a refrigerator, drawing out heat to leave the interior cool.

Split Wood, Not Atoms

Fire predates the wheel as one of the great inventions of the stone age. New entrepreneurs have the technology and systems to keep the home fires burning today while cutting the costs of space heating, displacing fossil fuel imports, reducing acid rain pollution, reversing global warming, diverting tens of millions of cubic yards of wood waste from landfills, creating local jobs and enhancing future wood suppliers. A tall order, but it's already happening in homes and institutions, and even to provide power for utilities. Fireplace inserts, zero clearance stoves, pelletizer machines and wood-chip combustion units have what it takes to take the hearth to where the home is.

Roasting chestnuts on an open fire isn't the way to heat a home. Couples have to snuggle up because traditional fireplaces lose heat.

The fire sucks up oxygen, creating a draft as cold air rushes through cracks in the wall to fill the vacuum. Later, when the embers are dying, cold air comes in through the chimney. If Santa can get down, so can heavy, cold air. Traditional fireplaces also need frequent stoking and new log supplies, often in the middle of the night, discouraging their use except for special occasions. By contrast, fireplace inserts and zero-clearance stoves, for a cost of about $2,000, can be fed on pellets with a flick of the thermostat.

The pellets—clean-burning because they're pre-dried, of uniform quality and fired up at high temperature—can be ground out of crop residues, sawdust from furniture factories and construction sites, and other waste that now goes to landfill. According to a report in **Bio-Cycle** magazine, 16 million cubic yards of city tree tops and stumps are available every year in the U.S.[12] In Ontario, more than three million tons of wood waste is landfilled each year. Calgary-based Friendly Fuels is developing a portable pelletizer that can be hauled on a truck to furniture factories, construction and landfill sites. Ideal for a worker co-op, the pelletizer makes money by charging once for waste removal and once again for the sale of pellets. Pelletizing solves a global warming problem too. When wood rots in landfill, it gives off methane, worst of the global warming gases. When wood burns, the methane is consumed in the fire. The ash can be used in gardens or on slippery sidewalks in winter.

Some utility investors, logging companies and energy-smart municipalities are chipping away at the problem. In northern Ontario, independent power advocate Stephen Probyn has financed five wood-energy plants which use scrap bark from milling and pulping operations. One medium-sized sawmill in Cochrane supplies more than 100,000 tons of bark a year. The companies save $100,000 a year on the expenses of scrapping bark, and get to sell electricity to the public utility.[13] In Montreal, Secure Wood Chips charges clients $20 a ton to remove tree trimmings, stumps and wood scrap, $13 less than waste haulers charge, then turns the waste into wood chips and hauls them to nearby Chateaugay, New York, where the chips off the old blocks are burned clean for electrical power. The firm employs 15 people where one waste hauler was employed before.[14] In Vermont, Lou Brabakis invented a unit that burns wood gases, which is cleaner and more efficient than burning wood directly in industrial or institutional settings. His units supply a number of area schools. Wood heating for a typical school saves $6,500 a year in fuel costs, and displaces 35,000 gallons of imported oil with 600 tons of local wood. The city of Burlington also gets its electricity from wood burning.[15] In Prince Edward Island, two district heating systems and 20 industrial-class, bio-blast burners keep hospitals and schools warm, cut their former heating bills with oil by one-third, and create 15 direct jobs.

Chips for industrial and institutional use are a boon for farmers with marginal land or stewards of logged-over, scrub forests. Forests cut in the days of high-grading, when only the straightest trees were taken, are still "plugged" with scrub and deformed trees that survived because natural selection worked in reverse. The stunted growth left behind stands in the way of new seedlings that need light and space to grow. The process of natural succession is strangled. What's needed, says Ottawa ecological forester Ole Hendrickson, is a way to finance "low-grading" selective cuts that can speed up the healing. To take advantage of that opportunity, Sweden went into wood chips in the 1970s, and now exports combustion technology instead of importing fuel oil.

Blaaaaaak And Decker

Shepherds are making a comeback. To save on the costs of mowing 95 acres of parks and grounds, the city of Fort Saskatchewan in Alberta put a shepherd, two border collies and 235 sheep to work. Maintenance costs were cut 18 per cent the first year.[16] Many operations are switching from toxic herbicides to four-legged ones, and trading in fossil-fueled tractors for solar-powered animals. "Weeder sheep" are used in some California vineyards to crop clover and undergrowth. The sheep can climb into areas that tractors can't reach, the growers say.[17] Sheep are also used in B.C. to trim grounds along utility power corridors and to clear competing weeds from forest plantations. Groundskeepers don't have to be woolly eyed to see the benefits: lower costs for fuel, mowers and herbicides; a free supply of fertilizer, wool and meat; and an extra kids' attraction in city parks.

Unplugged

The chair is probably the only piece of household furniture that is not yet plugged into an electrical outlet. Other than chairs, baths and an Eric Clapton album, everything is wired. And isn't life so much easier, and don't we have so much energy left over to do worthwhile things, thanks to all these electrical appliances? Not! Women spend more time on housework now then they did at the turn of the century, when women didn't work outside the home as well.[18]

We're killing ourselves with inactivity. "We buy expensive fuel-costly devices promoted as energy savers," says fitness expert Dr. Lawrence Gross. "They're not saving us a thing; they're depriving us of the movement and exertion we need to live an energetic life."[19] When we're not killing ourselves with inactivity, we're doing it with what Dr. Milton Zaret calls "electronic smog," the electro-magnetic fields suspected of causing cancer and many other diseases. And it costs us a wad of money for something that renewable energy, sometimes called elbow grease, can do perfectly well.

Although the American Physical Society, with 45,000 physicists as members, says there is no evidence relating cancer to the electro-magnetic fields caused by power lines,[20] credible scientists from around the world beg to differ. There is "a powerful body of impressive evidence," linking even low-level exposure to human health problems, says the chair of the U.S. National Council on Radiation Protection, Ross Adey, who is a neurologist at the Veterans' Affairs Medical Center in Loma Linda, California and who was speaking about a council report leaked to and published in the British scientific journal, **New Scientist**. Compiled by a committee of 11 experts over nine years, the report cites studies which show that electromagnetic fields can alter the production of melatonin, which is linked with sleep and can protect against heart, Parkinson's and Alzheimer's disease. The council recommends a safety limit of 0.2 microteslas from each appliance, degrees of magnitude lower than the two to 20 microteslas received by a person standing one foot away from a vacuum cleaner or electric drill.

The studies are impossible to ignore any longer. A comprehensive study of 500,000 Swedes who lived within 300 yards of power lines found the increased exposure was linked to increased cancer among children. Researchers at the University of North Carolina at Chapel Hill studied the death records of 140,000 women and found that women who worked in jobs with high exposures to electrical equipment had a 38 per cent higher chance of dying of breast cancer.[21] Women in the garment trades, who work constantly on electrical equipment, suffer from Alzheimer's three times more often than the general population, reports Eugene Sobel, professor of preventative medicine and neurology at the University of Southern California.[22] McGill University's Ben Armstrong studied 223,000 men who worked for electric utilities and found a link between leukemia and exposure to electromagnetic fields of 60 hertz, the same level produced by household appliances.[23]

Electric utilities such as Toronto Hydro now advise customers to keep as far away from electrical appliances as possible.[24] This follows a responsible policy in cases of disputed science known as "prudent avoidance."

Many home appliances violate prudent avoidance and contribute to indoor air pollution. That's important in a society such as ours, which has so much free time, thanks to all those electrical devices, that we spend 90 per cent of our lives indoors. Even when we're not using appliances, many of them continue to run with instant-on functions, coffee makers with clocks, for example. Leaking electricity adds up. Video players are the worst offenders, consuming up to 10 watts in the off position. TV sets consume eight, doorbells six, microwaves four, answering machines three, clock-radios two. In fact, typical consumption in a house with a range of such appliances is about 50 watts. It costs most home owners about $35 a year to run these appliances when they're turned off.[25] That comes to about $3.5 billion across the continent for hot wiring that does nothing, enough money to hire 70,000 energy conservation workers each year. Did we hear someone say we didn't have the money to fund useful public works?

Then come the electric treats that make our lives easier. Egg beaters, coffee grinders, food pulverizers, vegetable choppers, electric knives, electric blankets, electric brooms, electrically driven window blinds. Outdoors is for power mowers, leaf blowers, weedwhackers and snow blowers that make all those hours at work worthwhile. After that comes the electric workout equipment to get rid of the flab brought on by a 40 per cent decline in natural exercize over the last decade.26 The payoff for not shoveling, grinding and bending is 15 minutes free to pace along an electric treadmill. Beam me up Scottie, there's no intelligent life down here.

There's got to be an easier way to take it easy. There are business opportunities galore serving unplugged homes, and saving something in the area of $7 billion a year on useless energy. There are devices that turn lights on with motion detectors. Someone should be able to invent a device to turn off radios and TVs when no-one's around— though it is admittedly hard for a machine to discern motion even when someone is around. Air fresheners made with pine, juniper and cedar twigs are crafty alternatives to plug-in, scented petrochemicals. So are clothes lines that substitute for a dryer and make for a pleasant few minutes outdoors. As are quilts that use the body's calories instead of the energy from a coal-fired plant to power an electric blanket. Thermoses keep coffee hot and save it from getting bitter on the heater. People who enjoy messing around in the kitchen and who like to hear themselves think, perhaps even to talk while they're working, need designers and manufacturers who can revive and refine hand-operated kitchen appliances. Imagine the health benefits, the workouts, the sensual aromas, the chance to talk without a buzz in your ear, the appreciation for your food that comes from manually grinding coffee or grinding spices with a mortar and pestle. Think of what you could do with your free time when you no longer have to clean out your veggie and fruit smashers and slicers. Knead bread dough while you're practicing to control your temper.

Essence Of Night Soil

Solar methods can wipe up after bums as well as storms. The trick here is to find uses that close the loop on the product of the human body, without mixing it up with toxins and dumping it in water, on the land or incinerating it and dumping it in the air. This isn't any way to treat a natural resource. But it is a good reminder of Greg Allen's maxim, borrowed from composting toilet manufacturer Abby Rockefeller, that "waste is a verb, not a noun."

There's an upswing of interest in what's called "beneficial use," applying municipal sewage sludge—biosolids is the nice name for it—to the land. Supporters of this alternative cite a 1989 U.S. Federal Register Report which claims that the public risk of exposure to toxins from sewage applied on non-agricultural land is 0.02 in a million, compared to 3,000 per million for sewage sent to dumps, and 50,000 per million for incinerated sewage.

An entire branch of the public relations' industry has grown up around "beneficial use" of "biosolids" or "black gold"—exposed in John Stauber's and Sheldon Rampton's **Toxic Sludge Is Good For You: Lies, Damn Lies and the Public Relations Industry**—and communities need to exercise caution. True beneficial use centers on re-use of nutrients in human waste, not disposal of the biological pathogens and chemical toxins in the 11 million tons of sludge that get flushed through North American sewage systems each year.

The possibility of making money from biosolids makes elimination of toxins and contaminants from sewage a profitable objective such as Tacoma, Washington. But biosolids should not be used on agricultural lands. The E.P.A. is involved in a campaign of "linguistic detoxification," **In These Times** writer Joel Bleifuss charges[27] and has merely lowered safety standards to make sewage sludge seem safe as an agricultural fertilizer. Which begs the question about the safety of agricultural fertilizers. "When you look at the contents of biosolids," says Karey Shinn of Toronto's citizen group, Safe Sewage, "you have to compare them with what we're currently putting on the land in the way of artificial fertilizers and pesticides." Shinn hopes that proper controls can produce the essence of night soil, without household or industrial residues, so that human waste can be recycled on agricultural lands, as in many traditional agricultural societies. This is a tall order, however, given the flush-and-forget mentality that goes with sewers. Even with strict controls on industry, it's hard to guarantee that sludge is free of contaminants from household paints, solvents and cleaners.

As a transitional measure, Shinn believes remediated biosolids can be used to rehabilitate soil degraded by mining or logging, where trees are the primary recipients of the heavy metals and toxins. And, in locations where there is no likely contamination, excrement can be turned into a recreational resource. By crossing the processes for making ice beer and artificial snow for ski hills, Delta Engineering of Ottawa turns effluent from the Sugarloaf ski resort in Maine into snowfluent. When a fine mist of effluent water and compressed air is frozen, the ice crystals kill any pathogens and force chemical impurities out of the crystal, the company says. When the snow melts in spring, clean water percolates into the water table, the ammonia gas vaporizes and the phosphates fertilize growing grass. If the snow is stored on a parking lot, the phosphate can be gathered and sold as fertilizer. The system is now being piloted in Westport near Ottawa, where it's expected that construction will come in at half the cost of a conventional plant, while operating costs will run at one-quarter the standard.[28]

Communities that want to start with a clean slate should begin with source separation, according to Clivus Multrum president Rockefeller. Wash water or greywater can be piped to lawns and gardens where it provides free fertilizer. Excrement can be handled by odor-free compostiing toilets. Such complete systems are already cost-competitive for the many cottages and rural homes faced with non-functional septic systems. For mid-sized communities facing the costs of a new sewage system, on-site reuse of wash water and composting toilets provide superior service at lower cost. "Black boxes" may well do for recycling and reuse of human waste in the late 1990s what "blue boxes" did for waste packaging in the first half of the decade: turn it into a valuable product. The old term "night soil" suggests how well solar methods can work even when the sun isn't shining. As human waste is plugged back into the cycles of life, solar fertilizer will replace petroleum-based fertilizers and once again demonstrate the power of nature's systems to replace fossil fuels.

Ivy League

When it's too crowded to start at the bottom, there's no excuse for not starting at the top. That's how rooftop gardens got where they are. They're the hottest trend in solar technologies that grow food or ornamental plants, cool buildings in the summer, help keep them warm in the winter, keep rain water out of the sewers, and turn city neighborhoods into nature galleries.

Europeans, used to being thrifty with space, are ploughing ahead. In Holland, all the houses in the new futuristic community of Ecolonia[29] have sod planted on their roofs. The sod keeps the top floor warm in winter, cool in summer, requires no maintenance, and absorbs rain that would otherwise run off into sewers. The plantings also create what's called a "microclimate," cranking down city temperatures better than air conditioners. That's why utility bills in these neighborhoods are from 10 to 30 per cent below average, more than enough to offset the extra 10 per cent in construction costs of topping up with a roof garden. In Germany, several cities have bylaws requiring vegetation on all new flat-roofed buildings. Rooftop gardening is also looking up in Britain, where the firm Architype builds sod covered homes that use a waterproof membrane to prevent moisture from leaking through the ceiling.[30] In Switzerland, developers are required to relocate any green areas displaced by a new building onto the roof. Even old buildings are required to convert 20 per cent of their roof space to what one enthusiast calls "pasture."[31]

Almost all North American buildings with flat roofs are made to order for gardening. With new techniques, urban farmers will have no trouble making their plot thicken with food, displacing much of the fossil fuels used to transport and package food. Condensed gardening methods can produce 200 pounds of vegetables in a five-foot-by-five-foot plot, or 1,000 pounds from a 10-foot-by-10-foot plot, according to Duane Newcomb's **Small Spaces, Big Harvest**. Intercropping, placing quick and slow growers beside each other, lets two plants live as cheap as one. Dynamic planting puts plants that grow well together side by side. Succession and companion planting are other tricks of the trade. Many plants can also be trained to produce more in less space through the use of containers. Some plants, such as peppers, seem to grow better on roofs, where the sun shines strong all day. One large housing co-op in Toronto is making a rooftop greenhouse pay by using it to grow plants for ground-level flower beds from seed, thereby avoiding the cost of buying seedlings in late spring.

"There are as many ways to do rooftop gardens as there are buildings, people and budgets," says Monica Kuhn, an architect and member of the Rooftop Resources Group in Toronto. Sloped roofs in Europe often boast sod that nourishes a few goats, supplying the family with

milk and meat. The most common form in North America is the par-
kette atop an underground garage; just because it's at ground level
doesn't mean it's not a rooftop garden. The birds attracted to the
greenspace don't know the difference. Some warehouse roofs in New
York bear the weight of virtual forests. For roofs where weight is a
problem, the Danes have developed Groden, ultra-light rock wool
that anchors the roots and retains moisture and nutrients. Such green
roofs extend the life of the original roof membrane, Kuhn says, by
shielding it from the harsh elements and UV rays.

The wall is another neglected site for urban agriculture. Walls are
great for sunflowers, and all sorts of creeping plants and vines that
keep the sun's direct rays off the building proper, which otherwise
stores the heat and keeps people tossing and turning through the
night. Keeping cool as a cucumber has just been bumped up to edible
air-conditioning, courtesy of solar power.

Dare To Succeed

Jeff MacInnis is one of the world's great explorers and adventurers.
He was the first person to cross the Northwest Passage by sail, on a
400-kilogram catamaran. He was part of the first team to make an
overland trek atop Russia's share of the Arctic across to Alaska, then
on to New York. In 1996, he plans to take a 21-foot Hobie catmaran
around the world in a "race to the sun." Powered by wind and electricity generated from 18 solar panels and two wind generators, his
boat tour will dramatize a voyage to the future. "Solar power needs a
flagship," he says.

The mission, should you choose to accept it, is to excite youth with
"a big picture, not a big stick," he says. MacInnis works with a team
that puts out **POP, Protecting Our Planet**, "an environmental newspaper for kids and grownups (but mostly kids)" that promotes a strategy to Dream, Dare, Do. "What Disney has done for fantasy, I'd like
to do with reality-based ideas," he says.

MacInnis learned respect for nature in the Arctic. It taught him that
"nature must be ridden, not driven," that a flexible catamaran could
get places where big ships couldn't, and that a slalom course could
find a way around seemingly impenetrable obstacles.[32] He hopes his

world tour will dramatize the message that the sun supplies earthlings with the equivalent energy of 60,000 billion tons of oil a year. Those who think solar power belongs to the distant future might want to calculate how long petroleum and uranium would last if the sun went out, forcing us to heat and light the world from scratch instead of topping up what the sun already does. If only one-twentieth of a per cent of solar energy were tapped for high-grade power, the whole world could enjoy North American standards of technology without pollution.[33] "As with life, relationships, ideas and sailing, it's the invisible forces we have to harness," MacInnis says.

Home Delivery

Principle 8

Reveals how the values, value-added and "technology pull" of home suite home go together in community-based family firms and farms

"Thus the highest realization of warfare is to attack the enemy's plans; next is to attack their alliances; next to attack their army; and the lowest is to attack their fortified cities."
2nd Century B.C. military strategist, Sun-Tzu[1]

"Knowledge as the key resource is fundamentally different from the traditional resources of the economist—land, labor, and even capital."

Management guru Peter Drucker[2]

North American society is homesick. The superwoman of the 1980s is burning out. The organization man of the 1950s wants to be more of a family man. Both are looking into home businesses that give them more control over their time and life. The economy, community and environment are waiting for them, says home business expert Wendy Priesnitz.

The demographic tide has already turned in favor of home suite home, the cottage industries of the new economy. The home front is site of a multi-billion-dollar industrial and service sector that now offers about 20 per cent of North American workers the chance to be their own boss.[3] The trend is transforming the home renovation business, as people spruce up their basements or a spare bedroom instead of their bathrooms, the one place where conventional working families got to meet before dashing out the door. Only the 1960s sociologists and the career social planners they trained still put any stock in "modernization" theory, which holds that economic development and social liberation come from punching a clock away from the stifling influences of home, family and neighbors.

For Wendy Priesnitz, editor of **Natural Life** magazine and author of **Bring It Home**, placing workplaces where the heart is can balance economic independence with family and community. "Home business is definitely the leading edge of community economic development," she says. "It has created a new paradigm of self-employment—one that goes beyond growth and increased economic activity to include quality of life issues as well as environmental and economic sustainability."[4] Though the cheap office space and non-existent fringe benefits of freelancers are open to abuse, home work is more of a challenge to old ways of doing business than a cheaper way of maintaining it.

Low-cost fiber optics and miniaturized and digitized electronics do to behemoth corporations what the printing press did to giant cathedrals ruled by a medieval priestly caste that once monopolized the powers of literacy and long-distance communication. For less than $3,000, a computer, e-mail and Internet package gives a grungy basement the same reach as a corporate office, at a fraction of the transaction and overhead costs. The costs of real estate, receptionists, janitors, security guards, plush rugs, commuting, parking, car insurance, work clothes and dry-cleaning are orders of magnitude less. The performance from flexibility of hours, personalized attention and quick response time is orders of magnitude higher.

The big companies know this already. About 250,000 Canadians and three million Americans are telecommuters, plugging into, rather than driving to, work. Bosses find it increases the productivity of work time and office space by over 25 per cent. That's not a good thing if all it means is that piece-work is done in isolation, hidden away from union or government officials that can enforce decent standards. But the dynamic trend-line favors independence from the head office brass, most likely through indirect competition in niche markets. The worst days of home business are over. A variety of software programs helps home businesses overcome the "jack of all trades problem," says computer wizard Bill Gates. The worst days of the corporate megamergers are just beginning. Lean home-based companies will be competing with clunkers that don't know which end is up without calling a meeting. "Perhaps 50 per cent of the effort in a large company goes into co-ordination as opposed to doing things," Gates says,[5] a margin of inefficiency that home entrepreneurs should not have trouble beating.

The rage in niche markets creates a strategic sector for at least 10 per cent of the workforce which can keep busy customerizing operations for less than 200 choosy people. Sharpen a pencil and figure it out. When the average home owner spends $2,000 a year on repairs and maintenance, how many satisfied customers does a reliable renovator need? How many neighborhood streets does an organic lawn-care specialist have to walk along to find 70 customers at $500 a season? At $250 a subscriber, how many subscriptions of a season's worth of fresh veggies does a market gardener need to make $25,000 in half a year? Once the subscribers are in place, how many of them would need to have infants before it was worthwhile to turn on the cuisinart and sell organic veggies and fruit at 50 cents a returnable mini-bottle? How many neighborhood customers are there who love bread straight from the oven and want it delivered to their home for supper at $2 a loaf? What about direct sales of yogurt, kefir and tzaziki, relish, or fresh pasta? And, what if a local group of nutritionists and respected citizens checked up regularly on the quality and offered a Residents' Choice label to all who met the exacting standards, giving neighbors with a name and face a name brand presence in local groceries?

By concentrating on a small number of customers, home-based businesses can organize vertically to provide better service and to gain extra value-added opportunities and income. Baby-food processors, for instance, can grow their own produce, deliver it to customers and pick up the container for re-use, making or saving money at the production, transportation, retailing and packaging stages. Don't confront the distant corporations on their own turf, at the supermarket. Outflank them where they can't operate, in personalized service. That's how the small size of home-based businesses gets turned to advantage. "Do not undervalue your time trying to compete with products of lesser quality. It's a great temptation, but it is slow suicide," says Mark Musick, the guru of guerrilla food marketers.[6] Increasingly, local quality, reputation and servicing can even beat out mass production methods when it comes to price. The transportation, packaging, marketing and retailing embodied in most food containers costs more than the contents. The merger maniacs have painted themselves into a corner, and the chickens will soon come home to roost.

Ironically, this economic homecoming will counter trends toward home-alone cocooning and burrowing, which develop when the home is turned into a centre of pure consumption. Home entrepreneurs are easily spotted. Having saved a pile of commuting time, around mid-morning they get a bit lonely and can be seen prowling the streets, looking for neighbors to shoot the breeze with. Since home entrepreneurs rely on word of mouth and networks, rather than media ads and powerful connections to get their message out, they need to get involved. The same need that spawned all the Optimists and animal clubs of Lions and Moose in small towns across North America at the turn of the century is sure to foster social animals at the turn of the next. "Working at home is clearly more than another way of putting bread on the table," says Priesnitz. "It is a fundamental change in the way people organize and control the role of work in their lives."

"Rather than job training, we need philosophy retraining. We should challenge old, destructive orthodoxies about growth being good, bigger being better and new being always superior to traditional."

Nature artist Robert Bateman[7]

Home businesses aren't just smaller than big businesses. They're different. Right-sizing technology for home-based operations creates a whole new set of options. Don't look the gift of low input costs and high value-added in the mouth, a colorful band of new entrepreneurs with a lot of horse sense argues.

Defying the jeers of nay-sayers about their return to the horse and buggy days, the easy riders of the home-business set are hitching their wagons to one of the stars of the new economy—the horse. The workhorses of home-based farming, logging and retailing companies are doing laps around tractors, skidders and trucks, giving their drivers the flexibility, innovation and returns they need to stay in the race. They provide case studies of the technical and community innovations that will come to the fore when we take off the corporate blinders on technological development.

The secret behind the remarkable prosperity of old-fashioned Amish and Mennonite farm communities is a lot of horse manure. Aside from their religious opposition to tractors, they see no advantage in costly hardware that has no manure, no offspring, and doesn't feed itself. At 15 tons of manure per horse every year, they have all the free nitrogen fertilizer they need after pasture is rotated with other crops, and with less than half the pollution from nitrate leaching caused by petrochemical fertilizers.[8] Pasture is a useful way of giving the land a year off, and a way of working marginal land that can't take the compaction of heavy-duty equipment. "Solar tractors" don't drain cash flow off the farm like fossil fuel ones, and that's not horse feed when it comes to balancing incomes and expenses. Horses also help add value to crop diversification into barley and oats. Horse-power is adapted to the job at hand. "The rather common sight of a $30,000 tractor doing a two-horse (less than $5,000) job makes little sense," Grant MacEwen, Canada's best-known writer of animal stories as well as a respected agricultural instructor, used to say.9 At $3,000, a horse-drawn harvester is less than the yearly interest payments on a mechanical one. Volume is less with horsepower, but it's the money left at the end of the day that measures success.

Horses are all-season, multi-purpose farm aids, unlike dedicated machines that spend the winter in the shed eating interest. With a horse and a $7,000 portable sawmill, Minnesota farmers could increase the value of their forest "cover crop" from $36 to $193 million a year, hard-nosed woodlot operator David Israel calculates.10

You can't lead a farmer to money, but when the subsidies and tax write-offs for fossil-fuel-based mechanization are cut out, horses will make a comeback. Bankers and bankruptcy auctioneers will be the only losers when farmers make the shift. But the spin-off jobs in rural towns will make up the loss. In Waterloo, Ontario, a relatively small community of Mennonite farmers sustains six harness and shoe shops, four buggy builders, four stable equipment manufacturers, four black-smiths, and a manure bucket factory, more support jobs than the one-horse towns created by high-tech imports. Who knows what could happen if there was a revival in the use of horse hair, once standard in heavy mattresses and insulation, or in oxblood, the pioneers' standard preservative and the paint on furniture that now gets top price at antique auctions?

Gene Logsdon studied the economics of the Amish capital in Mount Hope, Ohio, and calculated that horse-drawn methods keep $316 per acre in the community. "Rather than turning their farms into factories," he writes, the Amish "are bringing the factories back to the farm."11 The carriage trade might even rival the auto as a job creator. In 1890, for instance, Cincinnati had 9,000 workers in 80 companies, producing 130,000 vehicles a year, which looks good beside many auto towns today.12

In towns and even in cities, horses are well-adapted to the stop-and-go of door-to-door deliveries and pickups. After all, that's how jobs were done in New York and London until about 1920, when they were already bigger than most cities are today. Avon Dairy in Stratford, Ontario, the first independent dairy in the province since the 1960s, delivers with a horse-drawn cart, which the owner found a lot cheaper than a $50,000 gas-guzzling truck. The milk is sold in returnable bottles, which many people feel as nostalgic about as the horses. And the kids running out to gawk at the horses don't do business any harm either.

Horse and mule loggers are making a comeback, using methods that increase forest yields. In British Columbia's interior Cariboo country, horse loggers such as Lorne Dufour and Diana Geensen are working areas too fragile or hilly for skidders to handle, or too close to recreation areas that tourist towns don't want despoiled.[13] Horses can get in and out of areas that require expensive roads for heavy equipment. That's especially important after a fire or beetle infestation, when the value of stands can't justify the heavy-duty overhead. Sudbury, Ontario horse logger Art Shannon makes $600 a day dragging cordwood off damaged land and overgrown plantations too densely seeded or "plugged" to permit natural succession to the old growth stage. He keeps all but $12.50 for horse feed and $2 for chainsaw fuel to himself. Skidder operators are lucky to have that much left over after paying off their bank loans.[14]

When managed forests are cut the way gardeners thin out the onion patch—reducing competition for sun and soil nutrients, and thereby increasing the yield—skidders will be carted off to the local museum of bad ideas, where school tours will gasp at the stupidity of the old pre-horse days. Horse loggers leave no tracks, don't tear up the earth or crush saplings like skidders do. They reduce the damage clumsy skidders do to cut logs by 20 per cent. Smarter than smart machines, they leave behind a foundation for natural regeneration, much cheaper and faster than planting the scorched earth after a clear-cut. Métis horse loggers in Green Lake, Saskatchewan, have been thinning out their community forest for use in their community saw mill for 50 years, without reducing the volume of available timber.

But the real growth potential for solo horse loggers is in value added. Conventional methods aren't hard to beat. Strong like bull, smart like tractor, corporate logging mills churn out the volume but neglect quality, which is where the jobs are. Cutting and milling 30 board feet of lumber into 2 by 4's produces one job for one person for one minute, an unsustainable formula. The same amount of wood employs a cabinet maker for two weeks, an instrument maker for a year, forester Herb Hammond calculates. But B.C.'s mills can only spit out shingles, construction lumber and pulp. Only nine of 25 pulp mills produce paper from their pulp—B.C. actually imports more paper than it exports—and 86 per cent of what logging mills export are logs and crude lumber. On the U.S. west coast, one quarter of the cut during the 1980s was sold as logs, thanks to government subsidies to log exporters of $100 million a year. If those logs were merely cut into lumber, the same number of trees would have produced an additional 7,500 milling jobs.[15] The brute technology of giant mills is good for automating jobs, but dumb as a stump for adding value.

Jobs and forests will suffer this downgrading as long as giant forest companies monopolize huge tracts of land, leased at a price that makes low value and high volume pay. Smaller lease areas issued by community controlled forest licensers will let horse loggers bid on hillside patches of High Engelmann Spruce, ideal for musical instruments, where a few acres cut with care give a year's liveli-hood.[16] This is how to reconcile greens and forest-based towns now at logger-heads while village idiots proclaim "Earth First! We'll Log the Other Planets Later." Patrick Mozza, a member of Oregon's Solidarity Network, is working to bring job huggers and tree huggers together for a future "of gentler exploitation, which assures more constant revenues for everyone and creates a new collective responsibility."[17] With community licenses granted to home-based horse loggers, that would be something to ride home about.

"The name of our proper connections to the earth is 'good work,' for good work involves much giving of honor."
Green essayist Wendell Berry[18]

Economics is all Greek to business leaders, who don't know the original meaning of the Greek word for "thrifty household management." Here are some trends to watch for as economics returns to its roots.

Home On The Range

Ward Sinclair and Case Peterson's 10-acre farm near Washington, D.C., puts them among the top 15 per cent of U.S. farm earners. They gross over $100,000 a year, selling 50 kinds of flowers and 70 varieties of vegetables grown from heirloom seeds to upscale restaurants and regular "subscribers," mostly journalists at the **Washington Post**, where the couple used to work.

Ignore the experts, especially when they tell you to grow more of the same, they advise. Diversity is the key to avoiding glutted markets that bring prices crashing down. "We grow unusual stuff. Then we sell it by helping customers understand what it is and how to use it." They've found "there are virtually unlimited market niches waiting to be filled."[19] Their voice of experience is reflected in a report from the Hudson Institute which found that U.S. policies, telling farmers what and how much of the "tried and true" crops to plant—rather than specialty items which garner higher prices—costs the agriculture sector up to $65 billion annually in lost sales. Instead of getting their money from the market, the "best" farmers in the current system get it from governments. Washington paid out $12 billion in direct subsidies in 1992, with 15 per cent of farms receiv-ing 90 per cent of federal payments. Farm-subsidy programs are the epitome of middle-class welfare: four of every five subsidy dollars go to households wealthier than the national average. The cotton farmers in particular gain from subsidies: a moderate cotton farm nets $200,000 a year in subsidies.[20]

In Radisson, Saskatchewan, where the climate is much harsher than in Washington, Darryl Amey tries to follow the philosophy of Stan Rowe, author of the lyrical classic **Home Place**, which teaches that "good agricultural practice requires a decline in production, not an increase." Mary Blease, a leader of the U.S. farm revolt of the 1890s put it more boldly: "raise less corn, and more hell." The huge farms that outdo themselves glutting commodity markets have dug farm communities into a grave, without the population base to sustain schools and hospitals or to service towns, Amey says. "If I can find a way to make a living feeding 100 instead of 1,000, there would be an opportunity for nine more people to do the same thing," he says. As a qualified heavy equipment mechanic, Amey makes more money from less crop by inventing machines to clean, hull and package beans and grains in his own barn for direct sale to subscribers and to a local co-op.21

Mass production agriculture has stripped down and de-industrialized the range of farm functions. Farmers are forced to work at the point on the food assembly line where skills are most specialized and easily gotten elsewhere, where value-added is lowest, market control least, and income consequently lowest. The dough is in bread, not wheat, so the trick to making farming pay is to diversify upstream, keeping the value added from packaging, preparing and retailing. Simple and low-cost electric grinding mills that fit beside a kitchen sink allow farm families to sell wheat, with the full flavor still bursting from it, as flour or bread, increasing keep-home pay tenfold. Better than farming out the profits to commercial bakers, who practice additive-value, which has the same relation to value added as there is bread in Wonderbread. Glenn and Linda Pizzey of Angusville, Manitoba went from growing flax for commodity markets to baking it in bread, and now sell 1,200 loaves a week to fairs, farmers' markets and stores. Linda Pizzey works out the math for other grain farmers: "10,000 bushels of wheat sold through the elevator would be worth about $30,000. Turning that wheat into bread mix would fetch $700,000. Producing bread loaves from the wheat, then selling them wholesale, would gross about $1.1 million. And turning them into pancake mix would bring about $1.5 million."22

When farmers start looking up the market chain, the markets will look up for farmers. Yvonne Kerouack and Robin Hannah of Bedford, Quebec cleaned up by using these methods with their six Nubian goats. The goats provide a creamy milk ideal for moisturizing soap that sells at $4 a quarter-pound bar. Each bar is hand-made with natural ingredients at their home, then sold out of their front door, at country farm booths, and, increasingly, at health and beauty shops.[23]

Home Plate

Anne Pomykala turned her hobbies into a living when her family bought a 12-bedroom Tudor mansion on 45 acres of farmland and woodlot in Stevenson, Maryland. She and her daughter run the Gromercy Bed and Breakfast, featuring the house omelet with home-grown cilantro, chives, calendula and shitake mushrooms. The garden herbs and mushrooms are also sold to specialty stores and to caterers serving weddings and parties held on the grounds.[24]

Bed and breakfasts, up from almost none in 1980 to about 25,000 across North America today,[25] are building blocks of eco-tourism. They're ready-made to introduce visitors to local hospitality. B and B owner-operators have a wide range of hospitality industry skills, and also get a return on their capital as well as their labor. Both factors help assure them a decent income. B and Bs also help keep more of the returns from tourism in the local economy, unlike hotel chains which import almost everything pre-packaged. This makes sure that the money to feed and house tourists doesn't leave the community as fast as the tourists. As a consequence, B and Bs can employ more people from a smaller visitor base, which helps preserve the local tourism asset instead of running it into the ground for fast turnover. One hundred stopovers a day can keep 25 families solvent in B and Bs, or provide minimum wages for 20 individuals in hotel and restaurant chains. Farms can also use a B and B to recruit workers for the busy season. Organic growers in Canada have a network that travelers can use to pay for their room and board with work in the field.

Family Values

Home offices get all the attention of a new fad, but old-time housework remains as inglorious and invisible as ever, perhaps because it's mainly done by housewives. Statistics Canada, world leader in recognizing and measuring the economic value of housework, rates the unpaid work as a $319-billion-a-year industry in Canada alone.[26]

Finding a way to give money for that value is far from the minds of
employers, who assume their workforce, unlike all other purchases,
comes through the door for free. Nor has the denial of housework's
value been raised by the neo-conservative family values crowd, which
wants to dump the workload from social service cuts on unpaid
houseworkers. Child-rearing took a big hit from Canada's neo-conservatives in the 1980s, when family allowances were clawed back. The
bugaboo of U.S. welfare bashers is single moms who endure poverty
to stay home with their kids. Alone in the western industrial world,
the U.S. government provides no maternity pay, and precious little
in terms of unpaid but protected leave. Canada funds 15 weeks of
maternity leave through unemployment insurance, a nice way to
classify full-time infant care. Conservatives honor family values like
tobacco companies honor sporting values—in their advertisements,
not their product.

Tax reform is one way to phase in support for this centerpiece of
home economics, especially during the early child-rearing years.
That's when, as Penelope Leach, the Doctor Spock of the fourth
wave, argues, deep and trusting primary relationships are critical to
emotional health.[27] One tax reform proposal comes from Gwen
Landolt, leader of Canada's REAL Women, a right-wing lobby
group.[28] In Landolt's scheme, the income of an at-home parent
would be counted for tax purposes as split evenly with his or her part-
-ner, bringing down the income of each parent to a level where little
tax is paid. Right now, by contrast, a two-income family netting
$50,000 a year pays $5,000 less taxes than a one-income family with
the same net. If the one-income family with a $50,000 net could get
the $5,000 tax credit during child-rearing years, it would suffer no
losses, since $5,000 is more than what is left over after the second
income is spent on child care and related expenses. Every time a parent drops out of the paid workforce, a job opening is created for a formerly unemployed worker. As a mass job creation scheme, it's almost
free, since the $5,000 shortfall is picked up by the new worker, who
also stops drawing unemployment or social assistance. The scheme is
readily adaptable to families where men and women take turns on
leave, or to families where both parents are low earners—in that
case, a negative income tax would top up the bulk of the family's net
loss of income. Job creation, it turns out, is a parenthood issue.

Another, more progressive, approach is to follow policies of continental Europe, where the left is not shy about boosting parental roles. Germany, Sweden and France—none of them slouches when it comes to international competition or deficit control—provide a year's paid leave to either parent. Sweden adds a $150-a-month support payment for each child under 16. France pays a little more, Germany a little less.[29]

Infant Industries

Babies need to be food-proofed before they're street-proofed. Don't trust strangers who offer sweets, or the officials who say "we're from the government, and we're here to help you." Whatever regulations there are for infant and toddler food, they don't seem to limit pesticide residue, sugar or cornstarch. The major brands are overpriced and overloaded with water, thickeners and fillers, charged Michael Jacobson, releasing a 1995 report by the Center for Science in the Public Interest, **Cheating Babies**. Sugar levels are so high, Jacobson says, that "these are the first junk-foods many American children will eat."[30] Over-processed, many of the clarified juices lack the enzymes found in pulpy or cloudy juices and frequently lead to diarrhea.[31] In 72 samples of leading baby foods, the National Campaign for Pesticide Policy Reform found pesticide residue in all vegetable samples, and multiple pesticide residue in all fruits—and that was applying lax U.S. Food and Drug Administration protocols to the samples.[32]

Governments don't set specific standards for infant foods, despite warnings from the U.S. National Academy of Science that threshold levels for growing children need to be 10 times stricter than for adults.[33] "Infants and children are subject to rapid tissue growth and development, which will have an impact on cancer risk," the Academy report, **Pesticides in the Diets of Infants and Children**, said. The Academy estimates that 55 per cent of a person's lifetime cancer risk may be due to pre-school meals, an estimate confirmed by the National Resources Defense Council.[34]

The Center for Science in the Public Interest praised organically grown Earth's Best, already the number three contender for infant food market share, Growing Healthy, and Beechnut. But going the extra mile for infant food security may not be the route to sustainable agriculture. Even without pesticides, the energy costs of transporting baby foods, most of which can be grown anywhere across the continent, doesn't make for a long-term solution. Perhaps leading organic labels might set up local franchises that couple brand-name recognition and reputation for strict standards with local produce. Infant food is a natural for home businesses to grow up on. With about 15 jars worth of sales per baby per week, home delivery in returnable containers can be featured, and a customer base of 400 is all that's needed to make a go of it. Even weirder, parents who don't have to be spoon-fed may try their hands at mashing fruit and vegetables with a fork.

By Hook Or By Crook

The east coast fisheries crisis is as much a problem of over-boating, too few people on too big boats, as over-fishing, too many people for too few fish.

Before the 1970s, most ocean fishing was done with hooks and line. Only older fish took the bait, leaving small fry and other species unharmed. Then came the government-subsidized factory trawlers, dragging their nets over miles, scooping everything in their wake. Factory trawlers are to hook and line what clear-cut logging is to selective cutting. Like military destroyers, they are equipped with sonar and radar, all the devices to track schools of fish and net them. The "killing power" of each boat increased by 50 per cent over the 1980s, says Karl Laubstein, director of industry renewal with Canada's fisheries department, and by 1989, the fleet had the capacity to handle five times what the ocean provided. Inshore fishers using hook and line and small nets still took half of the catch, but they employed 92 per cent of the fishery workforce. Then the biggest fishery of them all got away and the cod stocks collapsed, leaving east coast communities devastated and Canadian taxpayers on the hook for $2 billion a year in social assistance and retraining costs. No revival is expected for 14 years, according to an April, 1995 audit for the federal fisheries department. More proof that fish is not a brain food came from the west coast in 1994, where Canadians and U.S. trawlers had a fish war to see who could despoil salmon stocks best.

Two million less salmon than expected reached the mouth of the Fraser River for the last stretch of their famous spawning run. Despite quota cuts in 1995, the salmon spawning no-show persisted.

Just as with horse logging, old-fashioned boats may be as good as is needed for the stocks that are available, and may lay the basis for a less exploitive, more resourceful fishery. "Hook and line, or drag and die," chant Nova Scotia inshore fishers, fighting for their place in a sustainable industry and against the scheme of the government to drive them out. It's a different kettle of challenges from the factory trawler days, says Bernadette Dwyer of the Fogo Island fishers' co-op. The old cod fishery tossed overboard about 40 per cent of what it caught, then got bottom dollar supplying captive markets in the U.S., mainly school cafeterias and homes for the elderly. The new economy must center on a "value-driven, rather than volume-driven fishery," Dwyer says.

A Cut Above

A guitar takes 500 years to grow. But two board feet of wide, tightly grained spruce, only available from old growth, can be turned into a guitar that sells for $4,000. With three spruce logs, John Larrivée provides a year's work for 40 crafters in his B.C. guitar factory. By way of contrast, B.C. wood mills provide one job for every 1,000 cubic yards of trees cut, and U.S. mills provide 20 jobs for every million board feet of lumber.[35]

Three months before his shift was laid off by a Nanaimo, B.C. mill, third-generation lumber worker Mike Tardif visited Larrivée's factory and a number of other value-added companies. A film crew followed him, and brought out the contrast in jobs, not only in quantities of wood used, but also in pride of workmanship and pleasure of work environment. Hand tools and scraping don't create the screeching noise that forced Tardif and his crew to wear thick ear guards and still come home rattled. Still spry at 78, selective logger Merve Wilkinson showed Tardif the 77-acre, second-growth forest he started working 50 years ago. Wilkinson still has as much timber on his land as when he started logging it. With careful cuts and special lines that tow logs 200 yards to a clearing, he leaves no destructive tracks from roads or heavy machinery. Squirrels and wood mice do the planting for the next generation on the undisturbed forest floor. Wilkinson gets maximum value for each log by varying the end uses. Some parts go to fence posts, some for shingles, some for firewood, some for utility polls, some for lumber.

Tardif also met Mark Randen, who's set up his mill site under the forest canopy on Wilkinson's land. For $30,000, Randen bought a pickup truck and "wood miser" that can cut 2,000 board feet a day to a variety of custom-ordered sizes. He placed one classified ad in a buy-sell paper and has relied on word of mouth ever since. It's not fast-food forestry, Randen admits. "But I equate labor-intensive with jobs." Wilkinson calls his approach "continuous logging." If the big companies in B.C. were up to his standards, there wouldn't be nine million acres of prime forest land laying idle while clear-cuts heal and new trees grow back. That's enough land out of commission to employ 30,000 people like Wilkinson, and another 30,000 like Randen, in permanent second-growth logging. That's double the labor force now working on new clear-cuts of cherished old growth. Tardif's tour also took him to a boat builder, who, with a few hundred dollars worth of hand tools, fills back orders with 500 board feet of lumber a year. Tardif met a team of artisans making log houses, using in a year what a mill buzzes through in four hours.

But the guitar makers, boat builders and home builders all have the same problem. They can't buy logs for anything less than three times what the mills pay. When raw log exports are booming, they can't buy logs for love nor money. No-one can be bothered supplying such small orders. Right-sizing the logging industry of the future, helping it come out of the woods, means small leases from public lands, stewarded by small leaseholders who create sustainable employment. If government policy turns over a new lease, the methods are now here to log forests sustainably.36

The Last Straw

New home building methods and old materials now make it possible for almost anyone to try out the latest in home businesses—building your own home.

It already pays to take a year off work to build your own home. The savings in contracting and construction costs come to about $70,000, according to Harry Pasternak, who offers a nine-day course for do-it-yourselfers in Kingston, Ontario. The savings on lifetime energy and maintenance costs are just as high. His graduates do a better job than typical contractors, because they don't cut corners that lead to higher heating and water bills long after the builder has moved on. "Building is very repetitive and repetition leads to boredom, which leads to errors, which leads to lower quality," Pasternak says. "Owner-builders can build higher quality than the professionals." Some utilities offer special "feebates" to homeowners who build above standard, since every high-efficiency home can help utilities avoid building up to $50,000 worth of new supply. Many banks also offer discounted mortgages to owners of homes that are built to high energy standards. The banks reason that low energy bills make the mortgage easier to pay, and reward the owner with a low-risk mortgage rate. If all these savings are bundled together, owner-builders make more money than in the paid workforce, and get to enjoy a house they built for themselves to their own standards.

A revival of old building materials now makes this option available to everyone, including the unemployed who may want to make use of their free time providing "sweat equity" for their own home. One advance that's getting a lot of attention is straw-bale homes. From all reports, straw homes may be just what's needed to keep the wolf from the door, while benefiting farmers and the environment. Civilizations around the world have long used the materials at hand for their homes. England, for example, has used straw for centuries in its famous thatch-roofed houses but thatchers are finding modern-day straw is lasting only 10 years, instead of 30, because it's grown for grain and weakened by pesticide and fertilizer treatment. Research is underway to revive the Rivet Reed or Wheat which has been found at the bottom of 10-foot thick, 600-year-old thatch layers. It grows to 6½ feet and has a sturdy stalk, but is now only grown in Egypt and Italy.[37]

Straw-bale building was once standard in the Sand Hills area of Nebraska, where a shortage of lumber led turn-of-the-century pioneers to try building with a product that was readily available. Thanks to the new technology of baling, they were able to turn straw into building blocks. This building tradition was rediscovered in the 1970s by back-to-the-landers in the American southwest who were looking for a way to become self-sufficient.

Straw has captured the imagination of many, even for the construction of luxury dream homes. It is cheap, since it uses a resource available everywhere. It is environmentally friendly because it finds use for a product that farmers would otherwise burn in the field, causing more carbon dioxide emissions in many areas than cars. Builder Alex Wilson estimates 2.7 million, 1,000-square-foot, single-storey houses could be built each year from the waste straw generated in North America.[38] Straw also replaces the standard 42 trees used to build conventional homes. It is economical because it has outstanding insulation qualities. Levels of heat resistance in a straw bale wall achieve R-ratings of 40 to 55, better than those achieved by Canada's world-leading Advanced Houses, which have R values of 34 to 50. That makes them a good five times more energy-efficient than standard North American homes.[39] Straw walls make for healthy homes, since the straw insulation breathes and has no toxic properties. It is adaptable. Stramit-U.S.A. makes a type of drywall out of straw in Perryton, Texas. A Quebec company, ArchiBio, uses straw bales as a substitute for some of the more expensive, more energy-intensive and less healthy cement used in floor pads. Many cement kilns improve their cash flow by burning toxic waste, and homeowners are finding that connection a little too close for comfort.

Straw-bale construction is low-tech and labor intensive, lending itself to the same style of community building and skills transfer once common in old-fashioned barn raisings. "Women in particular like to work with straw bale construction," says Toronto architect Tom Ponessa. "They like how it enables them, the sense of self-sufficiency, the connection to nature, the community building that comes out of it, and a construction process that is inviting, not daunting." And the results are often stunningly beautiful, as can be seen in many of the catalogues put out by the industry.

In Tucson, Arizona, city leaders plan to encourage straw bale methods by tract builders, and are developing the first-ever building code to cover straw bale homes. The first buyer will be a low-income family paying off the mortgage with sweat equity. This concept, promoted widely by Habitat for Humanity, involves teams of skilled and novice constructors who get a low-priced home in return for helping others build their homes. When people build homes this way, they build communities as well as affordable housing. In this self-reliant scenario, professional tradespeople earn their keep as teachers and team leaders, not laborers.

Virtual Renegade

Dan Taylor is a competitive access provider on the outer reaches of the fiber-optic revolution. A rebel capitalist, he likes to scrawl graffiti on **Wired** magazine's Internet bulletin board: "support your local renegade bandwidth supplier." He spent a long time working with a local utility interested in supplying its ratepayers with fiber optic hookups. Capable of carrying 100 gigabits of information per second, the wiring lets subscribers sign on as energy misers, and have the bulk of their electricity supplied when rates are cheapest, usually in the mid-day and night, after the energy rush hours caused by cooking and showering. The smart wires can turn on the dishwasher and clothes dryer at 2:00 in the afternoon while subscribers are at work, turn up the heat at 5:00 before they come home for dinner, store heat in the dead of night when they are asleep and power is dirt cheap, wash the laundry at 3:00 in the morning, turn up the water heater at 6:00 for morning showers, and release the stored heat through a humidifier-type device while breakfast is served and when energy rates are high. The utility likes smart wiring because it can cut its purchases of expensive peak load power, and offers deep discounts to ratepayers who sign on. Some utilities are also looking to the day when their cables can carry signals from telephones and a million-channel universe, from Wayne's World to Highbrow, each with 1,000 subscribers who pay $2 a week for an hour of madcap humor or modern art critiques. Picture it as home video productions meet narrowcast audiences through fiber optics: Your local subdivision news, brought to you by and from Mike's Tavern. Subscribe through your local utility.

As the utility executives got down to the fine strokes of cutting a deal with Taylor, they wanted to know how many people he had on staff, besides himself and his number cruncher. Just us, Taylor said. One executive gasped. Of course, you can always choose a big company that's all optics, no fiber, and pay for the overhead and debt load they'll add onto the bill for the job, Taylor said. Corporations are just walls that keep debt in place, he said. Or you can choose us, a corporation without walls or debts, with the best of the best fiber and glass makers and installers brought together for their expertise at this one job. Taylor got the contract. He's since repeated his success elsewhere.

In the knowledge economy, the haves of the corporate world will become has-beens. They can't match the creativity, flexibility, customization, precision or prices of virtual corporations. Creative industries—film-making is the best-known example—have long run on this ad hoc basis where interests and alliances are always shifting and just the right people are brought together for a big job. That's also how northern Italy thrives with its hundreds of small co-ops and family businesses that control huge shares of the market in sectors as diverse as printing, cheese, ham and floor tiles. The best printer with blue ink hooks up with the best printer with red ink, each is independent, each is specialized, both get the high-class jobs. When people across town team up, they piggyback on the city's reputation and collective marketing. Parmesan cheese from Parma is the best-known product of this process.[40] "It's the basis for small and medium businesses being able to compete with big ones," says community economic development expert Robin Murray. "It's not small versus big, because they're part of a big system." The virtual corporation dances like a butterfly, stings like a bee.

Virtual corporations offer the best of both worlds for home businesses. They can have all the independence they want. And when they want to cut a big deal, they can join forces with a dream team. The virtual corporation is in line with today's economic needs for what an ad from investment house J.P. Morgan calls depth. "When your roots are deep in local markets, you see opportunities others may miss," the ad claims. "That's why investors call us—we trade ideas, not just bonds." Virtual companies are the only way to get real, say other companies. "The traditional, lumbering, top-heavy and multi-layered corporations of today cannot survive in the new chaotic marketplace," an ad from the Cable and Wireless Federation says. They will be replaced by "federations of smaller companies and groups free to move quickly and efficiently in an ever-changing marketplace."

Micro-enterprises and community-based businesses need virtual corporations as a counterpoint to the narrow experience and slim resources that sometimes go with small organizations geared to niche markets. Ginette Lafrenière, a professor of co-op business methods at Sudbury, Ontario's Laurentian University, says a community network that allows a more open flow of ideas offers "a womb with a view." Reverend Allan Reeve runs an economic ministry in Toronto's east end, where he works with the homeless, helping them set up craft-based businesses that let them work at their own pace. These homeless-based companies turned out excellent work with ingenious methods, using branches broken during storms for wood carvings, for example. But they couldn't handle high-powered marketing, nor could they afford sophisticated equipment. So they formed virtual co-ops, networking without hierarchy or uniformity. "By working together, small businesses can do big business in small ways," says Reeve, who's had more experience doing spreadsheets than delivering sermons. "Sharing space, equipment, skills and services can add up to a whole greater than the sum of its parts."[41]

"In Sumo wrestling, there's a way to win at the very last moment," says Japanese agricultural scientist, Masanobu Fukuoka, author of the permaculture classic, **One Straw Revolution.** "When a big wrestler pushes a little wrestler back, back, back, just as the little guy is back at the end of the ring, he uses the weight and power coming at him, and flips the big man over his shoulder, the big wrestler is thrown out of the ring and the little one wins."[42]

Easy Does It

Principle 9

Applies the power of positive thinking and the concept of
"social capital" to new ways of offering public and
business services

"*We have big business and big government.
What we need is big community.*"
Bioregional philosopher Whitney Smith

"To ask the biggest questions, we can start with the most personal—what do we eat?"
Food expert Frances Moore Lappé

A new brand of direct economic action is coming out of—surprise, surprise—not the private or public sectors, but the "third sector," the fastest-growing occupational grouping on the continent. The staff of volunteer organizations do for the community software of the new economy what **DOS for Dummies** does for beginners at computing: they make it easy to try something new and worthwhile without having to buy new hardware. Debbie Field and Rod MacRae have figured out how to break down a complex new food system into bite-sized pieces.

In a downtown basement office strewn with brochures and posters, the phone ringing off the hook, volunteers poking their heads in to ask for the nearest place where a desperate mother in the west end can get three days worth of food for her kids, Foodshare executive director Debbie Field excuses herself for a minute and hands over a copy of **Food Technology's** prediction of the top 10 trends for the 1990s. Almost all relate to demands for food that's fresh and healthy, more nutritious and flavorful, less microwaved and fatty. "The nice thing about organizing around food issues," Field says as she sits down again, "is that there isn't one thing people can do. There are hundreds." Her colleague, Rod MacRae, looks the part as the studious and considered holder of a doctorate in agricultural economics and head of the City of Toronto's Food Policy Council, but he has a zany sense of humor. He whips out a copy of the Manna Pesto of the Revolutionary Garden Party (organoanarchist-vangardenist) and recites its program: give peas a chance, zukes not nukes, soilidarity, overturn the compost, shake tabouli, hoe hoe hoe.

More projects and do-able dreams come out of this odd couple—the first woman to work in steel-mill coke ovens since World War II and a trained academic who footnotes more books in an article than most of us read in a lifetime[1]—than from anywhere else on the continent. They don't have time for boycotts. They're into buycotts. They're trying to transform markets. They serve as catalysts and go-betweens for organizations that do rooftop gardening, community gardening, school gardening, school nutrition programs, community kitchens where new parents prepare fresh food for their infants, community support agriculture where farmers link directly to customers, courses training welfare moms to work as caterers, good food boxes filled by a professional wholesale buyer and sold at cost to subscribers, field-to-table arrangements where market gardeners set up display trucks at low-income housing projects, special food boxes for people with AIDS... the list goes on.

The projects are one part Field's conviction that there's a "fast food plot. It's as if the medical system were run by the people who do facelifts," she says. "The nutritional crisis isn't just about being poor. Our children's taste buds have been kidnapped by the fast food industry. We are losing our shopping and cooking and mealtime social skills." So the linchpin of most projects is self-reliance. The projects are also one part MacRae's belief that by joining health, justice and environmental issues together, "you get this interesting alliance of underpaid farmers, the poor and environmentalists. It's actually possible to design a system that works on all problems at the same time." So, interdependence is the key theme in most of the projects. For Field and MacRae, the way to yes is outside the yes-men in the sanctioned food, medical, poverty and government industries. New skills and networks can break their monopoly grip on crucial intermediary roles.

This view is shared by Joel Salutin, a supporter of the progressive American farm journal, **New Farm**. "With new allies and a level playing field, we can regenerate the countryside," says Salutin. Government regulations hurt small operators who can't afford to work their way through the multiple layers of bureaucracy. "I can't even dress a pig in my backyard and sell a pound of sausage to my neighbor," he says, because of regulations passed with huge processors in mind. Salutin praises the U.S. Humane Society, which publishes the **Humane Consumer and Producer Guide** for its 1.6 million members. The guide outlines best practices, and gives the names of credible farmers, retailers and restaurants. This information highway bypasses the government-industry regulatory highway. "There are plenty of farmers and wanna-be's looking for value-added options. These people want to market their vegetables through pot pies, or milk 10 cows and sell butter to their neighbors, or dress a few pigs and make sausage for folks in town," he says. "We'll gladly connect with those customers and topple the icons of inappropriate agriculture and food policies."[2]

People like Field and MacRae personify what business guru Peter Drucker dubs the "third sector"—others call it the social sector—the catalyst of the knowledge economy. Jobs in non-profit and volunteer agencies are growing at twice the rate of for-profit and government jobs. Assets are huge, half those of the U.S. federal government. The third sector "already contributes more than six per cent of the gross domestic product and is responsible for 10.5 per cent of total national employment," Jeremy Rifkin writes in **The Decline of Work**. If volunteer time given through these organizations were calculated, an additional $182 billion a year would be credited. It's estimated that 90 million Americans give at least four hours a week to some voluntary organization.[3]

The third sector is a different creature from the traditional private or public sector. In clothing style, hours of work and intensity of commitment to their causes, third-sector workers have a lot in common with protest activists. But they raise funds in the real world, and deliver programs on very tight budgets. As policy wonks, they're at home with government bureaucrats. But they don't get a paycheck if they don't accomplish anything, and they define their constituency and mandate independent of government policy. They're the non in non-governmental organizations. They'll cuss the costs, waste and heavy-handedness of government bureaucrats with the best in business, but they do not believe in the divine right of markets. They can pencil in lunch appointments in double-booked agenda planners as well as the busiest of yuppies, but they arrange to meet in funky eateries that they can afford on blue-collar salaries. Their language is a dead giveaway. They have executive directors, not chief executive officers or supervisors. They advocate, not confront. They facilitate, not pressure. They network, not mobilize. They empower and enable, not lead.

They are the Sandinistas of the new economy. Roger Burbank and Orlando Nunez anticipated the third sector's pivotal role in their 1987 book **Fire in the Americas: Forging a Revolutionary Agenda.** The third sector does not come from the proletariat or peasantry. Members come from the educated classes, ethnic minorities, the women's movement. They are often profoundly spiritual, many inspired by a devout Christianity. They work through coalitions and partnerships, so tolerance for pluralism, the sense that it takes all kinds, is something they're comfortable with. They are less a force in politics than they are in civil society, which is why the media hasn't heard of them. Their bread and butter is issues that have no power base in the agendas of dominant institutions—issues such as peace, ecology, poverty and equality. Out of this social grouping, Burbank and Nunez argue, "we can begin to forge new alternatives, to build new values, to change the conceptions of daily life and of social relations."

The third sector is where the new economy will have its next growth spurt. The new economy has reached the point in its trajectory where it must jettison the rocket that blasted it off the ground. It is time to leave the counter culture that confines it to niche markets and marginal status. Few new entrepreneurs have been able to go mainstream, even when they're fixed up with sure-fire successes. That's because there's no more momentum in the counter-culture, which, when all is said and done, is defined by negativity, and there's no social space in the mainstream market. The third sector is making space for new entrepreneurs, and is offering them the hooks and ladders to get to it.

The social space occupied by the third sector is hard to define. It's the rich web of middle-level associations that Alexis de Toqueville identified in the 1830s as the secret success of American democracy, the force keeping it away from the brink of mass conformity and iso-lated individualism. It's what young kids used to do when they played outside, turning their parents from people who lived on the same street into neighbors. It's the no-man's land left idle by self-absorbed institutions, such as unions that limit themselves to the narrowest confines of industrial relations, or environmental groups that limit themselves to the preservation of nature. It's the chess clubs, singing societies, hangouts and mutual-aid groups that northern Italy used as a springboard for the public trust and cohesion underlying its economic renewal, according to the de Toqueville of the 1990s, Robert Putnam, in **Making Democracy Work: Civic Traditions in Modern Italy**. It's what former Soviet countries didn't have, "that set of diverse non-governmental institutions which is strong enough to counterbalance the state," and "prevent it from dominating and atomizing the rest of society," which is why, political scientist Ernest Gellner explains, these societies collapsed into self-destruction rather than bouncing back.[4] The market has proven no less destructive than the state. Huge corporations perform best when they use TV ads to leap over the thickets of groups, and make direct appeals to the lowest common denominator of mass marketing, one person at a time. Fat food, magic vans and Disney entered the breach with filler and fantasy. When that doesn't fill the social and moral void, uncharitable Christian fundamentalists step in, according to **Tikkun** editor Michael Lerner, one of the few leftist social critics in North America to identify absence of spirituality as the Achilles' heel of progressive politics.

Advanced industrial societies are "weak in the middle," according to pioneer workplace ecologist Eric Trist.[5] Without middling institutions between individuals and mass institutions, there are no equivalents to ecotones, the transitional zones in nature that are staging areas for rich growth and diversity. It's where salt water meets fresh, for instance, where marshes harbor nesting species from predators and offer dense nutrients that feed the greatest variety of species. The third sector is North America's best hope for social ecotones. The third sector is in the business of "social capital formation"—building up community linkages which let people work together effectively—that will allow the new economy to grow organically. As that social capital gets stronger, home-based entrepreneurs, vendors of local wares, and promoters of energy-conservation equipment will see their social set-up costs slashed. Once the buyers' club is up and running for good food boxes, for instance, the hard work has already been done for sales of the next item. New entrepreneurs will have the same access to the hearts and minds of consumers that mass marketing now monopolizes. The social side road will replace the information highway.

It's unclear how or when these new arrangements will topple the giants of North American mass marketing. We know that the overhead costs of some mega-corporations are so high that they don't start to clear profits until they make their last 15 per cent of sales. We know that the competition for retail space is so intense that products get taken off the shelves of high-volume outlets if sales drop just a few percentage points. So fairly small inroads via alternative production and distribution networks may create some healthy chaos. Just as dinosaurs may have been finished off by the impact of one stray meteorite or chance volcanic eruption, "systems as large and as complicated as the earth's crust, the stock market and the ecosystem can break down not only under the force of a mighty blow but also at the drop of a pin," argue chaos theorists Per Bak and Kan Chen. "Large interactive systems perpetually organize themselves to a critical state in which a minor event starts a chain reaction that can lead to a catastrophe."[6] The bigger they are, the harder they fall.

"The more I get into food issues, the more I get into democracy," says Debbie Field. "At first, I thought, my God, our food is poisoning us. Then I thought there wasn't enough money to go around to buy good food. But what we don't have enough of to go around is connections between self-reliance and interdependence. Those are the tools of the new democracy we are working for." This is the stuff of a citizen-led economic recovery.

"Rehabilitating American democracy thus requires much more than reforming the government. It means that citizens must reinvent themselves."
William Greider, **Who Will Tell The People?**

The new economy needs a government of, for, and by the people. To get there, it needs to declare its independence from the regulatory state and set out a new populist agenda based on carrots, sticks and honey. Bart Hall-Bayer works for a little-known agency in Arkansas that's earned the right to say "we're from the government, and we're here to help you."

Bart Hall-Bayer is the green thumb on the invisible hand of the government. He works for a federal agency with a big title, a small budget, and no legal muscle whatsoever. The office for Appropriate Technology Transfer for Rural Areas (ATTRA) has 20 staff, a telephone hotline, an Internet address, a photocopy machine, and access to the university library next door in Fayetteville, Arkansas. The office was set up in 1987 by the U.S. Fish and Wildlife Service when it figured out that wild life was threatened by chemical spill-off from farms, and that there was nothing that could be done about it under the law. There was no alternative to friendly persuasion. The word went out to farmers: call us about pests, and we won't bug you. If farmers want to think out loud about getting off toxic chemicals, they call.

Hall-Bayer and his colleagues, most of whom still have dirt under their nails from at least five years as working farmers, do their best to help. They place no demands on callers. "As long as they're more sustainable this year than they were last year, that's okay," he says. "Sustainability is a journey, not an end point." He calls ATTRA a "bridge between the farmer and rapidly changing farming technologies." Callers are put in touch with individuals and groups that can offer videos, courses or support. They get computer printouts from literature searches on particular subjects. For the most common questions, ATTRA has 40 of its own pamphlets covering nitty-gritty details of organic cultivation of blackberries and raspberries, hydroponic vegetable production, catfish aquaculture, cover crops and green manure. Many governments are caught in a logjam because they're wrong-sized, too big to deal with small problems, and too small to deal with big problems. By comparison, ATTRA is right-sized for people who want to change of their own accord.

At a time when governments aren't seen as up to much good, ATTRA's record speaks for itself. It helps 12,000 farmers a year become financially and environmentally sustainable. By kicking their chemical habit, Hall-Bayer reckons that farmers who've called in have kept 100,000 pounds of toxic chemicals out of the air, water and soil. There's been no need for a hard sell. Farmers know what they're paying for toxic-chemical methods. It's a minimum of $25 an acre just to spray for the most obnoxious weeds. For Florida tomato growers, chemicals account for about one-quarter of production costs, according to Alexander Csinszky at the University of Florida's Gulf Coast Research and Education Center. Then comes the extra machinery, the barn to store it in, the tools to fix it, and the time and fuel taken up spraying fields in the evening when the wind is low. Farmers also have an inkling of the health problems they're exposing themselves to.[7]

Many farmers are old enough that they don't need Hall-Bayer's history lesson. Fifty years ago, before the miracle petrochemical pesticides and herbicides, farmers lost 31 per cent of what they planted, while farmers of today, who are dumping one billion pounds of chemicals a year onto the soil, are losing 37 per cent of what they plant. A heavy investment in methods that cause a six percentage point drop in farm productivity doesn't tally up economically. But it does tally with mathematics. Mathematicians, working with biologists and zoologists, have applied chaos theory to pesticides, and come up with an analysis of why pests haven't been reduced by pesticides. It's so damning to the pesticide industry, it's no wonder it got no play in the media, despite having been reported in the leading scientific journal, **Nature**. The team found many cases where killing off of beetles led to a beetle population explosion, contrary to anything that linear science would anticipate.[8] The same pattern holds for efforts to exterminate coyotes. As predator control programs are stepped up, coyotes increase their breeding rate.[9] At any rate, when it comes to farm survival, "there's a much greater potential for long-term profit" by going off toxic chemicals, Hall-Bayer says.

Canadian research by Guelph University agricultural specialist Peter Stonehouse confirms ATTRA's experience. Farmers using organic methods do better than farmers who poison their land, for a number of reasons, Stonehouse shows. They get a premium price from specialty markets. They have a wider portfolio, because they raise animals for manure and pest control and get the meat as a bonus, or because they weave in a variety of crops that ward off each other's pests and deficiencies, and get to sell them all at the end of the day. Above all, Stonehouse found, organic farmers have lower input costs. Production costs for organic corn are about 40 per cent lower than production costs for farmers who pile on the fertilizers and pesticides.[10] The same pattern holds for farmers raising beans and cereal grains. "There is a potential to reduce rates of synthetic fertilizers and pesticides," Stonehouse concludes, "without jeopardizing crop yields or adversely affecting farm profitability."[11] He's more blunt speaking one-to-one. Farm subsidies are just a way of laundering government money to petrochemical companies, he says. Farmers can become self-reliant financially when they become self-reliant in their farming methods.

What else is there to say, other than helpful advice on how to get off the treadmill? ATTRA offers what Hall-Bayer calls a "whole system approach. We work toward long-term solutions rather than short-term treatment of symptoms." Then, he gets right to specifics. Have you tried starving out weeds with "living mulches" and "smother crops" like millet and barley? How about intercropping with buckwheat and oats, which also provide green manure for your main crop? Ever thought of "biological weed and pest control" with poultry and weeder geese? How about building up the organic matter in your soil so it holds one-third more water and you can irrigate less? Earthworms generate 57 pounds of nitrogen per acre, and aerate the soil as well, as long as they're not killed off by pesticides.[12] Ever think about how pesticides trigger "reverse succession," killing off pests that kill pests, requiring yet another pest killer?[13] Did you know that Nova Scotia tender fruit farmers use one-third less pesticides than others across the continent, and that's what's kept them afloat as low-cost producers? The rap falls a little short of stereotypes about government agents ramming something down your throat.

The withering away of the coercive state can be a many-splendored thing, ATTRA's record shows. There is a third option beyond the pale of the current debate on the regulatory state, which is polarizing conventional politics in North America in a lose-lose duke-out between the 19th century right and 19th century left. Leading political theorist and community economic development expert Robin Murray calls this option the "developmental state," one where government works with citizens as a facilitator rather than enforcer. When this option becomes better known and understood, we will come to wonder: why is it that the right, not the left, led the assault on useless and counter-productive agencies and programs?

Neo-conservative motives may well be suspect. Their program, as **Business Week** noted, amounts to a "reverse New Deal," not an alternative to the New Deal regulatory regime. It will remove limits on the power of big business. It will tear away at the social safety net and any sense of a mutual-aid society. But it will not lower deficits, as the ballooning national debts of the U.S., Britain and Canada under Ronald Reagan, Margaret Thatcher and Brian Mulroney suggest.[14] It will not revive the economy or create new opportunities for those outside the inner circle. That's because neo-conservatives are more into theater than policy. When they're not bullying children on welfare, they're suffering from Parkinson's second law. Most people have heard of Parkinson's first law, which holds that work expands to fit the time available. More important is the Law of Inverse Proportion, which holds that the smaller the issue, the more time will be spent on it, the bigger the issue, the less time. People can't cope with multi-billion-dollar military budgets, so they focus on a welfare mom who gets $76 extra a month for her third child, and lose their time and humanity whittling away at programs that account for less than two per cent of most government budgets. Politics that play to that human foible are diversionary, and should not be dignified with a title suggesting philosophical beliefs. Prominent conservative columnist George Will has slammed right-wing welfare cuts as "reckless" because they "could endanger the well-being of the poorest children in society in the name of untested theories about how people may respond to some new incentives. Surely," he wrote in the **Washington Post**, "a Congress whose majority proudly carries the mantle 'conservative' should be wary of risking human suffering on behalf of some ideologically driven preconceptions. Isn't that what conservatives always accused liberals of doing?"[15] That said, is it right or wrong to dismantle status quo agencies and programs with a proven track record of failure?

New entrepreneurs have better things to do with their time than the corridor crawl, trying to convince Washington or Ottawa to save some regulation. They have work to do growing resources in local communities and marketplaces. They have positive energy that shouldn't be squandered on whining and cat-calling. There may be an occasional victory from lobbying, but beware of geeks bearing gifts. The skill and power base of the new economy will not come from reacting to political power ploys and playing on the opposition's turf by the opposition's rules. That's like walking into a propeller. With his usual wit and wisdom, Canadian-born U.S. liberal John Kenneth Galbraith argues that liberals deserve neither the credit nor the blame for policies dealing with unemployment insurance, welfare, medical insurance, consumer and environmental protection. They just responded to the realities of an anonymous, urban-industrial, high-tech society without much in the way of natural cohesion, supports or free space that let people fend for themselves. "We liberals adjusted to circumstance, and we allowed conservative Republicans to believe that we were the force for change," he says. "They are now persuaded that they can reverse the tide."[16]

If the slate, and the state, are to be wiped clean by neo-conservatives, the challenge is to restore conditions in civil society that make ongoing government interference in the market unnecessary. Monoculture requires fertilizers and pesticides, whether in agriculture or society. The solution is not stepped-up chemical or political intervention, but organic methods that work when the soil is properly tended and diverse crops maintain their own balance.

Even if the political will were there, there's no future in the prescriptive regulations we have today. Very few of them improve behavior or even address real problems. For instance, building codes requiring a specific amount of insulation don't guarantee a house will use less energy. Zero tolerance of drugs has had full state backing for half a century. Why would anyone think that zero tolerance of chemical toxins or social inequality could do any better? Progress on regulatory reform is dead slow. It took the U.S. food and drug administration 25 years to restrict the use of carcinogenic red dye in food, for instance.[17] Since Canada's Environmental Protection Act was passed in 1988, 27 of 21,000 priority-rated chemicals have been regulated. Once the regulations get on the books, they stay in the books. Five hundred Fearless Fosdicks in Canada's environment ministry have collected $164,000 in polluter fines—permits would be more accurate—since 1988.[18] Read their actions, not their lips. There's not a lot of latitude for deregulation to be worse.

Regulations also suffer from a disease known as "capture." Regulators can't rule over a bankrupt industry, so they quickly move to set rules companies can live with. The line between regulators and regulated is especially hard to find when the lead players keep switching back and forth from a top job on one side to a top job on the other.[19] The trend to monopolies in the garbage industry only grew under regulation, which squeezed out small competitors, Harold Crooks shows in **Dirty Business** and **Giants of Garbage**. In 1995, Carol Browner of the EPA wrings her hands, lamenting that 30 years after Rachel Carson's powerful expose of chemical food poisoning in **Silent Spring**, "we have doubled the pounds of pesticides we use in producing the food we eat."[20] She might have mentioned that in 1982 the EPA approved 100-fold increases in pesticide levels.[21]

Regulations do one thing effectively, however. They suppress the new economy. Often as not, they make it illegal. Regulators insist that jam with natural sweeteners, such as grape juice concentrate, can't be called jam. Why don't they insist that fruit juice without any clouds from real fruit pulp be called "once-juice?" If they want to get picky, why not check out the regulations allowing 650 insect fragments and one rodent hair per 12-ounce jar of peanut butter?[22] Regulators insist that composter toilets have a hookup to septic tanks, even though it's known that septic tanks don't work, and that the cost of the hookup destroys the economics of composter toilets, which do work. Why don't they insist that septic tanks be hooked up to composter toilets? Regulators insist that urban homes be hooked up to utility lines, destroying the economics of contractors who build off-grid. Regulators insist that take-out food orders come in virgin packaging. Why don't they insist that food come from recently sterilized packages, including re-usables? Regulators insist that child-care centers scrub toys down with chlorinated cleaners. Why don't they insist on unchlorinated cleaners? Grading of foods is done by size and appearance, not nutrient content or absence of toxins. Get the point? Regulations repress innovation and diversity, and block new entrants to an industry. That has been the nature of the beast from the beginning, as Gabriel Kolko tried to tell 1960s new leftists through his classic histories, **Railroads and Regulation** and **The Triumph of Conservatism**.

The tragedy is that many of these regulations came with good intentions. And so have many roads to hell been paved. Regulations come from the era of mass production and scientific management, when one size fit all, and the further from the scene of action the decision-makers were, the clearer their orders would be. That's why regulations are standardized, in a world of almost infinite variety. That's why they're stuck on doing the right thing instead of doing the thing right. That's why regulations are heavy on prescriptive specifications, light on performance requirements, hung up on how much insulation to put where, not how little energy a home should use, for instance. That's why they're full of thou shalt nots, and why there are so many loopholes. "No shirts, No shoes, No service" doesn't say anything about No pants.

If politicians have an urge to do something positive, there are some obvious things they can do.

1.   They can cancel the subsidies and tax exemptions that pay corporations to do the wrong thing. There'll be no need to regulate those companies any more, because they won't be around for long. New companies in an equal marketplace will take care of that.

2.   They should give chemicals the same legal status as the people who claim redress before worker compensation boards. That is, they should be assumed guilty until proven innocent before a panel which includes those opposed to their interests. If that sounds too harsh, victims of chemical pollution can be granted redress on the same basis as toxic chemicals were

allowed to get into the environment, without any questions asked.

3. They should ban things which are known to be harmful. Biologist Barry Commoner has come up with a very simple rule: if you don't put anything bad into the environment, it isn't there. By contrast, he shows in painstaking detail in **Making Peace With The Planet**, levels of all regulated substances have gotten worse since they were regulated and given legitimacy.

4. They should move from complex specification or prescriptive regulations to simple performance regulations, which set out absolute goals, but don't prescribe how they're achieved. The government can speak for the public interest on, say, eliminating CFCs that destroy the ozone layer. People on the spot can use their ingenuity to figure out how to get there in their own way. That's how the Scandinavians got high levels of workplace health and safety with very brief laws and a small number of inspectors, and cottoned onto the principle of "minimum critical specifications"23—consultant talk for letting the people on the spot figure out the solutions. That's how the staff at Hughes Aircraft moved from CFC solvents to an ever-so complex solder cleaner based on lemon juice and water, saving themselves $750,000 a year for cleaners in the process.24 The idea is to keep pushing the performance up, not just reach the standard that was more often than not set by compromise, not science.

Once performance regulations have been set, the government may have a role facilitating their achievement, if that is requested. This is a process that the Japanese call kaizan, that new age consultants call continuous improvement, that Ted Gaebler and David Osborne call **Reinventing Government**, and that Robin Murray, the most thoughtful activist and theorist on this matter, calls developmentalism.25 To figure out what it means, call ATTRA and ask what you should do to get off toxic pesticides. Or check out what Murray did as director of Ontario's community economic development unit from 1993 to 1995. He didn't have any laws behind him to force people to develop communities, or force communities to develop economies. He had no levers, the strong suit of conventional governments, but he had a budget and a rolodex that let him travel to Windsor, meet a greenhouse operator who wanted to expand, and introduce him to auto workers who wanted to buy his produce, and to do something like that three times a day, every day. Follow through, as some already have, on Ralph Nader's ideas about citizen utility boards. All the government does here is require regulated monopolies and quasi-monopolies such as utilities and banks—which should owe the public something in return for their privileges—to include in their regular mailings to customers an invitation to learn about and join organizations fighting for consumer interests.

Developmentalism is the new populism. It's all about government from the commanding bottoms, not the commanding heights. Its relevance flows from a number of realities, expressed in a host of clichés. You can lead a horse to water but you can't make it drink. You can catch more flies with honey than vinegar. It takes two to tango. Don't tell me, show me. A rising tide raises all boats. Power over is a win-lose game; power to is a win-win game. All the king's horses and all the king's men couldn't put Humpty together again. Many of these clichés speak to long-standing North American orneryness about being bossed around. In Robert Frost's famous poem, **The Code**, a farm hand quit when the farmer told him what to do. "You weren't hinting," another helper explained to the befuddled owner. Many of the clichés also speak to an understanding of the complexity of human relations in a fast-paced society, and the need to work with chaos.

Everyone has a vested interest in saving money on fuel, but we all need some solid information on how to do it. The old dividing line between producer and consumer is irretrievably blurred, so manufacturers have to work with customers, and health experts have to work with patients to produce their own health, and garbage departments have to help people dispose of their compost in their own backyard. States no longer have a monopoly over specialized policy knowledge, and they gain in power to do when they share information and decisions with people they used to have power over. People on the front line know more about their jobs than people in management. There's more than one way to skin a cat, or as Murray, always adept at phrasing things nicely, puts it, "there's a rich ground for experimentation, for diffusion of best practices." The idea of one right way, he says, is a hold over from the Enlightenment obsession with pure reason abstracted from practice, a notion the left has accepted as dogmatically as the right. Development, in a word, is ongoing. Like communities. To succeed, says Hall-Bayer, ATTRA must face that challenge. It's not enough to fix soil health. "What we're about is stopping the decay of farm communities, strengthening the fabric of the rural landscape," he says. Developmentalism is thinking like a neighborhood.

"Next to environmental degradation, the disappearance of meaningful work is the most important problem facing Canada, the U.S. and the world."
Nature artist Robert Bateman[26]

Economics as if people mattered is a nice way of saying economics as if turkeys didn't. We've let the government and corporate turkeys create an employment problem, which is worse than the unemployment problem. They get us working full-time on things that are wrong, while volunteers are left to put them right in their spare time. Solving that employment problem, and the unemployment that goes with it, is what third sector jobs are about. Here are some trends to watch.

Salad Days

Modern consumers prefer a spot on their tomato to one on their lungs. Sales of organic food are soaring—$2.3 billion in 1994, up 22 per cent from the year before.[27] The **Popcorn Report** predicts organic food will soon be mainstream. "We will pay anything to Stay Alive," it says.

The demand for healthy food cannot help but up-end the production, processing and distribution methods of the current food system. Healthy food is fresh. Vitamins dissipate quickly once vegetables and fruit have been picked. Grains store better, which is a great hedge against famine, but we shouldn't press our luck. Dr. Antonio Constantini, director of the World Health Organization's unit that monitors mycotoxins in food, believes that fungi and molds that grow in stored grains are responsible for the spread of many degenerative diseases, including cancer. Several North American studies support him.[28] Likewise, illnesses from contamination in the under-inspected mass production food processing system kill 9,100 people a year in the U.S. Productivity losses from time spent staring into a toilet bowl, doing the dry heaves from food poisoning, cost North

Americans $7 billion a year.[29] That means food staples should be grown locally, and packaged foods should be minimized.

Modern shoppers also want more for their food dollar than cheap filler. They are HICCs, says Patrick Carson, vice-president of Loblaws supermarkets in Canada, "higher-inner-conscious consumers." They want the taste of justice in their food, and some sense of connection with where it came from. A survey by the Agricultural Council of America found that 89 per cent of people wanted a more direct relationship with the farmers who grew their food.[30] Soft customers are now defining markets as much as tough ones.

Healthy eating that's good for both the soul and the farmer accounts for the quick rise of community support or community share agriculture. There are now more than 500 CSAs in the U.S. and 200 in Canada. Here's how the new production and distribution system commonly works. Farmers sell a share of their future crop in early spring, using the advance payment to avoid a trip to the bank to buy seeds and tide the family over while crops are growing. With guaranteed customers, the farmers also avoids brokerage fees, time spent twiddling thumbs at stands and waste from over-production. These savings are passed on to the customer with organic food that's priced below spray-painted food at the supermarket. The food is delivered fresh-picked weekly. Last week's cuttings are taken back to the farm compost heap. It's a win for the farmer—a Saskatchewan study shows CSA farm families make about $3,000 a year more than conventional grain farmers, even though the latter enjoy $16,000 in subsidies. It's a win for the consumer, who gets fresh organic food at a good price. It's a win for the local economy, where local dollars multiply and spread the wealth. It's a win for the environment, since long-haul transportation, pesticides and garbage are eliminated.

But CSA is better than a good deal. "It satisfies members' more intangible desires for a sense of community and for re-establishing contact with the land," says Bruce Schultz, who coordinates the Celebrity Gardens Community Harvest Program near Kalamazoo, Michigan. Most of the 100 families that belong help out on the garden in return for a reduced fee. While the parents work in the vegetable plots, their kids play in the adjoining "country club," planting flowers to build a butterfly highway. Four potlucks and harvest festivals a year celebrate a "strong commitment to healing the earth and establishing a truly sustainable agricultural system," Schultz says. "We're adding some culture to agriculture," says Winnipeg CSA farmer, Dan Wiens. "We're putting some humanity back into it."

CSAs are a boon to what Patrick Carson calls "the most endangered species in North America— the farmer." Two market gardeners can make a go of it with less than 200 customers. CSAs help new farmers lower their start-up costs, and let immigrants, many with agricultural backgrounds, get their first plot by serving the community they know best. They are flexible, allowing members to donate more or less labor, more or less money, depending on their circumstances. They are easily customerized. Some CSA farms deal exclusively with pasta sauce or flowers. And they prepare the ground for new distribution networks that can be used by other local producers.

Down The Garden Path

New York City spends $500 million a year piling garbage on Staten Island's Fresh Kills Landfill. Believe it or not, it's now the highest mountain on the east coast of the Americas, as well as the world's largest garbage dump. Gray Russell is one of a team working to eliminate the costs of hauling away one-fifth of that load, made up of yard trimmings and kitchen scraps. They do not only recover value from organic materials that now foul dumps and contribute to toxic leachate. They add value to the community, one of the key features of the new infrastructure governments are challenged to create.

Russell is the compost project manager for the Bronx Green Up, an outreach program at the famous New York Botanical Garden. The BGU works with community gardening groups, helping them network with city agencies and supplying gardeners with plants, soil, compost, tools and training. They use the compost as soil conditioner for raised-bed gardens and car-tire planters. While the compost improves soil structure, it also helps to reduce the take-up of some contaminants common to the soils found in the 2,000 abandoned lots throughout New York City, some of which residents are re-claiming, Russell says. BGU also arranges for donations of plants from local nurseries, or floral collections that have finished their run at the New York Botanical Garden. Rockefeller Center's monthly floral displays, for instance, formerly tossed in the garbage, now brighten up these new self-help neighborhood centers that community gardeners are grow-ing in the Bronx. A community garden provides space for one of three demonstration sites Russell and his "compost crew" built to show the variety of composters people can build or buy. Composting clinics are offered at the three sites. Any questions can be answered by calling the 24-hour "Rotline" Bronx Green Up runs.

Russell's compost education coordinators have helped 400 teachers in 100 schools with presentations that have reached 10,000 inner-city school kids. Their "Wormshop" sessions start with a showing of red squiggly vermi worms that kids soon stretch out hands to touch. The worms thrive on eating kitchen waste, and Russell's team turns their composting ways into a biology lesson, now packaged as part of the science curriculum. When the worms finish converting leftovers into high quality, nitrogen-rich fertilizer, and teachers grow plants on win-dowsills using the vermicompost, "it really makes the lights go on, and kids understand that garbage can be made into un-garbage and that we can turn it into a valuable resource," he says.

Russell also works with ground crews who tend the 1,500 acres of lawn managed by New York City's housing authority. After attending a workshop Russell put on for 40 grounds supervisors, housing author-ity staff switched to mulching mowers that cut grass finely enough that it can be left on the ground. Mulching grass keeps lawns moist and fertilized for free—grass clippings are 85 per cent moisture and five per cent nitrogen—and eliminates useless raking. Since an acre of lawn produces six tons of clippings in a season, it eliminated 9,000 tons a year from being collected, hauled and dumped at NYC's over-burdened landfill. "Nine thousand tons from one seminar of one program in one borough…. Now that's a success story," Russell says. He's also set up a composting facility at the botanical garden, divert-ing another 500 tons a year from the garbage mountain. He's now working with restaurant and hotel owners, introducing them to the machines, invented by the Gaia Institute, that turn scraps into compost in 72 hours. It's a double profit center for the companies, says Russell. They slash disposal costs, and generate income from sales of finished compost.

A rotten attitude doesn't work with composting, says Russell. "When we stop asking where to put the garbage and start asking how we can use these resources, we are using a whole different, more modern mentality. The old New York City attitude 'This is the law!' won't work anymore. We need to provide incentives," he says. In the old economy, governments deskilled citizens, just told them which days to put out their garbage. In the new economy, where community skills and resources count for more than physical infrastructure, governments have to work with citizens as partners, he says, sometimes a big mental stumbling block for some sanitation managers.

Law 'n Order

Green lawns and sparkling floors illustrate the banality of pollution. But in the affluent west end of Montreal Island, 14 small local governments have cracked down on the use of pesticides since 1991. The campaign is spreading quickly, and the controversy will likely affect every municipal government on the continent by the end of the decade. Fifty boards of education and parks and recreation departments in Canada have already sworn off pesticides for their grounds. Dr. Michael Surgan, chief scientist with the attorney general's office in New York, favors elimination of known or likely carcinogenic applications "for purely aesthetic or recreational purposes." Though decorative poisons only account for a small portion of industrial-strength toxins in the world, the controversy highlights the public health, ethical, employment, and ecological consequences of cultivated tastes for whiter than white, greener than green, forms of species cleansing. When a company can openly call itself Chemlawn, we have some paradigm shifting to do.

An 11-year-old boy, Jean-Dominique Levesque-Rene, tours city councils around Montreal pleading for a stop to the spraying of parks and lawns with pesticides responsible for his cancer. His parents pass out an American Cancer Society pamphlet to others visiting their children in hospital cancer wards. The pamphlet says that "95 per cent of the pesticides used on residential lawns are considered probable or possible carcinogens by the Environmental Protection Agency," and that "children are as much as six times more likely to get leukemia when pesticides are used in the home and garden."

Citizens for Alternatives to Pesticides, led by public health expert
Dr. Merryl Hammond and backed by organizations of dentists, nurses,
physiotherapists and other health bodies, hops from council to council asking for a moratorium on pesticide use in residential areas until
they have been proven safe. So far, CAP has gone from one success
to another. First, it targeted the use of poison on municipal grounds.
Then it limited pesticide use by landscaping companies. In 1995, the
issue escalated to individual spraying. Dr. Jonathan Singerman got up
in arms when a neighbor started spraying while his daughter played
nearby. He ordered a computer printout of recent articles on pesticides, and found 55 reports linking them to non-Hodgkin's lym-
phoma, liver and brain cancer. The media ran with the issue. Popular
columnist Bee MacGuire dubbed municipal stalling of CAP requests
a Pestigate scandal, and started asking why the medical establishment
"has not been yelling blue murder about all this. Queer, isn't it?" One
possible reason, she says, is that half of all medical research is funded
by drug companies. "Now, guess who produces those pesticides? The
drug companies do." As word got out, parents freaked out when they
saw spraying going on near their children. "I think most people
would prefer weeds to cancer," said distraught mom Jan Murray, sur-
prised to learn that many politicians didn't agree. By early summer,
parents started chasing city workers with spraying equipment out
of parks where children played.31 The petrochemical industry is on
the run.

Pesticide bans raise some sticky enforcement and implementation
issues. Hammond, who's written up her experiences in a manual,
Pesticide Bylaws: why we need them; how to get them, says there's
no need for an army of inspectors and snoops. It's enough for cities to
clean up their own act, and to lend whatever moral authority they
have to the issue. The bylaws empower citizens who oppose spraying
to order a stop when neighbors put their kids at risk, she says. But
ultimately, the fact is that people are going to have to make some
personal choices about a piece of suburban technology, the lawn,
that's one of the biggest energy pigs on the continent after watering,
mowing, fertilizing, spraying and dumping of grass clippings from land
otherwise available for growing food are counted.

An experiment in North York, Ontario, suggests the kinds of grassroots partnerships and changes that can grow out of the new public

health consciousness. The Conservation Council of Ontario and Toronto Environmental Alliance teamed up with a government agency, the Environmental Youth Corps, and a number of retailers keen on keeping abreast of new lawn and housecleaning trends. Youth corps workers knocked on doors to find 1,000 households to commit to keeping toxins off their shopping list. It wasn't hard to get volunteers. They just watched for homes where kids and dogs were playing on the lawn, and showed parents the statistics on cancer. Parents were usually ready to listen when they learned that swallowing household pesticides and cleaners is the second most common cause of child poisoning, that most drain and oven cleaners can be found listed in Dr. Robert Gosselin's **Classical Toxicology of Commercial Products** as "extremely toxic," that even the government doesn't know what's in pesticides because the companies only have to list "active ingredients," not the inert solvents that are also problematic.

The youth corps workers offered a brief course on how to clean the home and maintain the lawn without poison, then provided a 24-hour hotline for people to call in with specific questions—what do I do to shine my oak table before my mother-in-law comes over? By going one-on-one, "we've unbought 60,000 liters of Killex this summer," says TEA chair Marcus Ginder. "How long do you think that would take the government?" The summer project paid for itself. Toxic waste depots cost cities $83 per family per year. Hospital emergency ward handling of child poisonings doesn't happen for free. With 1,000 people sworn off toxins, perhaps for ever, it doesn't take much to make these programs pay.[32]

Going non-toxic is easy, as soon as the information on alternatives is made available. What's hard is getting the information. The reason for that is simple. Non-toxic products and methods are too cheap for giant corporations to bother with, too plentiful for them to control. Are they going to put on a multi-million-dollar advertising campaign to push the merits of baking soda and vinegar? Will they spread the word about letting grass grow beyond the brush-cut stage, helping roots sink deep enough that grass can survive without fertilizers or pesticides? Is there a hardware franchise keen to pass around the recipe for non-toxic deck preservative that the U.S. agriculture department's Forest Products Laboratory uses to keep wood protected for 20 years, when the recipe is based on linseed oil, turpentine and paraffin wax?[33] What multinational will pay for ads telling you that compost made from grass clippings, autumn leaves, kitchen waste and nettles is a better soil conditioner than commercial fertilizer? What chain pooh-poohs fertilizer, and recommends planting clover to fix nitrogen in the soil? Does a gardening center push perennials or self-seeding native plants that don't need fertilizers or pesticides, and don't lead to sales of another batch of annuals next year? Companies only make money on artificial products when your needs are artificial.

But one company's poison is another company's meat. The future in home and lawn care, as elsewhere, belongs to information-intensive service companies. From the Montreal area, there's Ecoval, which produces a line of non-toxic fertilizer and pesticide alternatives that are beginning to sell briskly at high-end U.S. golf courses, which traditionally use seven times more toxins per acre than farmers. Neighborhood organic landscapers can make a go of it the same way organic farmers do, by keeping their costs low and quality high—pushing a lightweight lawnmower that cuts grass, instead of a noise machine that slashes it, for instance—so they don't need high volume to come out ahead. And someone should be able to figure out how to market a convenient collection of reusable bottles with the right mix of baking soda, lemon juice and vinegar for the 10 most common cleaning jobs, so a person doesn't have to rifle through a mound of fact sheets before cleaning the oven. To put the business mission in perspective, Michael Rossman has built his Toronto company, Kiddie Proofers, which targets the nine out of 10 childhood accidents that are preventable, into a $300,000 a year income.[34] Keeping pesticides off lawns and toxic preservatives off lawn-decks is as important as removing electric wiring from the reach of toddlers.

Organizing For Sunset

Greenpeace is known for daring stunts that manipulate the media into galvanizing public opinion behind the plight of cuddly and beautiful species. But if the truth be known, most Greenpeace staff and volunteers are hunkered down mastering the science of invisible toxins and building skills to manipulate the market. The strategy is known as "market transformation," and it's already well-advanced in

Europe, where chlorine-free paper, coolants and plastics are becoming commonplace. "The market moves faster than the politicians," says Charles Cray, a Chicago-based toxic campaigner with Greenpeace.

Cray likes to explain why Ken isn't as well hung as girlfriend Barbie is stacked, and why the only manhood G.I. Joe can grab onto is his rifle. These products are made from chlorinated or PVC plastic which release dioxins, shown conclusively to botch up reproductive organs, lower male sperm counts, and result in shortened penises.[35] At $2,000 a whack, not many men who grew up drinking the dioxin-spiked Great Lakes brew will be able to make up the inch they've lost with penis enlargements, though the shrinkage may lead to belated popularity for the green slogan "small is beautiful."[36] This contribution of dioxin toward reduction provides an easy way to measure dioxin's effects. "We have to stigmatize the product," says Cray.

There are other ways of inching toward progress. Ever since the blue ribbon International Joint Commission responsible for Great Lakes water quality supported the phasing out of chlorine in 1993, attention has turned to "sunsetting" the lab-made chemical, the only way to achieve "zero discharge." Sunsetting takes more than stigmatization. It requires, the IJC said in its sixth annual report, "a cooperative approach whereby the traditional regulatory approach is blended with consultation and dialogue among all stakeholders, using a range of mechanisms and partnerships." The Illinois-based Chlorine-Free Products Association is working on that. So are new "wet" or green cleaners who are using non-toxic solvents to give clothes something better than a dressed-to-kill look.

Cray has his finger pointed at the hospital sector, a high profile user of PVC products. Medical waste incinerators are the top generators of dioxin, according to the U.S. EPA. If hospitals ban cigarette smoking in their buildings, Cray reasons, logic requires they do the same for dioxin. But banning incinerator smoking in hospitals isn't a simple matter, Cray says. One inventor has developed a PVC-free IV bag. The Chicago-based Center For Neighborhood Technology is working on other product substitutes. There's more to the change-over than alternative products, however. Purchasing departments have to be brought on side. So do inventory control and accounting departments. Throwaways make for simplified billing, since an exact charge can be accrued to patients. That's a bit more simple, apparently, than when equipment is steam-sterilized for re-use. Even though sterilization and re-use are cheaper in the long run, there are front-end, start-up costs, different space allocations for both machines and the workers tending them. The market, Cray says, has to be "goosed." Once hospital dynamics are figured out, he says, "we'll pinpoint the economic incentive, avoid the whole EPA pollution control mess, and keep power in the local community."

The Chlorine Curse

Women entrepreneurs are finding a **Bagdad Café** of hidden business opportunities creating safe goods that old-style corporations take no interest in. A case in point is women's menstrual products. The conventional pads and tampons are laced with chlorine residues that cause a manufacturing problem, a waste disposal problem and a health problem, says Liz Armstrong, co-author of the industry exposé **Whitewash**, which links residues and certain fibers to toxic shock syndrome. Armstrong works with groups that try to mobilize women's purchasing power behind toxin-free and reusable materials. "We can't wait passively for governments to bring in legislation to protect our health," says Armstrong. "We need to use our economic power to bring in alternative products."

Willie Nolan, feminist and anti-poverty activist, as well as president of Bio-Business International, is selling a line of mass market and competitively priced alternatives. "Women in Britain insisted on and got product changes within weeks of a television documentary confirming the health and environmental damage caused by chlorine-tainted products," says Nolan. "It's time we voted at the cash register for groups and changes that serve our needs."

Look Before You Leak

A community economy needs matchmakers. When there aren't matchmakers, a purchasing agent ends up dealing with fast talkers and high rollers in town for the night. A retired politician has identified this missing link in the infrastructure of local economies, and has also figured out a way to put the matchmaker's role on a sound business footing.

John Sewell is a long-time leader of neighborhood-based urban reform, and occupied the mayor's chair in Toronto during the 1970s. He has since come to believe that governments are better at building bureaucracies than solving problems, so he set out to find a market-place solution to a marketing problem. Producers suffer from a home-town disadvantage when purchasing departments favor global firms that can bankroll expensive sales and bidding operations. That led Sewell to form his own company, Regional Sourcing, in an effort to meet the needs of purchasing officers who lack the time and resources to seek out local companies that might well provide them with superior quality or price. His procedure is pretty straight for-ward. He meets with the official who handles purchasing and asks for a list of product or service specifications. Then he hunts up a local who can enter a bid for the work, and charges a finder's fee if a deal is cut. It's that simple. Odd as it seems, budgets are so squeaky tight today that neither purchasers nor producers have any time to explore new clients and suppliers. That means an independent, honest broker and talent scout has a job to fill.

At first, Sewell thought he'd score his big breakthroughs with heavy and bulky products that cost a lot to transport. Local suppliers avoid that cost and should have a competitive advantage, he reasoned. He quickly found many other home-team advantages. When companies import goods from Asia, for instance, payment is due when the ship is midway across the Pacific. That means retailers of locally made goods, usually provided with a 30-day leeway, get up to 45 more days of sales before the purchase order has to be paid. On a $1-million order, that's an easy $10,000 saving in interest charges. Having a supplier close by also cuts down on the lead times needed to order fast-moving items.[37]

Then Sewell found the quality advantage. He started pestering a medical alert organization about having its identification bracelets manufactured locally. Can't be done, he was told, because no local firm makes that kind of metal. Before long, Sewell arranged a design competition for a new bracelet to replace the 40-year-old model. The new bracelet had to be distinctive enough to serve as a medical alert, modern enough to look fashionable, and made from materials that are readily available, the design competition specified. That experience opened a whole new world for local trade. It confirmed Jane Jacobs' pioneering study, **The Economy of Cities**, which shows how dynamic cities go forth and multiply through import substitution, using local talent to customize and innovate for the home market. Sewell now believes that the real competitive advantage of local firms comes from their willingness and ability to respond to precise needs, to bring together purchasers, designers, supervisors and tradespeople and negotiate continuous improvements, one customer at a time. Interface with a human face beats out the cookie-cutter imports. This process advantage outweighs all the other home-town offerings, Sewell now believes.

Most metropolitan areas can provide work for a host of independent brokers, each one a major job creator, a major reducer of transport pollution, a major spur to local diversity and creativity. Specialists in hospital supplies, working the billion-dollar-a-year market common in areas with five million people, may well be the ones to crack the monopoly of PVC suppliers, for instance, by hunting up contractors who'll deliver sterilized reusables. School board specialists can arrange purchasing partnerships for volume discounts, or find paper providers who'll agree to pick up paper waste for recycling. Restaurant supply specialists will match up chefs with farmers and processors, and arrange discounts for restaurant strips that combine daily deliveries from a centralized distribution depot. A junk dating service can zero in on unique suppliers and users of what's now waste, simply because a restaurant can't find a farmer who'll haul away organic waste, or a second hand bookstore doesn't know a recycler who can unglue paperbacks. There's really no need for government regulations on local purchasing when the real barrier is lack of con-tact points, not lack of government forms to fill out.

In today's world, the economic law of comparative advantage weighs in on the side of local suppliers. That's probably why multinationals rely on captive markets and funnel their global sales through their own branch plants. These internal transfers account for about half of global trade. But a monopoly that a parent multinational has over its servile branch-plant managers, few of whom have any authority to innovate, becomes a severe competitive disadvantage as soon as local economies develop the community software to connect productive partnerships.

While brokers like Sewell work on import substitution, others can work on export substitution. Tourism—a major drain on local earnings in most communities, as well as a cause of over-use of a small number of prized beach, mountain and wilderness destinations—is an obvious place to start. There's no infrastructure to support the notion that holidays start near home. The destination travel industry, now in the midst of merger-mania, makes an easy buck raking off a percentage of bookings on expensive holiday packages for accidental tourists. There's so much speculative profit from over-building new vacation hideaways, and so much over-capacity when speculators shift to a new hotspot, that the continental and global tourism industry can afford to give away free air miles and holiday points for use on off-days and off-seasons.

Why can't anti-travel agents be just as aggressive about developing and marketing local tourism to people who can't afford long trips, or don't want to spend one day of their holiday cooling their jets in airports? Have fun, won't travel, their slogan might be, as they issue ground mile points provided by neighboring communities. Some of the new anti-travel brokers might specialize in family holidays centered around recreational activities for kids of all ages, with baby-sitting during the evening included in the package. Some may specialize in local health spas—no need to fly for a day to get your colon irrigated or get mud for your face—or hiking trails that link to inns along the route.

It will often be necessary to coax local tourism operators into developing a modern industry. Hinterland areas surrounding most big centers have beauty, recreation and distinctive traditions to offer, though they're well hidden behind the facade of mini-putt and go-cart courses, fat-food strips and a chamber of commerce kiosk staffed by a bored teenage relative of the chamber president. Local operators need to sit down with a broker who'll level with them on what modern tourism is all about. From areas we've seen, many need tips on door signage alternatives to "no shirt, no shoes, no service;" regional cuisine supplements to Cheez Whiz on nachos; alternative landscape materials to pavement; and gift shops offering locally produced art rather than baseball caps made offshore but with the name of the local town printed on them. Anti-travel brokers, in other words, have to co-develop the local resource, not just take a percentage off sales.

For instance, the eight-day, 400-mile biking holiday promoted by the Grand Tour of Quebec now takes 2,000 people from Montreal to the colorful eastern townships and back. Most people who sign up want a low-cost (around $500) holiday that offers exercise, laughs, fresh air, quality time with the family, a chance to meet new friends and great scenery seen close up. Tour sponsors cater to novices and those who like to travel light. An advance crew makes sure meals and overnight stays are ready when bikers hit town. A "bus of shame" carries gear and provides lifts to those who get tired. We wanted to show people that cycling is fun, says tour organizer Linda Bouchard, and "to show that developing a bicycling infrastructure would provide economic spinoffs." The tour pumps $75,000 into every town it passes through, and helps keep 2,000 province-based bike and accessory makers busy with $600,000 in pre-tour sales.[38]

Banned Near Boston

Organic farmers need to protect their crops from parasites. That's true for organic human communities, too. Otherwise, pests swoop down on the fruits of others' labor and take without giving anything back. To create and maintain space for positive initiatives, a community sometimes has to draw the line.

Individual shops and restaurants give Cape Cod towns the charm and vitality that draw in visitors. Their owners work hard to keep their area franchise-free. They know that fat-food franchises bring down the neighborhood with their huge parking lots, garbage, greasy sewage, air pollution—Los Angeles fat-food joints, for instance, have been charged with creating more soot than all buses in the region combined[39]—and cheap wages that undercut family-owned restaurants which feature prepared, rather than processed, food. As merger-mania turns competition into a two-way fight—with mega-corporations that have patched up their differences in one ring and independent small businesses in the other—neighborhood groups are starting to rally against the destruction of community-based businesses. Junk-food chains are now as welcome in a neighborhood as junkyards. In Bexley, Ohio, residents seem to prefer having a smut shop over a golden arches chain. "We think fast food is equivalent to pornography, nutritionally speaking," says one community leader.[40] Junk-food chains are the underclass of North American business, and they can drag down community standards very quickly.

McDonald's is also suffering from gagvertising by vegetarians who denounce their offerings as damaging to health, destructive of the environment, and exploitive of workers. In Britain, the chain has sued two such critics, Dave Morris and Helen Steel, for libel. At the trial, which has broken records for longevity and been dubbed the McLibel trial, a witness for Coca-Cola testified that the drink   is nutritious because it contains water, "and that's part of a balanced diet." A McDonald's executive has testified that without fat-food waste packaging, "you will end up with lots of vast, empty gravel pits all over the country."[41] In the U.S., Cancer Prevention Coalition organizer Keith Ashdown co-ordinated protests at 3,000 outlets to mark the chain's 40th anniversary.[42] In Toronto, vegetarian chef Chris Sartor appealed a rap for mischief when he was found guilty of putting an **Adbusters**' "grease" culture-jam sticker on a sandwich board advertising a McDonald's. The judge admitted he had a point and quashed the charges.[43]

But truth in advertising standards in North America allow the company to print this message on placemats: "McDonald's offers its customers balance and variety with a wholesome menu of beef, potatoes, poultry, eggs, bread, vegetables and dairy products—the kind of good, nutritious food most people eat at home." And government nutritionists may soon testify that the four food groups are sugar, salt, animal fat and caffeine. What we have here is a failure to excommunicate.

Green Catalyst

"Criticism is fine, but it can't change a light bulb," says Keith Collins, key mover of Ontario's Green Community Initiative, one of the most successful projects yet developed to tap into the winning combination of job creation, community development and energy savings.

Collins spent years working up a government project that would work with community groups as equals and steer the environment movement from nuts and berries to nuts and bolts, before presenting the GCI package, co-developed with the activist Coalition for a Green Economic Recovery. The first slogan he gave the organization was "Harvest, Not Talkfest." A Rhodes Scholar and distinguished economist, he remains the son of a Nova Scotia farmer. "In the winter, farmers think and talk and talk about what just happened to them, and then they do spring planting, and in the fall they harvest, and have a measure of what they did," he says. "When we talk about environmental changes, we plan for three months, then we critique for three months, then we do another plan, and people wonder if we'll ever get to plant and harvest." He also reasoned that the missing link in popular adoption of environment-friendly technologies and practices was credible information from trusted deliverers. "At $10, low-flow showerheads will pay for themselves in two months, and over their 10-year life span can save homeowners $1,000," he says. "But people need more than a price signal. They need information and access. Advertisers will tell you that price is one of the top five motivators, but there's also brand name recognition, the credibility of alternatives and easy delivery." The Green Community Initiative came out of this search.

Partnership is what makes the venture work. Organizing begins by linking up local service clubs, utilities, environment and resident groups with the green initiative. The government covers half the salaries of trained home assessors to get the community outreach rolling. As a door-opener into the community, the assessors offer free water-efficient showerheads, faucet aerators, hot-water-tank blankets and composters to residents who invite them in for a two-hour house tour. The assessors point out areas where residents are losing money heating the outdoors, and make recommendations of cost-effective renovations that pay back within three years—usually some mixture of caulking, weather-stripping, insulation and high-efficiency furnaces and windows. They also provide a listing of reliable and qualified renovators, clear the way at a local bank that grants automatic approval and discount rates to all loans for green retrofits, and negotiate discounts with local product suppliers. The loan is packaged so that repayment costs less than the savings from the renovation. The banks are keen partners because they look forward to long-term relationships with customers who take charge of their energy bills and responsibility for their environment. Renovators and building supply stores are even keener, as are representatives of products that promote energy efficiency.

Now functioning in 20 Ontario communities, the three-year track record of the Green Community Initiative has been just short of spectacular. Residents have lower energy bills, less draughts and more comfortable rooms. Utilities avoid the heavy costs of installing new supply. Builders are working, doing skillful jobs with tomorrow's technologies. Building supply firms, especially those offering high-quality products, have a new outreach arm. Community networking quickly spreads to other projects, most often buying clubs for local farm produce, schoolyard naturalization and community gardens. The leverage of the government's investment in auditors is hard to beat. A routine home visit leads to $1,500 in loans raised from the private sector to cover renovations. To date, the government's investment of $8 million over three years has netted some $75 million in renovation contracts, which have generated 2,000 new jobs in high-performance contracting, and the manufacture and retailing of home-improvement equipment such as low-flow toilets. The province's return on investment is 400 per cent over three years, just counting increased sales and income tax revenue and reductions in social assistance payouts. Savings on avoided infrastructure came on top of this return. "The savings by the Green Community of Barrie alone, on deferred water and sewage treatment of $55 million, will exceed all government spending on the Green Communities," says GCI network coordinator Clifford Maynes.

Aside from seed financing, the initiative is independent of government regulation. This is a government operation that still makes housecalls. Participation is entirely voluntary, and groups are free to create a range of activities and practices adapted to their area. Some groups train social assistance recipients as assessors, some train environmentalists, some train science and engineering grads. Some groups spend a lot of time on composting, some on agriculture, some on alternative transportation and fuels, whatever the priorities of the particular community. "We offer a menu," says Collins, "but community groups select from and expand on it."

Collins, now a private sector consultant, sees the initiative as a new opportunity for government staffers to act as catalysts. "When the Berlin Wall fell, everyone saw it. But there's a whole lot of crumbling going on," he says. "The old parties, old systems, old ways, are crumbling very fast, and that's in no way restricted to the public sector. There's generational stuff going on here too. Young people feel there's no reason why any established institution should remain intact."

The old notion of public infrastructure was based on pouring concrete and providing one-size-fits-all solutions. "But now infrastructure has to be a lot smarter, more design and less gravel, more interactive with people and less hardware," Collins says. The new infrastructure makes connections. "When I first talked about linking waste, energy and water, it was like I said carpet, firetruck and man from Mars go together," he says. But by offering one-stop shopping, the GCI avoids costly duplication of home visits by several individual agencies. "It's a smarter way to deliver services," he says, "and for residents, it's a way to get customized information that fits with their needs." It's also people-driven. "Our overuse of water and electricity is a result of idiot-proof infrastructure that people use blindly. You can't have a community with idiots. Community takes creative, intelligent, disputing people, so we can't hardware the solution." As Collins sees it, "green communities are one way these pieces are being put back together. This is the kind of government creature we're going to see a lot more of, with results mutating so fast that in 10 years they won't look anything like they do now."

Cooking Up A Storm

Victoria Hogan has a lot on her plate. The Vancouver writer and former president of Canada EarthSave helps people eat their own words about healthy eating. To promote meals that are easy on the heart and planet, she offers a one-day crash course on low-fat vegetarian cooking, "quick and easy, for busy people." No taste is sacrificed when stir fries are sautéed in wine instead of butter, whipped cream is spun from tofu, vanilla and sweetener, or pate is ground from hazelnuts and mushrooms.44 One meal based on her recipes cuts out a ton of resources—just using flax seed oil instead of a pat of butter on bread relieves the heart and avoids contaminating 50 gallons of water, for instance. That's more water than can be saved with efficient appliances or wasting breath on politicians. It just takes knowhow.

Hogan bit off more than she could chew with speaking engagements, so she organized an EarthSave chapter of Toastmasters in Vancouver to train vegans, vegetarians and environmentalists in public speaking. She's also feels a potluck is worth a thousand words. With EarthSave, she fills a community hall with 200 people, once a month, and lets the taste speak for itself. Ideology is checked at the door. "Everyone finds their own way to healthier and more compassionate eating in their own time and comfort level," Hogan says. The way to the new economy's heart lies through the stomach.

Hogan has two favorite sayings. One comes from environmental broadcaster David Suzuki's 1988 interview with then-Senator Al Gore. "What can people do to help politicians like you?" Suzuki asked. "Don't look to people like me, don't look to business leaders," Gore replied. "If you want real change, you sell it to the grass roots. When people understand there is a problem, when they are given solutions and when they begin to demand it, people like me will jump on board without any problem," Gore said. "But it's the people who drive it, not leaders." Hogan also follows a motto given to her by a friend: "If you think you're too small to be effective, you've never been in bed with a mosquito."

What a Wonderful Life!

Principle 10

Replaces planned economies with the spontaneity of "community economies" and creates opportunities to take it easy, but take it

"We ask ourselves, 'Who am I to be brilliant, talented, fabulous?' Actually, who are you not to be? As we let our light shine we give others permission to do the same. As we are liberated from our own fear, our presence liberates others."
Nelson Mandela[1]

"Claiming I have a comprehensive list of principles for an eco-logical city would be like claiming I have discovered a list of principles for a tree."

urban analyst Terry Fowler

Joy, all too scarce in today's economy, will be the lubricant of the new economy, reducing the wasted energy of friction among moving parts. The pundits who tell us success comes from putting our noses to the grindstone just don't get it. The answer is right under our noses. It's in working to share the great moments of life that we'll rediscover our potential. Among the benefits of joy is openness to serendipity, the force that allowed us to evolve out of amoebas and down from the trees, according to Stephen Gould's **What a Wonderful Life.** The serendipity of good deeds saved Jimmy Stewart's life in the classic film rendition of chaos theory. It's helping Montreal succeed in the new economy without really trying.

By rights, Montreal should be declared the North American city least likely to succeed in the new, green, co-operative economy. The growing season is short, the topsoil is thin, and the former centre of market gardening in nearby Laval has been paved over for suburbs. The downtown core is getting sleazy.[2] The old factories that employed inner city workers have shut down. Unions are the most aggressive anywhere. There's chronic tension over Quebec separatism. And English has no official status, though the economy counts on nine million U.S. tourists a year who get lost looking for the Pont bridge, think the French quarter is a weird currency and expect a bellhop at the Hotel de Ville.[3]

But Montreal keeps getting picked as the best big city in the world to live in. It's also the place to watch the new economy come together. What it has going for it is a certain *je ne sais quoi*. Call it *joie de vivre*.

Economics don't mean a thing if it don't have that swing. It's the quality of life, stupid.

"If I were Billy Graham," health and environmental scientist and crusader René Dubos once said, "I would preach to people that the best way to save their souls is to save the environment of cities like New York." The statement can be understood on many levels. It can be felt during a walk along the Dubos Point Wetland Park, the wildlife refuge he saved from the expansion of Kennedy International Airport in the 1970s. It can be sensed by gazing at and tasting what Dubos described as "starless skies, treeless avenues, shapeless buildings, tasteless bread, joyless celebrations," the losses a society suffers when it forgets that "we do not live on the planet earth but *with* the life it harbors and *within* the environment that life creates."[4] It can be taken as a challenge to find meaning and spirituality in the commonplace that people have created together. It can also be acted on as an opportunity for economic renewal.

From the good-to-see-you kiss on both sides of the face to the cafés that are hopping all night, this is a city where people embrace life and celebrate their place in it. *On est bien ici*, they say, life is good here. That's why there are few poor areas in Montreal, though there are many areas where people have too little money. The Pointe St. Charles district has rarely known good times in 150 years, but it is the birthplace of hockey, of community legal clinics, and of community health clinics. It's celebrated in playwright David Fennario's **Balconville** for the way people hang out of balconies, yards and doorsteps to yak, yell and help out. Old working-class row housing is caught up in gentrification from below, as co-ops renovate and name themselves Co-op of Hope, Co-op of Stars.

Collective life is celebrated in world-famous jazz and comedy festivals that stretch through the muggy days of summer, drawing 200,000 people a night into the downtown, a 50-mile bike tour of the island that draws 45,000 people each spring, national holiday demonstrations that draw 400,000 in the early summer, and a televised New Year's Eve celebration of local talent that is watched by everyone. Where people cherish the city, see it as a place to play as well as work, see it as a habitat, an ecosystem as beautiful and dynamic as any wilderness, as effective in bringing out what is good in people as solitude, the new economy has a fighting chance. A city where everyone minds their own business does not have a buoyant service sector. There can't be new economic players if noone is playing.

Montreal is widely misunderstood as a European city, the Paris of North America. It is, in fact, the most North American of cities, with roots that go back to the 1600s. That is one of its secrets. It took its form in the age of the foot and canoe, not the car. Housing development was intense. The city of 1,000 steeples is based on parishes, where churches, parks and shopping were within walking distance, where religious, commercial and social life intermixed. Front lawns are few, but there are pocket parks and squares for resting and people-watching. City governments are under constant pressure to give neighborhoods direct control over budgets that affect them. Mayor Pierre Bourque, elected on a platform that partially turned on city beautification, makes grants of $50,000 available to neighborhood groups that carry out planting and related schemes. The attachment to non-motorized transportation is reflected in the popularity of bikes, despite steep hills and cold winter temperatures. The ranks of feet firsters now include 230,000 bladers, the outlaw voyageurs of a new transit system. The texture of city buildings comes from locally quarried stone, and adds to that juxtaposition of chaos and order that urbanist David Engwicht has defined as the essence of city beauty.

To give credit where credit is due, the city owes much to bad luck. The downtown moved uptown from the port in the 1800s, as commerce moved to center around the railroad rather than canoe docks. The St. Lawrence Seaway of the 1950s let ships bypass Montreal. Thus, the historic core was saved from urban renewal, and remains a working harbor, worked by buskers and renters of sidewalk book and print stalls. There are throngs of visitors every night to fill restaurants, cafés and shops. A mountain in the middle of the city stood in the way of rational street engineering, so prime downtown space had to be wasted on parkland, and homes had to be built one at a time to fit the contours of the land. That's where the well-to-do still live, preserving the city as a place for all walks of life. Thanks to corruption, the wave of progressive reform that swept through most of North America at the turn of the century never got much of a foothold in Montreal. So modern city planning, Puritanism wedded to scientific management, has had less impact. There are cafés and variety stores, called depanneurs, in the middle of residential streets. And there is no stigma against loitering, hanging out. Thus there are many mile-long stretches where people do nothing better than waste their evenings eating, walking and talking. Fast food does not sell well when dinner takes all evening.

With more than its share of hard luck, Montreal has also been blessed with derelict land that planners and developers haven't been able to clean up and ruin. There are miles of untamed land along railway tracks that provide habitat for bikers, joggers and food foragers. "Heard about multi-tasking environments?" asks city columnist Barry Lazar, describing one stretch where food pickers come for wild grape leaves, milkweed shoots and dandelion leaves in spring, wild flowers in summer, grapes in September, vine boughs for the Jewish festival of Succoth in late fall and Christmas festivals at the depths of the winter solstice.[5] And untamed land in the city centre keeps getting turned from an eyesore into a social oasis. Sculptor Gilles Bissonet turned one derelict lot into a stage for his art and a speakers' corner. That way, he says, "people will really understand what a vacant lot represents."[6]

Like most of urban North America, Montreal is a city of immigrants. Bioregional food—other than poutine, a combination of french fries, cheese and gravy that is either loved or hated—includes the Montreal bagel, the best in the world according to the **Washington Post**, and Montreal smoked meat. Both come from a Jewish community that has produced Leonard Cohen, Mordecai Richler of **Duddy Kravitz** fame, and Irving Layton, and which sustains one of the few Yiddish theatres on the continent. Jackie Robinson, the first Black ball player allowed to play major league ball, got his start in Montreal. Oscar Peterson perfected jazz piano in working class St. Henri, before leading the first integrated jazz band through the U.S. deep south before the civil rights era. French-speaking Haitians, Africans and Vietnamese have settled in more recently, and non-whites account for 18 per cent of the population. As long as there are immigrants in a downtown core, it will be maintained and vibrant with people who live on hope. If only because immigrants must make a virtue of necessity, they find their way up through, not out of, their neighborhoods and roots. Community gardens that dot city parks have fed immigrant families for generations. Whatever blocks the homogenization and dependency of mass markets cannot help but benefit the new economy.

Montreal is a mainly French island in the English sea of North America, an island with few natural resources of its own. They must support their own, *nous autres*, which they do, sustaining a film, music and literary industry said to be impossible among five million people in an era of globalization. And they must work things out. The unions are intent on giving up none of the gains they won in the aftermath of a 1972 general strike, the biggest ever on the continent, carried under slogans such as "rely only on ourselves," and "the state: agent of our exploiters." Employers talk tough. But they know that one set of unions controls a Solidarity investment fund with $800 million available for local firms that offer workers some say in decisions. They know that credit unions control $40 billion, which they do not hesitate to use to bolster the local economy against takeovers or shutdowns. And since the late-1980s, unions, community organizations and businesses have been meeting in what are called "concertations" to iron things out. "These were places where the things people had in common were brought to the fore," says Henry Milner, who launched the journal, **Inroads**, to spread the good news about dialogue to Anglo-America. As many as 1,500 people have met in single sessions of public hearings to thrash out an economic future over the past decade. It may lead to what one Catholic magazine, **Relations**, calls a "communitarian state," where unions, co-ops, public investment funds, governments and private employers knock heads until they come to an agreement on the way forward.

One little project comes out of Concordia University's Institute in Management and Community Development. It trains people in low-income neighborhoods to start their own community businesses, sets up revolving loan funds to lend them start-up funds, and has access to government grants to buy up community land before speculators get to it. "We're not here to assess a community's needs simply so it can manage its poverty better," says director Lance Evoy. "We want to transform the barriers that keep people in poverty."

Montrealers are a people who have not forgotten how to sing together. Their favorite song is Gilles Vigneault's *Gens du pays*, people of the country, an unofficial nationalist anthem that is sung at all celebrations, including birthday parties. "It's your turn," the chorus goes, "to let yourselves talk of love." The new economy will be second nature here.

"The three L's, learning, loving and laughter, bid us reclaim our birthright from the shadow of consumerism."
Writer Mike Nickerson7

In the new economy, we may have trouble finding where the rubber hits the road. When we get into serious restructuring and re-engineering, roads will be about improving access and strengthening community, not increasing traffic mobility. When people, not tires, hit the road, local businesses will take off. The word on the street, says traffic expert Tom Samuels, is that neighbors and local companies will revive on their own when they figure out their places in the world.

Tom Samuels trained as an accountant and landscape designer before he figured out that bean counters and planners couldn't solve city traffic problems. "I'm a Virgo, and I like neatness and order," admits Samuels, the leading advocate of "living streets" in North America, "but I'm getting over it." He's gaining a hearing from safety experts, fitness buffs, mainstreet enthusiasts, neo-traditional architects, downtown business associations and roads department officials across the continent. But the new kid on the block of traffic planning looks to the street smarts of residents' groups for this new vision of city life. He hopes Not In My Front Yard will do to traffic dumping in the 1990s what Not In My Back Yard did to garbage dumping in the 1980s.

The $100-billion-a-year, going-nowhere-fast sinus headache known as traffic jams is mainly about bad trips, the accountant in Samuels says. About three-quarters of all car trips are "discretionary," he reckons, short errands of less than two miles, mostly for shopping. Even in rush hour, as many as 60 per cent of the cars are crawling to a non-work destination. This is why no one has been able to build a solution to the car overpopulation crisis, least of all the "predict and provide" school of traffic engineers, who've blown hundreds of millions of dollars in the effort. Adding more traffic lanes adds more dri-vers. Adding more High Occupancy Vehicle lanes adds more cars. Adding more buses adds more debt to transit authorities. This is what traffic engineers working with a mindset from water hydraulics don't get. Traffic does not flow like water, bursting through barriers if there is not enough space. Traffic is like bureaucracy. It expands to fit the space available. That's what accounts for the highway planning mys-tery known as "the case of the missing traffic." When lanes or entire roads are taken out of service, traffic jams don't get worse. Less peo-ple take their car. They find another way to do what they need to do. Drivers obey the law of supply and demand. This pattern has been confirmed so many times that Samuels and the Ontario-wide Better Transportation Coalition he worked for have drawn a line on the pavement. No more roads, they say.

Now traffic policy starts to get interesting, especially since Samuels isn't anti-car. Samuels is more pro-street. He favors streets that bring shops to the people, so they don't have to drive to shops and lose the wealth of human exchange in the process. That means seeing streets as conduits of neighborhood life, and through traffic as extensions of the front porch and not the garage. In the process of putting the planning shoe on the other foot, cars are integrated into street life as guests, but the affirmative action is for pedestrians so drivers are no longer kings of the road. That's the only way to get to the sunny side of the street, Samuels says.

Most of Samuels' work is with residents' groups, upset that their tran-quillity is lost to a stream of traffic and that their kids' safety is at risk—one child in 10 is struck by a car before reaching the age of majority. The residents usually start out with standard roadblock gim-micks. They prohibit turns onto the street during rush hour. They add some extra stop signs and speed bumps to discourage dragsters. These deterrents don't do much because they don't bring people onto the street, and people are the best traffic barriers yet invented. Then Samuels pulls out his bag of traffic-calming tricks. They're designed to take the high road with drivers, to invite them, not ban them, but to play with the rules of the road that now marginalize residents to the sidewalks.

Here are some of his common proposals for re-inventing the street.

1.   Play with car drivers' head space. Perception isn't reality. If roads are wide, lanes are wide, vision is clear, drivers think it's safe to speed. That's why police set speed traps on wide and bare roads when they need to meet their ticket quotas. But if roads are narrow, lanes are a tight fit, the view to the side is busy—perhaps because cars are parked diagonally, instead of parallel to the curb—drivers slow down of their own accord. Hold a pavement mural party and complete the visual overload.

2.   Throw drivers a few curves so they stay alert. If there's no natural bend in the road, take a chip off the old block. Switch street parking from one side to the other halfway down the street. Install a pinch point or choker, perhaps a potted tree by the curb. Put a park bench or a permanent chess board behind it. Anything to modify homogeneity and provide openings for other users.

3.   Build ramped speed tables at intersections, raising the road to sidewalk level and driving home the point that pedestrian comfort and safety come first. Put basketball hoops over the stop signs. Paint hopscotch lines on the table, or whatever it takes to get people to put their feet up on the table.

The same hijinks work with neighborhood business districts. Conventional ignorance holds that main street businesses have to compete with malls by becoming more car-friendly. So they think they have to offer lots of free parking and introduce one-way speedways for extra driver convenience. They think they need big stores with big signage to attract interest from passers by. But check out the insides of malls first, Samuels advises. Once people have driven there, the malls feature a pedestrian environment, traffic calming at its best. They know they'll catch more customers with the slow touch, so they make it inviting to slow down. There are places to sit and gawk. "People want a pedestrian scale, an environment that recognizes them as human beings," Samuels says. This is where main streets have it over sterile malls. They have more nooks and crannies, more points of interest. The object is to slow traffic, not speed it up, draw people out of their cars if they want to be part of the action.

Hire models to stand in the middle of the sidewalk if that's necessary. Get away from the highway idea. Highways are the neutron bombs of main streets. They leave the buildings standing, but remove all the people.

Aside from neighborhood groups, Chicago has shown the most interest in Samuels' approach. It's suffering badly from suburban sprawl. Since 1970, the city's population has increased by only four per cent, but the amount of land taken up by housing has increased 40 per cent and the land taken up by commercial space by 74 per cent. Meanwhile, there are 2,000 vacant commercial-industrial buildings in the downtown. This is jobless growth. In the inner city, problems came to a head with the summer heat wave of 1995, when more than 400 people died. Mayor Richard Daley has a handle on the dimensions of the problem. He knows about the "heat island effect," the fact that black asphalt intensifies and stores sweltering heat. He senses that seniors who had neighbors check in on them weathered the heat better than home-alones, and that for neighbors to check in, there have to be neighborhoods. The city is also looking for ways to revitalize downtown neighborhoods, and to make the old streetcar suburbs appealing to middle income groups willing to give the city another try. Traffic calming looks like a way to accommodate all interests. "What Chicago has going for it," says Samuels, "is history and culture. It can't hit bottom because it has that to draw on." The city of broad shoulders has been home to generations of community organizers, from Jane Addams of Hull House fame at the turn of the century, to Saul Alinsky of **Rules For Radicals** mid-century infamy, to today's apostle of from-below organizing, John McKnight.

And this is what living streets need, says Samuels, a culture that can bring people out of their cars, not his bag of tricks for keeping cars off the road. City building, says the original theorist of traffic calming David Engwicht, now an advocate of people-calming, is about turning space into place by creating close encounters of a different kind. The tragedy of our modern cities, he writes in **Reclaiming Our Cities and Towns: Better Living with Less Traffic**, is that "we have turned places into destinations, or converted them into traffic corridors. We have forgotten that transportation can be more than a means of getting to a place—it can be an experience of place in itself." That puts politics in its place too, gets it more into hand-shaking, less into earth-shaking. John Barber, one of Canada's leading urban commentators, has followed Samuels' career closely, and thinks it speaks to the new politics of the 1990s. Forget about deficits, he says. "The important issues of the nineties—the ones you have power to influence—are different. They concern such weighty matters as where to buy milk, and how you get there." After Samuels led a successful campaign to block a highway widening in a prototypical suburb called Etobicoke, Barber wrote: "You start by wondering how your children will ever get to school if they have to walk across a roaring six-lane highway. You end up changing the world."

"What excites me," says Samuels, "is the way this empowers ordinary people, gives people belief in themselves instead of giving that up to experts who 'know,' and who will solve our problems for us." The new road map is about saving bags of money on useless highway expansions, saving scads of time in traffic jams, and saving the world from global warming. But it goes beyond the agenda of environmental protection, and opens a future of living with the environment, including the wonders of human habitat. "It's not just about getting back to Mother Nature," Samuels says. "It's getting back to human nature, and our need for street life and neighborhoods, which we've forgotten."

"The trouble with knowledge is that it is so much more difficult to manage than capital: fixed in the heads of pesky employees, rather than stored in the bank, and infuriatingly volatile and short-lived to boot."

The Economist[8]

Getting to the new economy is half the fun. The entertainment industry won't be hived off from other productive enterprises in an economy that weaves art and sociability back into the fabric of the workaday world. Here are some trends that speak to the core economic virtues of the new economy—creativity and zest for life—which can also put reduce, reuse and recycle in their proper place in the environmental hierarchy, quite a bit below party hearty.

Carpet Beaters

Designers' Walk is where the top interior decorators in Toronto hang out to see what's new. Ed Lowans, president of the Environmental Health Association of Canada, comes here to meet with building consultant Brian Greenberg and textile artist Joan Kritz, a typical new economy merger of health, cost-effectiveness and design.

Like most health experts, Lowans, himself sensitive to a score of allergens, turns up his nose at thick wall-to-wall carpets. Mites, dust, fungi and mold hide out there, millions of microorganisms per square foot, snug as a bug in a rug, until washed with toxic biocides. "House dust smog," as home health expert Dr. Alfred Zamm calls it, can't be vacuumed up or swept under the carpet.[9] Under the carpet is reserved for toxic or allergenic adhesives and matting, which off-gas into the air, mostly when first installed. In a conventional sealed building, the toxins join the micro-organisms in the heating system, and then circulate through the building. There's a reason why the air is thick enough to cut in many offices, and why most hospitals insist on hard floors. In 1993, the American Institute of Medicine fingered carpets as the biggest culprits in indoor air pollution. They may be responsible for the doubling of asthma rates since 1990.[10] Nice and soft for baby, Lowans sneezes. It's a good thing for manufacturers that carpets are just regulated for flammability, not toxicity of smoke. Building codes are so out of touch, Lowans says, "it's as if they specify the color of the car and think that means it's safe."

Like most designers, Joan Kritz likes the subtle textures and high resolution colors of woven fabrics, rather than tufted plastic. She has to spend some time deprogramming clients. "Most people don't know that nylon is plastic," she says. "If I said 40-ounce plastic was a luxury, would you believe me?" Most of her customers are people who put the savings from not buying quantity of wall-to-wall for the quality of something that stands apart. Kritz' work is showcased in one of Toronto's downtown five-star office complexes, which needed a face-lift to take on competition from a new state-of-the-art building. Thousands of feet per day tramp over her art, the sound of their scuffles and the glare of light muffled by a multi-colored carpet made of natural materials. The colors hide the dirt, the material washes easily, and the complex has kept its five-star rating.

Like most building consultants who advise managers of office towers and malls, Brian Greenberg has a sharp eye for lifetime costs, as well as the mood-setting and other functions of flooring. Well-heeled is for the punishment flooring has to take, not the prices managers will pay. But with conventional rugs, building managers are taking more and more punishment. They have high maintenance costs for cleaning. They have high dumping costs every eight years when the carpets give out. The cost of dumping can only rise when someone in the building regulations department finally gets around to telling someone in the sanitation department that old carpets belong in toxic waste sites. And, Greenberg says, building owners are starting to get stuck with some of the health costs of carpeting that has three toxic lives. There are heavy off-gases for three months after installation. Then the mites and dust settle in. Then come the off-gases from cleaning biocides. Any time a worker is off on compensation or disability because of problems related to carpets, building tenants get angry. If some of the indoor air pollution cases now making their way through the courts set a precedent, cheap rugs will be a financial disaster.

Greenberg is not anti-carpet. Carpets provide traction for seniors and they absorb glare and noise. But smart operators are looking at advance-design materials, where the money goes to skilled labour and design, not adhesives and solvents. Sisal rugs with jute or hemp backing can be composted, rather than landfilled. Tiles can be made from cheap, low-energy materials such as crushed, colored glass available from recyclers for next-to-nothing, crushed ceramic from recycled toilets and recycled cardboard. A new composite made from soybeans and recycled newsprint is a dead ringer for granite. Linoleum is making a healthy high-art comeback as Marmoleum and Artoleum, made from linseed oil, natural resins, wood flour and jute backing, now available in 130 colors and any number of computer-generated patterns from the Forbo Group in Toronto.[11] All easy to clean, durable and fashion-conscious. It's the concept, not the material that's a challenge, says Greenberg. Super-graphics, what used to be called quilts, can be made from ends and pieces. "One of the great things about the 20th century is that we've been able to make things available to ordinary people that were once only for the elite," says Greenberg, a capitalist's capitalist. "I believe in the socialism of design. If it's designed properly, it can be universal and affordable."

Fashion Plates

Eating is believing, and organic farmers are lucky to have the most acclaimed chefs in the world eager to take their products. One of the few instances where leaders of a profession are spurring on the new economy, demanding chefs provide a quality-conscious, less price-sensitive market for organic growers, and a chance to explore a co-learning relationship.

Credit for launching "cuisine naturelle" probably belongs with Anton Mossiman, the former chef to Britain's royal family, who was booed when he gave a 1985 speech on the need to pay more attention to where food came from.[12] In Hawaii, top cooks formed the Chefs Collaborative 2000 to promote healthy eating, respect for cultural diversity in cooking, and to use their buying power to educate farmers to their needs.[13] The organization was hailed by Columbia University nutrition professor Joan Dye Gussow. A group with prestige and power "has finally come forward to be guardians of the food supply," she said.[14] The Culinary Institute of America trains future chefs to source as much local and organic produce as possible, and to divert kitchen scraps to the compost heaps of nearby farms.[15]

Food for thought and a feast for the eyes is featured in the annual Feast of Fields in Toronto, a tournament of the province's best chefs, growers and brewers. Smoked trout sesame blinis with fresh horseradish and green apple compote vie with woodland risotto, topped off by wild peach and black raspberry in maple-almond tartellettes, or another jaw-teaser, brandy-macerated sour cherries in hot maple taffy on almond cookies. And it's even politically correct.[16]

The teamwork between chefs and growers wins by a country smile. Restaurateur-turned-grower David Cohlmeyer supplies Toronto's most discriminating chefs with red Russian and purple Peruvian potatoes, red, white and even orange carrots, and winter kohlrabi and Dahlba root, to keep customers coming back. He has a newsletter, **Cookstown Greens**, to remind chefs that his organic vegetables "contain more essential oils (to reduce the need for fat), more minerals (to reduce the need for salt), and more dissolved solids (to reduce the need for sugar)."[17] In British Columbia, Herb Barbolet has the leading hotels hooked to his Celebrity Salad, with 30 different ingredients, including three kinds of kale, two kinds of mustard, chickweed, petals and the odd piece of lettuce. In his garden, he works to achieve "cut and come again" continuous cropping, picking pea tendrils for garnish while waiting for the pea, for example. By reducing the chefs' waste and labor time, and by sharing cooking tips others follow, he's won a loyal customer base. Barbolet is also founder of Farm Folk/City Folk which promotes better town and country understanding. "Eating food is an agricultural act, and we all eat for a living," he says.[18]

The post-harvest season poses a few extra challenges, but the Grisold Inn in the northeast has a winter menu featuring "Connecticut Bounty," including squash soups and roasted root vegetables.[19]

Reclaiming Heritage

Guerrilla growers with the Cariboo Community Enhancement and Economic Development Society in interior British Columbia have their hands on some hot potatoes. Potato heads in Agriculture Canada have delisted the local Cariboo potato because it doesn't take to mechanical harvesting.[20] That's its only sin, but it now has to be sold through the potato underground.

The industrialized food system craves uniformity, the key ingredient in high volume processing, packaging and marketing. This unnatural process of corporate selection of the fittest has got to the point where about 90 per cent of what we eat today comes from 20 plants. Prior to European settlement, Iroquois farmers tilled 20 varieties of beans and 16 of corn. Now, two varieties of peas and beans dominate the North American market. Early European settlers often had two dozen vegetables in their salads. Now we call lettuce and tomato a salad. Since 1900, 86 per cent of apple varieties and 2,300 pear varieties have vanished. Since 1984, a blitz of takeovers, mergers and bank-ruptcies in the mail order seed industry has resulted in a 23 per cent decline in the number of firms, and close to a 50 per cent decline in the availability of non-hybrid vegetable varieties.[21] Consumer choice is dwindling rapidly, and 57 varieties now refers to additives not veg-etables. Even more worrisome, the gene bank so necessary for diversi-ty and adaptability in the face of disease is being rifled.

Putting all eggs in one basket is good for petrochemical companies. They patent and create hybrid seeds, gaining ownership rights they could never get over seeds in the public domain. Their seeds sell for several times the price of traditional, open-pollinated varieties. Hybrid seeds, often genetically screened for ease of transport and packaging, are also drug addicts, coated with pesticides long before they go into the soil and requiring a constant supply of pesticides and fertilizers. Produce is then hauled an average of 1,300 miles per item. The companies win coming and going in this vicious circle of petro-chemical dependency.

To restore farm independence, groups across North America are working to preserve heritage seeds. In the U.S., backyard guerrillas are organized under the Seed Savers Exchange, in Canada under the Heritage Seed Foundation. Private groups such as the Joywood Farm

Rare Breeds Conservancy in southern Ontario preserve livestock at risk of extinction because they don't respond well to the crowded indoor conditions of factory farms. Woodwinds Nursery sells over a hundred varieties of apple and pear trees from its Ontario farm, including several hardy species that can survive in cool climates. A $20-billion-a-year market in specialty foods across North America serves the natural craving for variety as the spice of life, a craving that could eat away at the agribusiness agenda. For farmers, this diversity offers a chance to get away from the intense price competition of standard issue goods, and link to alternative retailers who can turn their small size to advantage in an age of discriminating customers.

The struggle against corporate genetic uniformity is most marked in India, where almost a million farmers have demonstrated against multinational seed companies that are buying up the many varieties of rice seeds once hosted there (there were once 30,000 varieties grown), and replacing them with 10 hybrids.[22] Vandana Shiva, author of **Monoculture of the Minds**, has made traditional seeds a symbol of hope and resistance, akin to the hand loom used by Indian liberator Mahatma Gandhi 50 years ago. A simple seed that can be held in the palm of a hand "embodies diversity," she says, and "the freedom to stay alive. Seed freedom goes far beyond freedom of the farmer from corporations. It indicates freedom of diverse cultures from centralized control."

Flower Power

It's insulting to flowers when people like them only for their good looks. Many qualify as edible landscape. Flowers sprinkled on salads and soups or frozen in cubes smell good, taste good, and are even good for you. Chrysanthemums, squash flowers and day lilies add color and zest to salads. Nasturtiums give salads a peppery taste, radish without the bite, while pansies taste like lettuce. Marigold petals are great in soups, cheese dips and ice cubes. Violets and pansies make good jelly. Rose petals blossom on fruit salads and ice cream, and can be boiled with honey and lemon juice to make rose petal syrup. Lavender and apple blossoms are yummy in cakes.23 Anyone with a green thumb, small acreage and a kitchen can go into the food decorating industry. This bud's for you.

Logging Off

The shutdown of a logging town is not a pretty picture. Chemainus, B.C., was threatened with ghost town status until it got into murals, and became the first community in the world to use an outdoor art gallery as the linchpin for economic survival. Mainstreet walls were turned into a blaze of larger than life paintings of the larger than life days of pioneer logging. The town is now a standard bus stop for tours going up the coast, and attracts $27 million a year in tourism revenues, mainly from sales of high quality local crafts. British Airways gave the town an award for tourism innovation.24

Au Naturel

Infrastructure for "the wonder years" means the intimacy of magic forests, bravery on the high seas of mud puddles, leaping over boulders and escaping to secret hideaways. Naturalized parks offer kids rooms of their own where they can discover the outside world without losing their sense of inner-directedness, and explore fantasies of their own making without getting hooked on the gateway commercial drugs of Mario and Mickey Mouse. Kids' craving for places to let their minds go wild can't be satisfied by formal playpens in recreational complexes, claim Gary Nabham and Stephen Trimble in **The Geography Of Childhood: Why Children Need Wild Places,** one of the best child-rearing books ever. Since play is the child's way of communicating, their need for a wild-habitat play partner deserves constitutional protection on par with adult free speech, they suggest.

It's child's play to accommodate them. Lay off the herbicides and grass mowers, let fallen logs lie, put the savings into some stumps, boulders, bushes and ponds. Parks departments may also want to sponsor the Woodcraft movement, precursor to the cubs and scouts, now going through a revival. Ernest Thompson Seton, the author of world famous nature stories, including the **Bambi** story, founded

Woodcraft and gave it the motto "fun not bought with money."
He believed Woodcraft taught kids that life should be "drunk while
it's fizzin."'25

This does not appear to be the thinking of those who design school
playgrounds and free space, most of which look like prison exercize
yards. For a remarkably low cost, naturalized school grounds provide
an outdoors classroom where students can do field trips for biology
and zoology. The Evergreen Foundation has published **Welcoming
Back the Wilderness: A Guide to School Ground Naturalization**,
based on experiences in more than 575 Canadian schools. A Montreal experiment has already shown many benefits. Putting sand in
equipment areas reduced the harm from inevitable falls. Vandalism
has been reduced, as kids take more control and responsibility.
Learning opportunities have multiplied. Kids have gained confidence that they can nurture a new and better world.26

Big people can also benefit from naturalization. A suburban train
station in Burlington, Ontario, hired restoration architects to spiff up
a parking lot for 712 cars. The lot features trees, shrubs and wildflowers that shield cars and drivers from direct sun and wind, and which
clean the air from a nearby dump. Ponds and catch basins save on
costs of sewage drainage, and provide moisture for bulrushes and
ornamental grasses.27 Naturalization fits with designing parks with
women's needs in mind, says planner Reggi Modlich, founder of
Women Plan Toronto. Parents and child-care workers, mostly
women, enjoy pleasant "passive open space" for sitting, chatting and
connecting while their kids are in the playground. As it happens,
that's also ideal habitat for butterflies. Park design around nature's
call also takes into account the fact that pregnant and elderly women
need ready access to safe and clean washrooms, Modlich says.

Free Range Kids

It's a shame that youth has to be wasted on the young, Mark Twain
used to say of a generation that whiled away its time playing outdoors. But, to speak plainly, a lot of parents, educators and planners
should be hanging their heads in shame at the way youth is being
wasted today.

Parents keep their kids inside, doing safe things like watching TV violence, because they're afraid of the perverts that lurk outside. The most dangerous perverts, statistically speaking, are car drivers. They kill about 500 kids a year in Canada, and 3,400 in the U.S., most within half a mile of home. They injure many more. The government's response? Elmer the Safety Elephant, and research budgets that spend 10 times more on cancer and six times more on heart disease than is spent on researching readily preventable child deaths.28 U.S. state governments spend less than one per cent of their health budgets on accident prevention. Something is being protected here, but it's not kids.

It's so easy to reduce the child death toll. We could reduce speed limits on residential streets to 20 miles an hour, a rate that lets 95 per cent of car accident victims survive, albeit with serious injuries. At 30 miles an hour, half of accident victims live, and at 40 miles, less than 10 per cent survive. But then, speed limits would be controlling drivers, not kids.

Tom Samuels is working on two projects that make streets safe for kids. As a stopgap measure, he helps organize "human buses." This is an ever-so-complex, high-tech and costly initiative. Volunteer parents take turns picking up kids on school routes and they all form a walking bus. For the long term, he tries to organize Safe Routes To School, based on the success of an experiment in Odense, Denmark which reduced traffic accidents by 85 per cent. The idea is to involve kids, parents and teachers in mapping out key routes kids take. Those streets and areas are calmed. Speed limits are set low. Foot prints are painted along the road to remind drivers why they are going slow. In case they miss the subtle hint, there are speed bumps and speed tables to shake a little sense into them. But then, this puts the onus of responsibility for safety on parents, schools and local governments, not kids, so it may not be acceptable.

Safe Routes To School measures are probably the best health and educational reforms a local government can enact. It's well known that kids today are 40 per cent less active than they were 30 years ago. Overweight among kids aged six to 11 has increased 50 per cent over the last 15 years. Forty per cent of children have at least one risk factor for heart disease. If parents want to keep their kids off the gateway drugs, they should shut off the TV, spend some of that quality time they keep talking about, and start throwing their weight around on the street. Streets are for hockey, baseball, basketball, hopscotch and street parties. Cars are just the invited guests who never left, and it's time to call them on it.

Turning streets into romper rooms is even good for grades. A six-year study in Trois Rivières, Quebec, showed that kids who exercised regularly had improved concentration, memory, creativity and problem-solving skills.[29] Play is how kids glom onto "generalized learning strategies," say Drs. Marcel Bouffard and Sandy Romanow at the University of Alberta in Edmonton. "Kids who play games involving a ball or a puck, or who engage in movements such as those required in gymnastics or playing on monkey bars in the park, are actually learning indirectly about movement, direction, distance, angles, force, velocity, acceleration and torque," says Romanow. That's all germane to physics, math and graphic design.[30] "For the child, work is play," says Samuels. "All we are doing is protecting their workplace on the street."

Diamonds In The Rough

School dropouts can't get no respect in today's society. But a training center operated by the Energy Conservation Society of Ontario gets it and gives it while upgrading what are called "severely marginalized youth"—most with histories of chronic abuse, addiction, crime and unemployment, and few with more than public school education—for work in energy-efficiency construction and renovation. "Our job is to find the jewel in the rough and polish it," says ECSO director Glenn McKnight. "It's not a boot camp here, but it's not warm and cuddly either," he says. "We teach that there are no rights without responsibilities, and there's no use seeing yourself as a victim if you suffer from your own nihilism."

Students get a top-up on welfare to attend, less than the cost of halfway houses, but a financial incentive to good attendance. The 26-week course begins with six weeks of problem-solving and life skills, including sessions on buying and cooking nutritious foods. Each student has a buddy and a mentor, usually a retiree from the

construction trades. By the time formal instruction begins, discipline
has evolved from cowboy anarchism to self-regulation, with a code so
strict that the school has not lost one item from its open tool shelf in
its two-year history.

Formal education is surprisingly high-tech. Interactive video and
multi-media slide presentations on computer let students set their
own pace at mastering healthy home construction methods. "This
is an age group raised on TV and video games," says instructor John
Sneyd, who helped design the learning modules. "They like stuff
that's quick, flashing, moving." A student peers up to tell an onlooker
that "the house is a whole system, not just windows and doors," then
adds "You have to know what you're talking about, and know how
to explain it to a customer. You can't just use street talk like a lot
of guys."

In week 20, students are sent to work as volunteers, renovating
women's shelters or building from salvage with Habitat for Humanity,
which helps disadvantaged people build their own homes. "The students see the value of giving back to society," McKnight says. Sneyd
says the environmental angle helps get the lessons across. "If we're
going to teach them to be responsible, we have to show them they
have a future in an industry that's responsible about waste and energy," he says. "They're going to turn an industry with a bad reputation
into one with a good reputation."

To date, the school has placed all its graduates in jobs. Dennis Wilks,
who came to the program an illiterate, has published a pamphlet
Struggle for Success, and is working on a full-length book about the
pain of growing up in families separated by immigration. "If you have
a downfall, you must rise again or fall deeper," he says.

Yankee Come Home

The Yankees are making a comeback. Believe it or not, Yankee
was once a compliment. It meant hard-working, thrifty, self-reliant,
inventive, righteous, neighborly, the qualities that distinguished
fierce democrats with a sense of the New England common wealth
from British aristocrats and genteel southern slave-drivers. It may be
that the stars of the emerging economy, companies such as Tom's of

Maine, Ben and Jerry's, and Green Mountain Coffee, owe some of their success to the continuing vitality of these core values in New England, which was largely bypassed by the second and third stages of industrialism. Lacking coal, New England missed out on heavy industry. Lacking major population centers to the north, south and east, it missed out on mass distribution. Intuitions are therefore more attuned to the new model of entrepreneurship.

Some take delight in finding fault with the new companies. A cone of Ben and Jerry's is an efficient way to consume a weekly load of animal fat and sugar in one sitting, and there's no flavor that features the taste of real sprouts. The natural plant flavors replacing saccharin in Tom's toothpaste don't come from organic farms, and the packaging on the deodorant is a problem. Coffee from reasonably paid plantation workers still doesn't qualify as a bioregional drink.

Such criticisms miss the point. There is no economic equivalent to the virgin birth. If we have to measure new companies against perfection, let's not bother starting.[31] Vermont Businesses For Social Responsibility tries to build lobbying clout for the new economy, but admits its members are "neither granola-flakes nor money grubbers" and "neither perfect angels nor ethics police."[32] The learning curve of the new economy is steep, and no-one gets to start at the top. These companies have climbed far enough to confirm some secrets of success. The record shows that companies with less than $15,000 in start-up capital can make their mark on the big time inside of 10 years. The results show that this can be done with humor and humanity, and without a subsidy or a huge advertising or marketing budget. Pillsbury found out the hard way in the 1980s when it tried to escalate the cold war in the premium ice cream market by leaning on retailers, suggesting they carry all Pillsbury or no Pillsbury. "What's the dough boy afraid of?" Ben and Jerry fired back on a bumper sticker distributed to supporters. "The American Dream?" Pillsbury backed off. The upstarts confirm the presence of a significant customer base for premium products with values-added. The new companies are conscientious about sourcing their products, going to great lengths to find quality suppliers based in self-help and co-op organizations. They give their staff a fair shake. They donate significant amounts to community groups and causes.

They've been rewarded by "share of mind," loyal customers who want values for their money. In the words of Michael Treacy and Fred Wiersema's business advice book **The Discipline of Market Leaders**, these companies "choose their customers," though not in the same way as Treacy and Wiersema's consultancy did, according to one report, by buying up 10,000 copies of their own book to get it listed as a bestseller.[33] "Relationship marketing," as it's called, creates an interaction that makes space for entrepreneurs who are true to themselves, who are committed to what Tom Chappell calls an "upside-down vision of capitalism" or "common good capitalism," and what Ben Cohen calls interconnectedness. "Like individuals, businesses can conduct themselves with the knowledge that the hearts, souls and spirits of all people are connected," he wrote to shareholders in 1992, "so that as we help others, we cannot help helping ourselves."[34]

What these companies have going for them is context. Vermont, home base for Ben and Jerry's and Green Mountain, raises its citizens in a tradition of town hall democracy that respects natural places and human eccentricities, the mother of more inventions than necessity. It's where Murray Bookchin, the sometimes cranky but always pushing founder of social ecology, learned to marry social to ecology. The Maine seashore is where Rachel Carson was inspired to write her classic books on the environment, where the Colony Hotel took the lead in environmentally responsible tourism management, and where towns like Kennebunkport build their charm and reputation as a meeting place of ocean beach and pre-auto streetscapes. Working to preserve this charm from an invasion of tourist cars is Barbara Cook, who started the Seabird Shuttle Service in 1995. Stopping for anyone who flags them down, the 17-seat mini-buses give tourists the run of the town and beach. Tourists sidestep the congestion. The town center doesn't have to fight traffic jams. And it gives Cook and her staff a job driving out pollution. "Everybody's happy," she says. "What more can you ask for?"

True Grid

Mass transit can't compete with the car for the simple reason that cars have changed the rules of the road. Traffic patterns bear as much resemblance to cow paths as they do to the grid lines laid out for subways, streetcars and buses. In a city where trips are best simulated by pouring spaghetti on a map, public transit is stuck in the rut of fixed routes to a few destinations, apparently based on the theory of build it far away and they will come.

To be successful, alternative transit systems must accommodate four realities.

1. A motorized transit system inevitably favors the car, which goes directly where the driver wants to go, when the driver wants to go. "Follow that car" works for cabs, not public transit. Land use reform which brings essential services closer to consumers, so they can walk or bike, is more effective than mass transit locked into sprawling city forms dictated by planners who zone for single use. Main streets, corner variety stores, bike paths and walking trails are the main vehicles of a public transit system because they are an alternative to a motorized access system. Often, this will mean increasing density of housing arrangements—two- and three-story apartments over retail shops, for instance—so we can increase street traffic while decreasing the space taken up by roads. This will free up a third of the space in most cities, and give it over to other public uses such as recreation, which again reduces the need to drive elsewhere for entertainment.

2. Public transit cannot function effectively as long as the car infrastructure of roads and parking continues to be subsidized. When car travel is artificially under-priced, home buyers and businesses move farther afield to where land is cheap, unraveling the density needed for main streets and public transit. That's why public transit has to be subsidized whenever cars are subsidized. Chasing the city form created by car infrastructure always leaves public transit one step behind the car. By contrast, cars are left behind in city environments built for walkers, strollers, people-watchers, bikers, bladers and transit riders.

3.   Public transit has to offer a competing experience to the car. We've put the car on easy street. Cars get the parkways, transit riders get a subway. Cars go express. Buses do milk runs. Cars provide private space. Public transit invades private space. Driving is safer than walking or biking. Drivers have air conditioning. Bikers breathe in their pollution, and bake on un-treed blacktop. Any need to wonder why drivers won't give up their cars?

Inventors at Winnipeg's KOR Product Design have come up with a version of public transit that's part sports car, part roller coaster. Passengers hop into a stylish two-seater waiting in the station, and an electric motor carries them to the main track. The track, enclosed to protect customers from the weather and minimize wind resistance, offers so little rolling friction to the car's steel wheels that passengers simply push a foot pedal to maintain the momentum of 15 miles an hour—the same speed drivers in Los Angeles are soon expected to reach. Sensors prevent rear-ending. The car pulls off at whatever station the driver wants to stop at. The system is ultra-cheap by mass transit standards. There's no tunneling. There's no heavy construction, since the load the track has to bear is quite light. Pedal power keeps electricity demand low. There are no drivers to pay, and a coin-op turnstile eliminates the need for ticket takers. The system is best suited, says KOR manager Bob McLeod, for short trips on low density routes on the way to rapid transit stations—reducing the need for parking lots beside transit stations—or for trips to major amusements such as zoos and water parks, allowing places that are off the beaten track to be designed as car-free zones. "The ride becomes part of the venue," says McLeod. "Kids will harass their parents to take it." A pilot project is in the works for Winnipeg, where the KOR kars will take people from downtown hotels, across a series of city parks to a favored tourist riverside lookout.

4.   To deal with the reality of freewheeling traffic patterns, public transit has to be de-massed and de-railed, freed from the grid mentality. Big buses haven't been able to accomplish this. They have to carry too many passengers to allow them to take advantage of their flexibility and go down side streets to pick up or drop off passengers. Though buses can theoretically go anywhere, they may as well be rail cars for all the convenience they offer customers.

Peugeot-Citroen is testing a scheme based on electric mini-cars in Tours, France. Subscribers to the service pick up rental cars at a charging station and drive it to the recharging station nearest their destination.[35] Jitney vans are probably better adapted to North American sprawl. Jitneys can be hailed just like taxis, but they cost the rider the same as public transit, because they carry several passengers. They offer convenience, personalized service, speed and comfort that buses can't match. They're also cheaper to buy and run than buses. They can be easily adapted to run on farm-made ethanol fuels. They are ideal for bringing suburbanites to rapid transit stations.

We blame suburbia too often for the transportation ills that are more properly blamed on the gridism of transportation planners.

Swap 'till You Drop

The cause of poverty, it's said, is lack of money. That's a poor excuse, says novelist Tom Robbins. It's "akin to a starving woman with a sweet tooth lamenting that she couldn't bake a cake because she did not have any ounces. She had butter, flour, eggs, milk and sugar, she just didn't have any ounces, any pinches, any pints." Money's legacy, Robbins writes in **Skinny Legs And All**, is that "the arithmetic by which things were measured had become more valuable than the things themselves." This predicament "was indicative of the extent to which reality had been distorted by the abstract lens of wealth."

For as long as money has made the world go round, people have tried to get around it. Cranberries first came on the world market in 1677, when Massachusetts settlers shipped 10 barrels to King Charles to cool him out after he threw a tantrum at the news that the Pilgrims had minted their own Pine Tree shilling.[36] Uniform national currencies weren't standard in North America until the 1870s. Until then, merchants and churches fairly commonly issued tokens for local use. Indebted farmers and manufacturers wanted money divorced from the gold standard for many years after:[37] witness William Jennings Bryan's run for the U.S. presidency in 1896 saying "we shall not be crucified on a cross of gold," or the notoriously subversive **Wizard of Oz**, a populist classic from Kansas that exposed the smoke and mirrors behind the big money power. Experiments with currency "multiply with social change," argues Princeton sociologist Vivian Selizer. "People will segregate, differentiate, label, decorate and personalize it to meet their complex social needs," she writes in **The Social Meaning of Money**.

Since the 1980s, a new computerized money-free system developed by Michael Linton in Courtenay, B.C., the Local Employment and Trading System or LETS, has been taken up by more than 500 regions around the world.[38] England has about 350 systems, Holland over 50. In Australia, it's government-sponsored. LETS is virtual money for the post-scarcity information economy, Hazel Henderson argues in **Paradigms In Progress**, where "information 'flows' and is not 'scarce'." Issued by communities to facilitate local economic transactions, the system encourages "the use of money as a means of exchange, rather than as a tool by which people can exploit each other," says development expert David Weston, founder of Vancouver's Community Exchange and Nanaimo's Widget Exchange.[39]

Once money is recognized as information—a way of keeping track of swaps but otherwise not worth the paper it's printed on—communities can set up a range of systems, from the cashless to the cashful. Money, after all, is just a convenient fiction that stores no value in and of itself. It acquires value only because it's accepted as good coin by someone else. Once there's popular agreement, anything can be used to record transactions, from seashells to gold to IOUs to baseball trading cards to paper bills to checks to credit cards to columns on a computer to pogs.

Ithaca, New York, has multiples of an HOUR note with "In Ithaca We Trust," and "Time Is Money" printed on it, a welcome break from In God We Trust, all others please pay cash. The HOUR is valued at $10, the average hourly cash wage in the area. It's accepted by 1,200 vendors, including doctors, credit unions, theatres, bowling alleys and market gardeners, who are all free to charge what they want, just as with conventional money. As more people join or more goods are traded, the "local reserve" issues more money. The system was started, says organizer Paul Glover, because people got tired of watching "fed-

eral dollars come to town, shake a few hands, then leave to buy rainforest lumber and fight wars."[40] Toronto follows a "purer" system,
where no bills change hands, and debts and credits are simply
phoned into a central number. Members can charge part "federal dollars" and part "green." Renovator Brian Milani, who classifies energy-
efficient construction as "ideology with thermal mass," charges regular money for the thermal mass materials he has to purchase, and
LETS money for his own labor and ideological time. This allows people to contract him for work before they've salted away enough to
pay down the whole job, a nice benefit when times are slack, and
keeps him rolling in massages, yoga and tai chi lessons, and gets him
into a range of food outlets and theatres.

Many other variations are possible. Budding financiers might set up
the Virtual Bank of Toledo, and so on, charging a small overhead fee
for the currency they issue, and start hustling to get as wide a range
of services on the system as possible so they can live their lives within the alternative economy. Business Improvement Associations can
issue neighborhood currencies and use them to pay for renovations or
entertainers, in effect getting work done for wholesale prices, and to
reward repeat customers. Municipalities can accept local money for
services and even taxes, then spend that money to buy local services
and goods. If the feds wanted to cut their losses in the production of
money—a penny costs three cents to make, there's a loss on dimes
and quarters too—they could stop issuing small change, anything less
than $5, and make a big difference for local currencies, which could
fill the vacuum. Over the next 10 years, we'll witness the biggest real
estate dump in history, as banks replace community branches with
automatic tellers built into the wall of convenience stores and recep-
tionists from anywhere who handle unusual transactions over the
phone. With information technology, there's no longer a need to live
close to customers to shake them down. As prized buildings in prime
locations become vacant and available at fire-sale rates, there will be
an unparalleled opportunity for community currency exchanges to
move into good digs and fulfill a service role now monopolized by
banks.

The only people who stand to lose once community currencies catch
on are central bankers, money traders and counterfeiters. Despite all
the hoopla about the need for a strong dollar, the weaker the dollar

is, the stronger the economy. A strong dollar is the root of all evil. It creates scarcity where none exists in the real world, a place full of needs and skills that are withering for lack of connection and exchange. Because it's scarce, centrally issued money creates win-lose relationships where win-win possibilities abound. It's no sweat off my back to tutor your daughter in history. I like it, and I'm not doing anything else with my time. And it's no skin off your nose, ozone layer permitting, to give me a basket of tomatoes, because at harvest time you have more than you know what to do with. Even if I insist that my time is worth twice yours, you'll just give me a second basket of tomatoes, which you would have had to give away anyway. It's easier to raise historical consciousness and tomatoes than money. As soon as we talk money, there's not enough to go around. You have to sell too many tomatoes to make it worthwhile to hire me and I'm out of a job.

Scarcity is what gives the moneyed interests their control over the economy and keeps the poor in chronic dependency. Poor communities have what it takes to become hives of economic activity. There are more than enough needs and skills to go around. But I can't sell you my book and you can't cut my hair until someone with money gets a haircut from you and buys a book from me so that we can pay each other. In the meantime, all we have to trade is hard-luck stories. Money is the enforcer of the trickle-down economy.[41]

A strong dollar drives up interest rates, because a strong dollar is one that's in demand, or scarce. But if our local virtual reserve issues money in harmony with exchanges actually taking place—that is, lets economic exchanges keep currency in balance, rather than the other way around—there's neither inflation, nor deflation. We pay each other for our work, not our money or our interest payments. And if someone gets maxxed out on their community credit line, all they have to pay back is the principal, not the compound interest, which represents a saving of $1,000 a year for most families now paying 18 per cent for the illusion that plastic is the only bona fide currency.

A strong dollar is the power tool metropolitan regions use to ride herd on have-not regions. If Newfoundland or Alabama had their own currencies, their dollar might be worth 90 cents on international exchanges. That's a 10 per cent price advantage for exporters, a 10 per cent cost advantage for local producers competing with imports, and a 10 per cent penalty on banks that invest local savings outside the region. There'd be no need to lure in outside companies with grants or promises of cheap labor and weak environmental laws to overcome the disadvantage of a dollar that's overpriced for the region.

Local currencies flip the financial system in the same way as energy conservation flips the power companies. With energy conservation, as we saw in Principle 2, the trick is to redefine power as service. It doesn't matter how much a kilowatt hour of electricity or cubic meter of natural gas costs. It's what energy service is required to keep rooms warm and showers hot. A more open-ended question gets a lower-cost answer: insulation and solar water heaters. In the same way, once money is redefined as a service to facilitate economic exchange, the challenge becomes to make it more, not less, accessible to people with trading needs.

Let the central bankers worry about what active local currencies do to their pals. They can figure out a way to turn their skill at juggling numbers on a screen into a useful trade, or else find honest work. Let the rich pay. All others should swap. Why let a little thing like money stand between us and a beautiful thing?

Eat, Drink And Be Merry

It's hard to doubt the strength of John Robbins' convictions about food. He gave up his claim to the Baskin-Robbins ice cream fortune because of his health, environmental and ethical beliefs about meat and dairy products. But the author of **Diet for a New America** and **Diet for a New World** says that "the person who eats beer and franks with cheer and thanks will probably be healthier than the person who eats sprouts and bread with doubt and dread." He warns fellow vegans that in Hindu spiritual centers, "there's what's known as the 'sin of scrupulosity,' in which a person becomes holier-than-thou, becomes self-absorbed in his own attempt to achieve purity to the extent that he is no longer able to relate well to others."[42]

For Robbins, grace is the most important part of any meal, and Thanksgiving needs to be celebrated more than once a year. Grace "is a way to slow down, relax, to let go of the busyness and worries of the day," he says. "It enables us to acknowledge and bond with the others with whom we are sharing the meal. It is a way to join with them and all the people and elements that have made our meal possible."

Grace is a bigger challenge to the economy and culture of our food system than veganism. Two-thirds of Americans eat while they drive, the other third don't drive or are lying, **Prevention** magazine reports.[43] Breakfast ritual for many is a coffee, a cigarette and a pee. The dining room is "increasingly the least-used room in the house," says University of Pennsylvania food anthropologist Saul Katz.[44] Fake food thrives in this setting, where chains market "solutions to meal-time," not food,[45] and couch potatoes eat whatever can be cooked up during ads. "Social manners may be more effective in promoting balance, moderation and variety," in eating and farming, says renowned food critic Margaret Visser, "than the conscious efforts of individuals, often eating alone, subject to commercial blandishments, who seek to control their food intake."[46] Scarfing is nature's way of making fast food go down, but no one scarfs a home-grown tomato.

Mealtime is for breaking bread. It is for yakking and laughing. It is for kids to be seen and heard, to show food and teach us that meals are about play and art and goofiness. It is for showing off what each person helped prepare and present. It is for friends to drop in without any special invitation or occasion, to bring wine, which, if an excuse is needed, has enzymes that fight heart disease by increasing the level of good cholesterol.[47] It is a time to bring out the beeswax candles, to set the right mood and, at the rate of one meal by candlelight per week, to balance out about 100,000 tons a year of carbon dioxide now produced by coal-generated electric lighting.[48] It is a time to rejoice about what makes us happy, to remind ourselves what we are working for and toward, and to think about the changes we need to make to honor life's cherished moments.

"It has been a joy to learn how many times the foods that are healthiest for the human body are also the healthiest for our environment and create the least suffering for other creatures," says Robbins. "It affirms for me that nature can be trusted, and that we can yet learn to live in peace and harmony with the rest of the living Earth community."49

Get A Life!

Get a Life! gets personal with economics. It's about aligning human needs for fulfillment with productive social and natural systems. When people follow their inner light, a lot of details fall into place. When biology and sociology are integrated with economics, productivity comes to life. When these untapped sources of renewable energy are fired up, good things start to happen.

Get A Life! doesn't mean get lost or get off my back. Get A Life! means the dishes and laundry can wait. Life is a relationship with mystery, not an ordering of tidy piles. Mess it up a little with backyard weeds, composters and rain barrels, try an odor-free composting toilet at the cottage, lobby for a combined café, public-access Internet, library and convenience store in the middle of your block. Be at home with chaos, and its deep patterns and laws will work with us.

Get A Life! means taking laughter and giving back beauty. Grow a garden on your roof. Plant beans up your walls and wildflowers in your lawn, play road hockey on the street or bake bread at the community oven in your neighborhood park while you tend your garden plot. Have some serious fun.

Get A Life! takes inner resources. Your boss won't get you a life. Neither will the government. Want to slow down, spend more time with friends and family? Work a four-day week, and make your car last an extra year. Want to feel healthy? Walk more, enjoy yourself and eat less animal fat and sugar. Want to give your new baby a head start? Breast feed. Change will not come from the commanding heights, but the commanding bottoms.

Get A Life! means losing our fear. That's what the debate about jobs and the environment boils down to. We don't need jobs that are a death sentence. Good jobs work with life's cycles. Sewage can be turned to fertilizer. Trees can double as air conditioners. Breathing walls beat polyvinyl chloride. Effective builders work with natural materials. The new medicine works with the body's instincts and immune system. Most of the chemicals and drugs we need can be grown. We can make our lives count, make a difference.

Get A Life! means the power's there for the taking. That's what the challenge of global competitiveness is really about. The multinationals have no power if you buy your food through community support agriculture, exchange your skills through local trading systems and currencies and save and borrow at a credit union. A five per cent drop in sales knocks most products off the retail shelves and a 15 per cent drop in sales of a leveraged company sends their stocks tumbling. Is it their power, or ours, that frightens us?

Get A Life! means the time has come. The technology is ready. The logistics are in the making. The experience is building. If you like the idea of basing your business on coming trends, check out the exponential growth in home business, bike commuting, walking, holistic medicine, vegetarianism, recycling, premium quality products, authentic goods, natural textiles and cleansers, fresh and healthful food, spiritual exploration and ethical purchases and investments. If you know 200 people and can keep your costs down, you can make a go of it in food preparation, lawn care, renovation, or toxic-free cleaning.

Get A Life! means believing in yourself. Don't let the system take away your confidence and responsibility as well as your job. It won't be easy, but let's not make it harder than it is. The dinosaur corporations are only on top because our tax dollars put them there.

Get A Life! means the more the merrier. We're not in this alone. Micro-enterprises bespeak a new economic individualism. Helping them bespeaks a new economic support system. If we stick together, we can combine economic prosperity with social justice. We can start by sharing what we learn on the way up. Keep in touch. Good luck!

Endnotes

AP—Associated Press
BN—Broadcast News
CP—Canadian Press
FP—Financial Post
G&M—Globe and Mail
Mtl. Gaz.—Montreal Gazette

NYRB—New York Review of Books
NYT—New York Times
ROB—Report on Business
Tor.—Toronto
Van.—Vancouver

Introduction

1   CP, Oct. 5/93
2   EcoCity Cleveland, Feb./95

Overview

1   New Shoes
2   The Globe & Mail, August 21, 1995
3   Cf. J. Myles, Studies in Political Economy, Summer 1988
4   L. Dobyns, C. Crawford-Mason, Thinking About Quality: Progress,
    Wisdom and the Deming Philosophy
5   The Economist, Feb. 4, 1995
6   Ross, op cit; Economic Reform, March 1994; Progressive, February
    1995; New York Review of Books, Nov. 17, 1994; Economist, Jan.
    14, 1995; E. Mann, Taking on General Motors: a case study of the
    UAW campaign to keep GM Van Nuys open
7   Toronto Star, May 14, 1995
8   Boston Sunday Globe, July 16, 1995
9   Fortune magazine, March 8, 1993
10 Globe & Mail, Feb. 22, 1995; Nation, Feb. 20, 1995; R. Reich,
    The Next American Frontier
11 Nation, Feb. 20, 1995
12 Financial Post, May 18, 1995
13 Economist, Feb. 4, 1995; Globe & Mail, May 23 and 31, 1995
14 Globe & Mail, June 1 and 7, 1993
15 NYRB, Sept. 21, 1995
16 Globe & Mail, Feb. 22, 1995
17 Toronto Star, Apr. 20, 1993; Financial Post, July 8, 1994;
    Globe & Mail, June 7, 1993

18   P. Hawken, The Ecology of Commerce
19   Toronto Star, June 14, 1994
20   G. Easterbrook, A Moment on the Earth: The Coming Age of
      Environmental Optimism

Principle 1

1   M. Elvin, London Review of Books, Oct. 19/95
2   T. Berry, The Dream of the Earth; M. Fox, Original Blessing
3   C. Merchant, The Death of Nature; M. Berman, The Reenchantment
      of the World
4   D.Reid, Paris Sewers and Sewermen, Realities and Representation
5   R. Carson
6   P. Carson, Green is Gold
7   FP, April 24, 1993; See SolPlan Review, Feb./Mar, 1993 for list of
      plants
8   J. Gleick, Chaos, Making a New Science
9   Van. Sun, Aug. 5/94
10   The Collapse of Chaos: Discovering Simplicity in a Complex World
11   Economist, Nov. 19/94
12   Alive, # 146
13   Mtl. Gaz. July 4/95
14   G&M, Aug. 23/95
15   G&M, Sept. 30/95
16   Natural Life, July-Aug./95
17   Shape, July/93
18   Maine Sunday Telegram, July 16/95
19   How to Live Longer and Feel Better
20   G&M, July 29/94; Wholesome News, Oct./Nov./94
21   Mtl. Gaz. Aug. 16/95
22   B. Jensen, Foods That Heal; E. Mindell, The Vitamin Bible; P. Hausman,
      J. Hurley, The Healing Foods
23   G&M, Aug. 19/94
24   Reuters, June 15/95
25   G&M, Aug. 7/94
26   G&M. Oct. 8/94
27   Tor. Star, July 1/93

28 CP, Aug. 21/95

29 Cookstown Greens, May/94

30 Mtl. Gaz. July 14/95; P. Hausman, J. Hurley, op cit.

31 G&M, Sept. 7/95

32 Tor. Star, Sept. 18/95

33 G&M, May 5/93

34 Health Watch Canada, Winter/93; Mother Earth News, Feb./Mar./95; Common Ground, Autumn/95 re: garlic

35 J. Lexchin, The Real Pushers, Economist, Jan. 28/95

36 Scientific American, May/91

37 Alive, Feb./Mar./95; W. Crook, The Yeast Connection: A Medical Breakthrough

38 Mtl. Gaz. July 21/95

39 Common Ground, Apr./95

40 Economist, June 28/95

41 J. McVicar, Jekka's Complete Herb Book

42 Journal de Montreal, June 25/95

43 Compleat Mother, Summer/95

44 Economist, Oct. 22/94

45 Thanks to CBC Radio reporter Lori Stahlbrand who supplied her background notes and tapes from the convention.

46 Cf. for example, the Canadian Task Force on the Periodic Health Examination, The Canadian Guide to Clinical Preventive Health Care; Mothering, Spring/94

47 Mothering, Spring/94

48 Mothering, Summer/93

49 Mothering, Winter/93, Fall/94

50 Mothering, Spring/95

51 Mtl. Gaz., June 13/95

52 Health Watch Canada, Winter/93; D. Krieger, Accepting Your Power to Heal: The Personal Practice of Therapeutic Touch

53 Flare magazine, Oct./94

54 Mtl. Gaz. June 4/95

55 Reuters, Apr. 29/94

56 S. Meakin, Hazardous Waste Management: Canadian Directions

57 Clive Ponting, A Green History of the World; NYRB, Oct. 6/94

58 Alive, # 144

59 Cf. Mtl. Gaz., Aug. 18/94

60   G&M, Oct. 20/94

61   Alive, # 144

62   G&M, March 31/95

63   Cf. Pollution Probe, Canadian Green Consumer Guide

Principle 2

1   Tor. Star, Oct. 13/94

2   A. Lovins, Soft Energy Paths; Toward a Durable Peace; Energy/War: Breaking the Nuclear Link

3   ibid., May/95

4   Progressive, May/95

5   M. Jacobson and L.A. Mazur, Marketing Madness: A Survival Guide for a Consumers Society, Tor. Star, July 8/95

6   C. Long, Life After the City: A Harrowsmith Guide to Rural Living

7   Home Energy Retrofit in Canada, Mar./94

8   NYT, May 21/93

9   Van. Province, Aug. 3/94

10   G&M, May 8/95

11   Great Lakes Pollution Prevention Centre, At the Source, Sept./95

12   G&M, May 14/93

13   Tor. Star, June 8/93

14   Mtl. Gaz. July 16/95

15   New York Energy Plan, vol. 2

16   M. Lowe, Alternatives to the Automobile, New York State Energy Plan, vol. 2

17   M. Replogle, Transportation Conformity and Demand Management

18   G&M, May 24/95

19   G&M, May 31/95

20   Adbusters, Spring/Summer/94; D. Engwicht puts the cancer figure at 30,000, the EPA at 1,500: Reuters, May 10/93

21   New York State Energy Plan, vol. 1

22   Van. Sun, Aug. 19/94

23   Car and Driver, Sept./94

24   NYT, Mar. 17/94

25   The Ecologist, July/Aug./93

26   Beyond Sprawl: New Patterns of Growth to Fit the New California; G&M,
      June 2/95
27   Cf. International Institute for Energy Conservation, Integrated Transport
      Planning: A Sensible Path to Roads Less Travelled
28   Cf. Jim Iverson, NYT, Aug. 20/95
29   Cf. International Institute for Energy Conservation, op. cit.
30   G&M, Sept. 1/94
31   Cooper Institute, Report on the Impact of the Withdrawal of Marine
      Atlantic Ferry Services from Prince Edward Island, G&M, Dec. 7/93,
      Tor. Star, Dec. 9/93
32   Good Work, June/95
33   A Millennium of Family Change, Feudalism to Capitalism in Northwestern
      Europe; Weathering the Storm, Working Class Families from the Industrial
      Revolution to the Fertility Decline
34   Tor. Star, Dec. 3/94
35   Prevention, Nov./94
36   Tor. Star, Aug. 9/93
37   Tor. Star, Oct. 16/95
38   New York State Energy Plan, vol. 2
39   G&M, Mar. 18/94
40   Canadian Tax Journal, Winter & Spring/93; FP, Sept. 1/93
41   Tor. Star, Dec. 14/93
42   USA Today, May 12, 14/95
43   G&M, Mar. 23, 25/95; Tor. Star Apr. 5/95
44   Endnote on circadian rhythms and general health effects: Canadian Centre
      for Occupational Health and Safety, Rotational Shift Work: A Summary of
      Adverse Effects and Improvement Strategies; International Archives of
      Occupational and Environmental Health, vol. 49, # 2, C. Zenz, ed.,
      Developments in Occupational Medicine; American Industrial Hygiene
      Association Journal, Nov./86
      Endnote on shifts and accidents: Labor Studies, Winter/88; Proceedings of
      the Human Factors Society, 1988; J. Harrington ed., Recent Advances in
      Occupational Health; International Archives of Occupational and
      Environmental Health, vol. 49, # 3
      Endnote on pre-term babies: British Journal of Industrial Medicine,
      Mar./89 (based on Montreal data)
45   G&M, Dec. 11/93, July 1/94
46   G&M, Oct. 1/94
47   Tor. Star, Dec. 26/94

48 G&M, Oct. 7/94

49 G&M, Sept. 22/94

50 Tor. Star, Mar. 9/95, G&M, Mar. 13/95

51 Labor Studies, Winter/88

52 Cf. Tor. Star, Nov. 5/94

53 G&M, July 1/94

54 J. Schor, Overworked Americans

55 W. Rybzynski, Waiting for the Weekend

56 G&M, June 2/95

57 Tor. Star, Dec. 17/94; Statistics Canada, Why Has Inequality in Weekly Earnings Increased in Canada; Mtl. Gaz. Aug. 10/95

58 Chicago Tribune, Apr. 3/94

59 Snow Country, May/June/92

60 Cf. G&M, Aug. 9/95; Cf. Statistics Canada reported that Canadian employers pay out somewhat less in payroll costs than U.S. employers, placing 13th, in comparison with the U.S., at 12th position, in a ranking of nations

61 G&M, Sept. 22/95

62 FP, June 11/94

63 Toronto Social Planning Council, Social Infopac, Feb./93

64 G&M, Mar. 1/94, Jan. 18/95

65 Cf. G&M, June 5/95

66 Men's Fitness, Apr./94

67   Peat Marwick et. al., The Cost of Transporting People in the British Columbia Lower Mainland

68 Consumer Reports, Feb./95

69 Economist, May 7/94; UN., Reality of Aid, 1993, UN., Human Development Report, 1991; London Review of Books, Aug. 18/94

70 P. Adams, Odious Debts

71 Guardian Weekly, June 26/94

Principle 3

1 Signs of Hope, Working Toward Our Common Future

2 Report on Business, G&M, Oct./95

3 Mtl. Gaz., Aug. 24/94

4 See R. Knack's superb overview in Planning, July/94

5   Mtl. Gaz., Aug. 15/95

6   Grow T.O.Gether, Apr./94

7   Vegetarian Times, Sept./95

8   E. Fowler, Building Cities That Work

9   Community Greening Review, 1992

10 The term comes from Sean Cosgrove, executive member of the American Community Gardening Association, who also shared his extensive files with us

11 House on Pooh Corner

12 G&M, Jan. 28/92

13 The most comprehensive and finely tuned statistics on these matters come from Scotland's Department of Transportation's Killing Speed and Saving Lives, which shows that every one-kilometer-an-hour decrease in car speed lowers traffic accidents by five per cent and fatalities by seven per cent. The more conservative estimates used in our text come from Ontario Ministry of Transportation tabulations of police accident reports, which are commonly considered to under-report speed as the dominant factor in accidents

14 At its November, 1990 meeting, the Canadian Council of Environment Ministers adopted a report (which has not been implemented, needless to say) estimating a 10 per cent reduction in carbon dioxide and nitrous oxide emissions from enforcing speed limits. Since cars cause about half of global warming emissions, this measure alone could meet five per cent of targets.

15 Global ReLeaf Fact Sheet

16 NYT, June 7/94

17 NYT, June 7/94; Mothering, Summer/95

18 J. Robbins, May All Be Fed

19 M. Klaper, Vegan Nutrition

20 Our Times, June/July/94

21 CP, Apr. 18/93

22 L. Pauling, How to Live Longer and Feel Better

23 S. Watson, Sugar Free Toddlers; Dr. W. Crook, The Yeast Connection: A Medical Breakthrough

24 Only 56 per cent of Americans eat breakfast regularly, compared to 74 per cent of Canadians: Tor. Star, Nov. 25/93

25 Good Food Book

26 AP, Apr. 24/95

27 Tor. Star, June 8/93

28 Vegetarian Times, Nov./94

29   G&M, May 17/94
30   R. Bullard ed., Confronting Environmental Racism:
      Voice From the Grassroots
31   Tor. Star, Aug. 25/95
32   E. Fowler, Building Cities That Work
33   Cf. G. Mulgan, R. Murray, Reconnecting Taxation

Principle 4

1   Guardian Weekly, Nov. 27/94
2   Cf. NYT, Mar. 21/94
3   G&M, Oct. 6/93
4   A. During, Ecological Wakes: The Story of Six Everyday Objects
5   U.N., Food and Agriculture Organization, 1995
6   Cornucopia Project, Empty Bread Basket: The Coming Challenge to
      America's Food Supply and What We Can Do About It
7   J. Rifkin, Biosphere Politics
8   Reuters, Dec. 7/93
9   Cf. The Ecologist, Nov./Dec./92
10   F.M. Lappé, op. cit.
11   F. MacKinnon, Posture and Politics: Some Observations on Participatory
      Democracy
12   H. Girardet, J. Seymour, Blueprint for a Green Planet
13   Canada Mortgage and Housing Corp., Co-Generation Systems in Multi-
      Unit Residential Structures
14   Food Service and Hospitality, June/92
15   Agro Alternatives
16   Cf. G. Coates ed., Resettling America
17   L. Riotte, Carrots Love Tomatoes
18   Reuters, Apr. 20/94; Nature, Apr./94
19   G&M, June 1/94
20   Cf. R. Hart, Forest Gardening
21   Manchester Guardian, Apr. 2/95, reports on French use of this method for
      premium chicken prices
22   J. Seymour, Changing Lifestyles: Living as Though the Wild Mattered
23   Mtl. Gaz. May 3/95
24   AP, May 9/93

25 G. Burrill, I. McKay, eds., People, Resources and Power

26 Saskatchewan Research Council, Some Agricultural Implications of Feed Fiber Fuel and Industrial Feed Stocks

27 G. Peabody, Forestry; J.R. Smith, Tree Crops

28 Robert Costanza of the University of Maryland's International Society for Ecological Economics estimates that a forest has a value seven times that of the lumber it produces and suggests that value be used as a bench mark for depletion taxes to be charged against logging companies

29 N. and D. Goldbeck, Choose to Reuse

30 BioCycle, July/95

31 In Context, # 37

32 Thanks to Lori Stahlbrand of CBC Radio who provided her background notes and tapes

33 W.C. Liebhardt, ed., The Dairy Debate, University of California Sustainable Agriculture Program

34 R. Gottlieb, Forcing the Spring: The Transformation of the American Environmental Movement

35 Tor. Star, Oct. 31/91

36 W. Ashworth, The Late Great Lakes; Co-operative Institute for Limnology and Ecosystem Research, Great Lakes Environmental Research Laboratory, The Ecological Approach to the Zebra Mussel Infestation of the Great Lakes

37 Annals of the Earth, 1993, # 2

38 Cf. B. Berglund, C. Bolsby, The Edible Wild; L. Peterson, Edible Wild Plants

39 Tor. Star, June 30/93, June 29/94

40 In Business, Oct./92; G&M, Sept. 5/94

41 G&M, Nov. 24/94

42 Journal of the American Medical Association, Mar./94

43 Tor. Star, Oct. 8/94

44 Prairie Progress, vol. 3, # 1

45 Tor. Star, Nov. 19/94

46 Alive, # 149

47 Outdoor Canada, Oct./94

48 Mtl. Gaz. Sept. 11/94

49 A Vogel Journal, Apr./June/94

50 G&M, Aug. 24/94

51 A. Gore, Earth in the Balance; S. Watson, Sugar Free Toddlers

52 Mtl. Gaz., June 29/95

53   Mtl. Gaz., May 3/95; G&M, Dec. 7/94

54   Alive, # 150

55   Cape Cod Life, Oct./Nov./93

56   Sustainable Farming, Summer/93

57   G&M, June 30/92; Planning, Dec./87

58   A, Matthews, Where the Buffalo Roam

59   Tor. Star, Dec. 19/94

60   Tor. Star, Dec. 20/93; Harrowsmith, Dec./92

61   In Business, July/Aug./94

62   Pollution Probe, Canadian Green Consumer

63   G. Coates, ed., Resettling America

64   J. Kolko, Restructuring the World Economy; F.M. Lappé,
     Diet for a Small Planet

65   Prairie Progress, vol. 3, # 1

66   Mtl. Gaz., July 2/95

67   J. Brody, op. cit.

68   G. Griffen, World Without Cancer: The Story of Vitamin B17

69   In Context, # 39

70   Cognition, Fall/92

71   Good Food Book

72   City Palate, Sept./Oct./94

73   G&M, Mar. 24/94

74   Cf. C. Derber et. al., Power in the Highest Degree: Professional and the
     Rise of the New Mandarin Order; Cf. H. Bailey, Vitamin E, Your Key to a
     Healthy Heart

75   Business Week, Apr. 12/93

76   M. Rachlis, C. Kushner, Strong Medicine: How to Save Canada's Health
     Care System

77   NYT, Aug. 20/95

78   Public Citizen, July/Aug./95

79   Dollars and Sense, May/June/95

80   G&M, May 8/95

81   M. Reisner, Cadillac Dessert; G&M, Nov. 8/93

82   FP, Jan. 14/94

83   R. De Genarro, op. cit.

84   R. Ferguson, Compare the Share, Phase III; Economist, Feb. 11/95;
     Mtl. Gaz., July 4/95; Dollars and Sense, May/June/95

85   G&M, Dec. 7/94

86   Dollars and Sense, May/June/95; Cf. also G&M, Oct. 6/95
87   G&M, Nov. 2, Nov. 22/94, Nov. 15/95
88   eye, Sept. 8/94
89   Time, Nov. 22/93; G&M, May 17, Aug. 17/94
90   R. De Genarro, Earth Budget, Making Tax Dollars Work for the
      Environment; Dollars and Sense
91   Hazards Communication [Western New York Council of Occupational
      Safety and Health] Winter/92
92   Dollars and Sense, May/June/95
93   Cf. G&M, Jan. 1/94
94   F.M. Lappé, Diet for a Small Planet
95   Vegetarian Times, Sept./95
96   Tor. Star, May 29/95
97   Economic Reform, Apr./95
98   Nation, Feb. 13/95
99   Alberni Valley Times, Mar. 18/94
100   Tor. Star, Aug. 10/93
101   R. Kehl, Studies in Political Economy, Summer/94

Principle 5

1   International Institute for Sustainable Development conference, Spring/94
2   The Progressive, Jan./95
3   Canadian Living, Mar./94; G&M, Aug., 12, 14/94; New England Journal of
     Medicine, Sept./94
4   Cf. American Journal of Public Health, Sept./94
5   Mtl. Gaz., July 24/95
6   Imprint, Spring/95; Canadian Guide to Clinical Preventive Health Care
7   G&M, July 1/94; Health Naturally, Feb./Mar./95; Dr. Carolyn De Marco,
     Take Charge of Your Body: Women's Health Advisor
8   Wholesome News, Oct./Nov./94; Mtl. Gaz., July 24/95
9   G&M, Aug. 13/94; Tor. Star, Aug. 27/94; Cf. The Canadian Institute for
     Advanced Research, Why are Some People Healthy and Others Not?
10   G&M, July 13/94
11   G&M, Mar. 6/95
12   Nation, Jan. 9/95
13   Economic Reform, May/94

14   USA Today, June 21/94

15   G&M, June 2/95

16   Mtl. Gaz., Aug. 15/95

17   FP, July 27, Aug. 13/94; Newsweek, July 25/94

18   Tor. Star, Nov. 6/94

19   NYRB, Mar. 3/94

20   G&M, Apr. 3/94

21   Tor. Star, Sept. 9/95

22   Tor. Star, Aug. 7/94

23   Nation, Jan. 9/95

24   CP, Jan. 24/94

25   Annals of the Earth, 1992, # 3

26   Mtl. Gaz., Aug. 17/95

27   Tor. Star, Jan. 15/94

28   Boston Globe magazine, July 16/95

29   R. Douthwaite, The Growth Illusion: How Economic Growth Has
     Enriched the Few, Impoverished the Many and Endangered the Planet

30   eye, June 2/94

31   WorldWatch Institute, Vital Signs, 1994

32   Tor. Star, Apr. 2/93; Tor. Star, Oct. 6/95

33   G&M, Sept. 7/95

34   G&M, Nov. 2/94, May 22/95; Economist, Dec. 3/94; Mtl. Gaz.,
     Sept. 22/94, May 22/95

35   Tor. Star, Mar. 18/95

36   Economist, Dec. 3/94

37   G&M, Aug. 20/94; Reuters, Apr. 7/93

38   Georgia Straight, Aug. 19/94

39   Mtl. Gaz., June 28/95

40   Tor. Star, Feb. 11/95

41   W. Ashworth, The Late Great Lakes

42   J. McPhee, The Control of Nature

43   EarthSave News, vol. 3, # 1, 1994

44   G&M, Apr. 2/94

45   N. Grove, Preserving Eden

46   Audubon, Aug./94

47   Equinox, Sept./Oct./95

48   Cf. Phoebe Cutler, Public Landscape of the New Deal

49 G&M, Jan. 8/94
50 G&M, May 23/94
51 Van. Prov., Aug. 2/94
52 USA Today, June 22/94
53 Mtl. Gaz., Sept. 23/94
54 H. Henderson, Paradigms in Progress
55 G&M, Sept. 10/94
56 Tor. Star, Apr. 21/93
57 Chicago Tribune, Apr. 24/94
58 Progressive, May/95
59 Journal of the National Cancer Institute, Sept./94; Mtl. Gaz., Sept. 21/94, May 23/95
60 Tor. Star, Sept. 21/94; Mtl. Gaz., Sept. 21/94
61 Prevention and Nutrition, Summer/94
62 G&M, Nov. 25/92
63 New Scientist, July 9/94
64 G&M, Aug. 9/95
65 G&M, Mar. 21/95
66 Mtl. Gaz., June 14/95; Y.W. Shurtleff, A. Aoyagi, The Book of Tofu
67 AP, Jan. 18/95
68 G&M, Mar. 15/94, Mar. 3/95
69 Tor. Star, Jan. 4/95
70 New England Journal of Medicine, May 20/93, Aug. 3/95
71 Chatelaine, Feb./95
72 Mother Jones, Mar./Apr./95
73 J. Robbins, Diet for a New America; Tor. Star, Feb. 11/95
74 American Health, Dec./94; Health Naturally, Dec./94 - Jan./95; J. Robbins, op. cit.; Mtl. Gaz., July 12/95, July 24/95; New England Journal of Medicine, June 15/95; G&M, July 13/95

Principle 6

1 G&M Oct. 12/95
2 V. Shiva, Staying Alive
3 Van. Sun, Aug. 15/94
4 Pediatric Research, 1993; CP, Dec. 8/93; Reuters, June 8/95; Common Ground, Spring/94

5   Pediatrics, May/93
6   British Medical Journal, 1994; New England Journal of Medicine, Summer/92; Compleat Mother, Summer/92
7   Mothering, Winter/94; Tor. Star, Feb. 20, July 30/92
8   Mothering, Spring/95
9   Mothering, Sept./93; Beach Metro News, Aug. 1/94
10 Infact Canada Newsletter, Spring/93
11 Mtl. Gaz., June 19/95
12 Tor. Star, Sept. 17/95
13 G&M, Sept. 18/95
14 Compleat Mother, Summer/95
15 Tor. Star, Sept.. 2/94
16 G&M, Apr. 19/95
17 Fitness Walking
18 Shape, July/93
19 Tor. Star, July 12/93
20 Mtl. Gaz., Aug. 15/95; G&M, June 17/93
21 Flare, Oct./94
22 Tor. Star, Aug. 20/95
23 With thanks to Herschel Hardin
24 J. Brody, op. cit.
25 A. Leung, Encyclopedia of Common Natural Ingredients; Tor. Star, Apr. 21/93; Shape, Apr./94
26 Alive, # 148
27 Organic Gardening, Nov./82
28 H. Griffith; Complete Guide to Vitamins, Minerals and Supplements
29 Vitality Magazine, Dec./94-Jan./95
30 Alive, # 148; Griffith, op. cit.; Globe, Oct. 14/94
31 Vitality magazine, June/93
32 G&M, Mar. 26/94; Vitality magazine, June/93; S. Weed, Healing Wise
33 Botanic Recorder, Summer/89
34 Mtl. Gaz., May 3/95
35 Mothering, Spring/95
36 G&M, Oct. 5/94
37 Harper's, Sept./93
38 Guardian Weekly, Aug. 27/95
39 G&M, June 21/95

40 G&M, Sept. 14/94
41 M. Lamb, Two Minutes a Day to Super Savings
42 G&M, Mar. 15/94
43 Tor. Sun, May 12/93
44 G&M, Sept. 6/95
45 Tor. Star, Sept. 28/95
46 G&M, June 1/94
47 G&M, Aug. 9/94; Van. Sun, Aug. 12/94
48 Nation, Jan. 9/95; American Health, Nov./94
49 Health Naturally, Dec./94-Jan./95
50 G&M, May 27/94
51 Time, Aug. 22/94; FP, May 10/94
52 Tor. Star, Oct. 3/94
53 Tor. Star, June 9/95
54 Reuters, Nov. 8/94
55 FP, Aug. 27/94
56 Victoria Times-Colonist, Aug. 7/94
57 Reuters, Sept. 7/95
58 Alive, Feb./94
59 G&M, Aug. 3/94; Van. Sun., Aug. 24/94
60 Walking, Mar./Apr./94
61 Reuters, June 8/95
62 Tor. Star, Nov. 10/94
63 G&M, Mar. 1/94
64 Psychology Today, Mar./Apr./93
65 G&M, Mar. 8/93
66 Mtl. Gaz., reprint, July 15/95
67 Mtl. Gaz., June 3, 18/95
68 The Suburban, June 26/95
69 Mtl. Gaz., July 6/95
70 Cf. M. Replogle, Transportation Conformity and Demand Management

Principle 7

1 Recycling Council of Ontario Update, Apr./95
2 RCO Update, Apr./95

3   Annals of the Earth, 1992, # 3

4   Institute for Local Self-Reliance, Replacing Petrochemicals with
    Biochemicals: A Pollution Prevention Strategy for the Great Lakes Region

5   S. Rowe, Home Place: Essays on Ecology

6   S. Ebenreck, Shading Our Cities

7   Horticultural Science, June/78

8   AP, July 4/94

9   Friends of the Earth, Global ReLeaf Fact Sheets; G. Moll, S. Ebenreck,
    eds., Shading Our Cities

10 Windsor Canadian Auto Workers, Labor Working Toward Sustainability,
    vol. 1, # 2

11 Horticultural Science, June/78; NYT, July 18/89

12 Bio-Cycle, July/95

13 Northern Ontario Business, Feb./94

14 Mtl. Gaz., May 25/95

15 REAP-Canada, Proceedings of the Wood Chip Combustion Workshop,
    Apr. 2/93

16 Alternatives, vol. 20, # 1, 1993; Wildflower, Winter/94

17 G&M, May 16/95

18 R. Schwartz Cohen, More Work for Mother: The Ironies of Household
    Technology From the Open Hearth to the Microwave

19 L. Morehouse with L. Gross, Total Fitness in 30 Minutes a Day

20 G&M, May 16/95

21 Health Naturally, Feb./Mar./95; American Health, Dec./94

22 Tor. Star, July 31/95

23 American Journal of Epidemiology, vol. 139, # 6

24 Toronto Hydro, Connections, Mar./Apr./94

25 Sol Magazine, Summer/94

26 Tor. Star, Feb. 2, Mar. 3/94; Van. Province, Aug. 15/94

27 In These Times, Oct. 16-29/95

28 Canadian Geographic, Dept./Oct./95; G&M, June 6/95

29 G&M, Mar. 9/94

30 Mtl. Gaz., July 3/93

31 Natural Life, Sept./95

32 Polar Passage

33 Earthkeeper, Dec./94

Principle 8

1 The Art of War

2 Atlantic Monthly, Nov./94

3 Mothering, Summer/94; G&M, Jan. 16, June 13/95; B. Orser, M. Foster, Home Enterprise: Canadians and Home-based Work; FP, Apr. 8/95

4 Home Business Advocate, # 33

5 Mtl. Gaz., July 5/95

6 Whole Earth Review, Spring/89

7 The Working Centre, Economic Justice Newsletter, Sept./93

8 W. Berry, The Unsettling of America, Culture and Agriculture

9 Heavy Horses

10 Mother Earth News, Feb./Mar./95

11 Draft Horse Journal, Winter/88; Whole Earth Review, Spring/86; M. Tellen, The Draught Horse Primer

12 C. Fix, Working Horses

13 Quesnel Advocate, June 22/94

14 Tor. Star, Apr. 8/95

15 R. De Genarro, op. cit.; Earthward, # 5; V. McLenighan, Sustainable Manufacturing

16 H. Hammond, Seeing the Forest Among the Trees; M.M. McGonigle, B. Parfitt, Forestopia: A Practical Guide to the New Forest Economy

17 Le Devoir, July 4/95

18 W. Berry, Sex, Economy, Freedom and Community

19 New Farm, Mar./94

20 G&M, Oct. 2/95

21 Natural Life, Nov./Dec./94

22 Natural Life, Jan./Feb./95

23 Mtl. Gaz., July 24/95

24 Mtl. Gaz., June 3/95

25 ROB, Sept./95

26 G&M, Apr. 17/94

27 Children First: What Our Society Must Do and Is Not Doing for Our Children

28   G&M, Dec. 4/94

29   L. McQuaig, The Wealthy Banker's Wife: The Assault on Equality in Canada

30   Reuters, Apr. 20. Aug. 20/95

31   Two papers by J. Koekstra, Free University Hospital, Amsterdam at International Symposium on Pediatric Gastroenterology and Nutrition, Montreal, June/95

32   Report, July/95

33   CP, June 28/93; AP, June 28/93; Van. Sun, July 21/93

34   G&M, Sept. 27, 28/93

35   IISD, Sustainable Development: Opportunities for Canada; Cf. G&M, Mar. 22/94

36   All About Us Canada Foundation, A Cut Above; Thinking Like a Forest: A Case for Sustainable Selective Forestry (video)

37   CBC Radio, Morningside, Oct. 6/95

38   The Last Straw, Summer/95

39   Cf. Earthkeeper, Oct./Nov./93

40   Cf. M. Best, The New Competition

41   Toronto Community Ventures News, Fall/Winter/94

42   Mother Earth News, Mar./Apr./87

Principle 9

1   Cf. for e.g.., American Journal of Alternative Agriculture, vol. 2, # 5, 1990

2   New Farm, July/Aug./94

3   Economist, Feb. 18/95

4   Conditions of Liberty: Civil Society and Its Rivals

5   Cf. A. Van der Ven, W. Joyce, eds., Perspectives on Organizational Design and Behaviour

6   Scientific American, Jan./91

7   Chemical Week, Feb. 10/93 announces a government study on the health impacts of pesticides on farmers, after reports that pesticide users suffer higher than normal rates for most cancers

8   Nature, May/95

9   W. Grady, The Nature of Coyotes: Voice of the Wilderness

10   Van. Sun, Aug. 20/94

11   P. Stonehouse, Economic Comparison of Farming Systems with Alternative Weed Management Strategies: A Case Study Approach

12 Sustainable Farming, Winter/93
13 Organic Gardening, Aug./82
14 D. Savoie, Thatcher, Reagan, Mulroney: In Search of a New Bureaucracy
15 Washington Post, Sept. 14/95
16 G&M, Sept. 21/95
17 W. Greider, Who Will Tell The People?
18 Canadian Environmental Network, CEPA, An Agenda for Reform
19 Cf. W. Greider, Who Will Tell The People?
20 AP, Apr. 21/95
21 D. Dickson, The New Politics of Science
22 C. Wade, The Paranoid's Handbook
23 G. Hunnius, The Politics of Labor Reform; J. Wilson, Bureaucracy
24 Economist, Oct. 1/94
25 Cf. his writings in S. Hall, M. Jacques, ed., New Times: The Changing
    Face of Politics in the 1990s; G. Albo, L. Panitch, eds. A Different Kind of
    State?, Marxism Today, May/91
26 The Working Centre, Economic Justice Newsletter, Sept./93
27 AP, July 24/95
28 NOW, Nov. 3/94; Tor. Star, May 21/95
29 G&M, Nov. 3/94; NYRB, Apr. 6/95
30 H. Henderson, Politics of the Solar Age
31 Mtl. Gaz., June 29, July 29, 30/95
32 G&M, June 5/95 discusses a similar project in Halifax sponsored by the
    Ecology Action Centre
33 Cf. Mtl. Gaz., June 24/95; Earthkeeper, Oct./Nov./93 prints recipe
34 Tor. Star, Sept. 11/95
35 Lancet, Apr. 15/95
36 IJC Reports, excerpted in Chlorine Free, Spring 1994; Broadcast News,
    Apr. 20/94; and Health Naturally, Aug./Sept. 1993
37 ROB, Nov./94, Sept./95
38 Mtl. Gaz., Aug. 6, 12, 13/95
39 Tor. Star, Apr. 29/95
40 Tor. Star, Dec. 28/94
41 Tor. Star, Aug. 14/95; Guardian Weekly, July 9/95
42 Guardian Weekly, Apr. 23/95
43 CP, Sept. 7/95; CBC Radio, Sept. 7/95
44 Cf. V. Melina et. al., Becoming Vegetarian: The Complete Guide to
    Adopting a Healthy Vegetarian Diet

Principle 10

1   Economic Reform, July/95
2   Mtl. Gaz., June 30/95
3   Mtl. Gaz., Aug. 14/95
4   Scientific American, May/91
5   Mtl. Gaz., Oct. 8/95
6   Mtl. Gaz., Oct. 6/95
7   M. Nickerson, Guideposts for a Sustainable Future
8   The Economist, unsigned, June 10/95
9   A. Zamm, Why Your House May Endanger Your Health. Cf. also L. Hunter, The Healthy Home; C. Venolia, Healing Environments
10   Reuters, May 3/93; Tor. Star, Dec. 3/94
11   Tor. Star, June 3/95
12   Tor. Star, Feb. 16/94
13   Successful Meetings, Nov./93
14   Tor. Star, Feb. 16/94
15   In Business, Feb./94
16   Tor. Star, Aug. 31/94; Cognition, Winter/94
17   Cookstown Greens, Dec./94
18   City Food, Oct./93
19   In Business, Feb./94
20   Van. Sun., Feb. 17/93
21   Alive, Jan./95
22   Tor. Star, Oct. 23/93
23   Organic Gardening, Jan./89
24   Van. Sun, Aug. 23/94
25   G&M, Aug. 12/94
26   Mtl. Gaz., Aug. 12/95
27   G&M, Feb. 19/94
28   Cf. Safe Kids Canada, fact sheet; U.S. National Safe Kids Campaign, fact sheet
29   Today's Parent, Oct./94
30   Homemakers, May/95
31   ROB, Oct./95
32   In Business, July/Aug./94
33   Economist, Aug. 5/95

34   T. Chappell, The Soul of a Business; F. Lager, Ben and Jerry's: The Inside Scoop; E Magazine, Aug./95

35   Mtl. Gaz., Aug. 19/95

36   Cape Cod Life, Oct./Nov./93

37   D. Montgomery, Beyond Equality

38   Harrowsmith, June/94

39   New Economics Journal, Summer/92

40   Boycott Quarterly, Spring/94

41   Cf. New European, 1991, vol. 4, no. 6

42   Vegetarian Times, Sept./95

43   Mtl. Gaz., June 21/95

44   G&M, July 12/95

45   Tor. Star, Mar. 10/95

46   G&M, Nov. 26/94

47   Tor. Star, May 5/95; Reuters, Aug. 21/95

48   Estimate based on 60 million, hour-long meals per week eaten under 100-watt bulbs and consuming 312 million kilowatt-hours of electricity

49   May All be Fed: Diet for a New World

Index

Voluntary Organizations
245ff

Waste Management
includes composting, incineration, recycling, source reduction, toxic waste

64ff, 107, 118ff, 168f, 263ff, 268ff